POVERTY STREET

The dynamics of neighbourhood decline and renewal

Ruth Lupton

The POLICY
P~P
PRESS

First published in Great Britain in November 2003 by

The Policy Press
University of Bristol
Fourth Floor
Beacon House
Queen's Road
Bristol BS8 1QU
UK

Tel +44 (0)117 331 4054
Fax +44 (0)117 331 4093
e-mail tpp-info@bristol.ac.uk
www.policypress.org.uk

British Library Cataloguing in Publication Data
A catalogue record for this book is available from the British Library.

Library of Congress Cataloging-in-Publication Data
A catalog record for this book has been requested.

ISBN 1 86134 535 6 paperback

A hardcover version of this book is also available

Ruth Lupton is a Research Fellow at the ESRC Centre for Analysis of Social Exclusion (CASE) at the London School of Economics and Political Science.

Cover design by Qube Design Associates, Bristol.
Front cover: photograph supplied by kind permission of www.third-avenue.co.uk
Printed and bound in Great Britain by Bell & Bain Ltd, Glasgow.

Dedication

To Emma Baker, for listening

Contents

List of tables, figures and boxes

Tables

Figures

Boxes

Acknowledgements

The study on which this book is based was carried out at the Economic and Social Research Council (ESRC) Centre for Analysis of Social Exclusion (CASE), based at the London School of Economics and Political Science. It was fully funded by the Centre's core funding from the ESRC.

I am grateful to many people at CASE who have helped with the study and the production of the book: Anne Power, particularly, and Howard Glennerster, for their ongoing guidance; Philip Noden, for his initial analysis of disadvantaged areas on which all the later work is based; Tom Sefton, for his help with labour market and house price analyses; Mairi Stewart, Joe Murray, Chris Hunter, Gerry Mitchell-Smith, John Houghton, Dan Monzani and Shirley Wilson, for their invaluable research and administrative assistance at various stages; Liz Richardson, Katharine Mumford, Helen Bowman, Martin Evans and other colleagues at CASE, for their ideas and encouragement; Julian Le Grand and Howard Glennerster, for helping with the fieldwork; and Jane Dickson and Rebecca Morris, for their administrative support. Anne Power, Liz Richardson, Rebecca Tunstall, Helen Bowman, Kevin Gill, Gerry Mitchell-Smith, Tom Sefton, John Houghton and John Hills generously gave their time to read and comment on the drafts, which were substantially improved as a result of their inputs.

The study would not have been possible without those individuals in each area who helped facilitate the study by showing me around, putting me in touch with people to interview and keeping me abreast of developments. In particular I would like to thank Patrick Leonard, Pauline Hickey, Karen Black, Christina Broad, Carole Evans, Jude Marks, Julia Crowley, Paul Gallagher, Val Cotter, Tom Flanagan, Lois Holden, Chris Waring, Dick Cartmell, Jan Bennett, Lyndon Ross, Craig Duerden, Neil Cawson, Pearl Hall, Jackie Pruckner and Anne Fox. They were endlessly patient and helpful. And last but not least, I am immensely grateful to the hundreds of other people: residents, frontline workers, service managers and policy makers, who gave their time to be interviewed for the study or to help me make contact with others, and from whose experience, knowledge and ideas I learned so much. Meeting and talking with them was a great personal lesson as well as an academic one. I hope I have reflected what they said in an accurate and helpful way and that this book will help others to gain some of the insights that they gave to me.

Photographic acknowledgements
Photographs on page 42 have been reproduced with the permission of the London Metropolitan Archives and the London Borough of Hackney, Archives Department.

Photographs on page 46 were taken by students at the Birmingham College of Art and Design. They were originally reproduced in Rex and Moore (1967) with permission of the principal of the College, Meredith Hawes, and permission to reproduce them in this volume has been regranted by her successor, the Dean of the Birmingham Institute of Art and Design, Professor Mick Durman.

List of acronyms

ABI	area-based initiative
CASE	Centre for Analysis of Social Exclusion
CCT	Compulsory Competitive Tendering
CDP	Community Development Programme
DETR	Department of the Environment, Transport and the Regions
DfES	Department for Education and Skills
EAZ	Education Action Zone
ESRC	Economic and Social Research Council
EZ	Employment Zone
HAZ	Health Action Zone
ICT	information and communication technology
ILD	Index of Local Deprivation
ILO	International Labour Organization
IMD	Index of Multiple Deprivation
IT	information technology
LMA	labour market account
LSP	Local Strategic Partnership
NCR	New Commitment for Regeneration
NDC	New Deal for Communities
NRF	Neighbourhood Renewal Fund
NRU	Neighbourhood Renewal Unit
ONS	Office for National Statistics
PAT	Policy Action Team
PFI	Private Finance Initiative
RDA	Regional Development Agency
SEU	Social Exclusion Unit
SRB	Single Regeneration Budget
UDC	Urban Development Corporation

Introduction

Bridgefields

"… a portrait of continuing government failure to understand people in poverty." (local vicar)

The journey that led to this book began in April 1999, in Bridgefields[1], Blackburn, Lancashire. Bridgefields is a 1970s council estate: modern three-bedroomed houses in neat cul-de-sacs, backing on to pedestrian alleyways and communal play areas. It is right on the edge of the town, and has stunning moorland views. A frequent bus service links the estate to the town centre, 15 minutes away. When I visited it, I found a strong sense of community, and a core of committed people, helping each other out and getting involved in estate life: running youth groups, social activities, pensioners' lunches, a food co-op and a credit union. The facilities available to residents were extensive: a modern and well-equipped community and employment centre, workshops, a family centre, health centre, library, youth centre, award-winning youth project, church-run community house, top-quality football pitch and hard court play area, as well as two primary schools.

"… lovely houses." (Bridgefields resident)

The primary school, with moorland views. "All this countryside, it's lovely." (Bridgefields resident)

But Bridgefields was not seen as a neighbourhood of choice for many people. In April 1999, more than one third of its 700 homes were boarded up, with some streets almost completely empty. Some houses had been seriously vandalised, with evidence of fire setting, missing roof tiles and fences and extensive graffiti. Piles of rubbish lay in the gardens of empty homes and there was litter around the estate in general. It was an appalling living environment.

Bridgefields residents also faced another disadvantage – the stigma attached to their address. A local employer described how some firms regarded estate residents with suspicion and declined to employ them; a community development worker related how children's self-esteem was damaged when they transferred to secondary school and were looked down on as "that

"If you live in a house where yours is the only one of six or seven not boarded up, what does this do to your morale ... just living in a place like this takes all your energy."
(Bridgefields resident)

"... a good estate gone to ruin." *(Bridgefields resident)*

"... a nice place to live is what people want. It would lift everybody's confidence."
(Bridgefields resident)

Bridgefields lot", and residents spoke of their difficulty getting insurance, credit or bank accounts. "I can't even get a TV on hire purchase, it's very degrading" (resident). When we asked residents and local workers what image people outside had of the estate, they said:

"Why don't they just put a wall round it and call it Bridgefields penitentiary?"

"Am I safe to bring my car on?"

"Giro city."

"The leper colony just outside the city where we visit occasionally and throw things at them."

I spent a week in Bridgefields, talking to residents and frontline workers, and to regeneration and housing professionals, learning about its history and its current troubles. It was a story of decline almost since the birth of the estate in 1974, when it was the last public housing to be built in the town. As was the case in many other towns and cities, the slum clearance programme that gave rise to estates like Bridgefields also created an artificial demand for housing, as large numbers of people were displaced from slum dwellings. With the programme complete, demand fell and within just a few years, homes on the estate became difficult to let. In fact, rumour has it that vacancies were advertised as far afield as Scotland. A number of 'problem families' with severe social problems and in real housing need moved in. One long-standing resident said: "It very quickly became seen as a place where you were put". Moreover, although some of the original residents remembered that the new houses and the estate environment were "lovely", it was also isolated. There was no bus service at the time, nor any shops, community centre, doctor's surgery or any other day-to-day facilities. Some of the original residents quickly moved away, thus fuelling the demand problem.

By the early 1980s, the population of the estate had already begun to change, and this coincided with severe job losses in the local economy, as manufacturing firms made redundancies.

"… local industry just collapsed. There was no local employment. The make-up of the estate changed from being wage earners to unemployed." (resident)

For a time, the estate experienced extreme poverty. Many families struggled on very low incomes and social problems abounded. Still there were few facilities. Juvenile crime escalated. A small number of extended criminal families dominated certain closes, intimidating other residents and even driving some away. Bridgefields gained local notoriety:

"The bad press image started [in the late 1980s] with weekly headlines. There was bad crime on the estate but the press really reinforced the bad image. People started to find that they couldn't get insurance. As the negative perception built up, the population changed because the only people who came here didn't want to be here. People came here intending to move off. That's when the money started to get pumped in." (resident)

"In 1988, when the family centre opened, people had no jobs. They couldn't afford to run their heating and some families had no cookers or carpets. It was much worse than other areas in Blackburn – a real culture shock for the social workers. We saw 163 families in the first three months. The problems were immense. There was a lot of crime and people were trapped. They all wanted to move off." (family support worker)

The late 1980s saw significant investment in housing improvements, through Estate Action, and in new facilities – the new community centre, library, health centre and shops. Although the facilities helped, the amount of money being thrown at Bridgefields added to its notoriety. Several residents commented that "no one stopped to ask what the problem was", that the improvements were "done to" the estate. The community was demoralised and the estate unpopular. It continued to be difficult to let.

Events of the 1990s compounded the problem. Council housing continued to decline in popularity, new homes were built on the edge of the town and the economy picked up, making it easier for people to move. Housing surpluses opened up on other council estates and in the older private sector housing in Blackburn. The number of empty properties on Bridgefields escalated. In 1998, the council decided to suspend lettings while the future of the area was debated. They entered negotiations with a private developer and a housing association about possible redevelopment, which would leave only about 250 homes in council ownership, some new homes for private sale, and some for housing association rent and shared ownership. Consultations began over the estate redesign, and plans were developed to turn the shops into a village centre, with new leisure facilities attracting people from further afield. While negotiations continued, many of the more transient and problematic families moved away, some by choice and others evicted. The estate 'quietened down', with only the longer-standing and committed residents remaining. Funding from the Single Regeneration Budget (SRB) was used to employ a community coordinator to manage the regeneration process and to develop resident involvement. A core group of active residents got involved in working groups looking at Bridgefields' physical, social and economic infrastructure. It became, in the words of one professional, "a strong community committed to changing things". Although the bad reputation remained, several workers described coming to the estate and thinking "what's the problem?", surprised to find little resemblance to the stories that they had heard.

Economic and social problems had diminished but were still higher than average. Many households were still on low incomes, with a large number of lone parents, and many men either unemployed or in part-time or temporary low-paid work. Staff at the employment centre reported the need for skills to be upgraded, but also on a lack of well-paid, secure work in the area: "It's not a benefit culture – it's just that the jobs aren't attractive, especially for lone parents, because the wages aren't enough to cover the childcare". Local headteachers reported low attendance and aspiration. One said: "Education is not on everyone's agenda. Some of them just expect to be on the dole. The school tries to encourage them and some have got on and really done well, but there aren't enough role models for getting up for work. Some Year 6 pupils seem to think 'what's the point, there aren't any jobs'". Staff at the health centre remarked on high levels of depressive illness, poor diets because people could not afford expensive foods, and high rates of infection due to weakened immune systems. Youth and family workers described the need for support with alcohol and drug problems, isolated parents struggling to cope, and angry alienated young people who felt undervalued and excluded. These problems did not affect every household, by any means, but they were significant in number and demanded intensive public investment to offer the support that was needed.

By the time of my visit in 1999, the uncertainty over the estate's future was having its own effect. As plans changed and delays mounted, many residents lost confidence in the ability of the council to secure their future. They felt that estate services such as housing repairs and street cleaning had been allowed to run down. Some suspected that the council had given up on the estate and would rather see the land sold:

> "What we want to know is what's happening to our houses. We're not being told the truth. Bridgefields has become a political battleground." (resident)

> "Lots of people are keen to stay if the houses are done up. But what will actually happen is that people will leave. They think the council

is delaying on purpose to make them move off. They've given up on the regeneration – there's a total lack of confidence in the council and people just don't believe it will happen. People are losing their pride. Maybe 70% would want to go now. People have stuck through some very bad times and now they're leaving – because of the council." (resident)

After all the past troubles, the uncertainty and powerlessness of the present was the last straw. Some long-standing residents began to leave. Others, determined to stay, planned a protest march on the Town Hall[2].

Bridgefields made a profound impression on me. In the space of 25 years, a place that had symbolised renewal, modernisation and a better living environment had come to symbolise disillusionment and dereliction. It was, in the words of one interviewee, "a place which doesn't meet the agenda of anyone anymore". The story of its rapid decline suggests that it had only ever done so for a very short time, if at all. Now, its future was uncertain, its environment poor, and its notoriety widespread. Its residents, many of them on low incomes, faced a double disadvantage: the disadvantage of poverty and the disadvantage of place. Events originating way beyond the neighbourhood – the decline of manufacturing industry, an increase in social problems, and an oversupply of social housing – had combined to concentrate poverty on the estate. Its social infrastructure had come under intolerable strain, and neighbourhood conditions had declined. People struggling on low incomes had to contend with crime, vandalism and an environment strewn with rubbish and litter. While a core of long-standing residents battled on, they acknowledged that social networks had shrunk as people became suspicious or antagonistic towards their neighbours, and increasingly reliant on established ties. The reputation of the estate in the outside world had plummeted, creating another barrier to success, and closing the neighbourhood in on itself. Deteriorating conditions and a sinking reputation made Bridgefields unattractive to newcomers, such that only those with limited financial choice came to live there, while many of those with more choice moved away. Thus the concentration of poverty had caused neighbourhood problems, which in turn both created obstacles to an escape from poverty, and led to further concentration. The effect of poverty and the effect of place had become intertwined. Public investment had been too little, too late, and while in one sense it had helped to tackle the problems of the estate, in another it had contributed to a sense of exclusion and demoralisation.

A widespread and growing problem

This was a depressing story but it was not an isolated one. Most estimates suggest that in the late 1990s there were several thousand neighbourhoods like Bridgefields. A Department of the Environment study found 1,370 deprived council estates (Price Waterhouse, 1997). The 1996 English House Condition

Survey (DETR, 1998) identified at least 3,000 neighbourhoods of one hundred or more homes with concentrated problems of run-down, vacant or derelict housing or vandalism and graffiti. The 'ACORN' market research classification of residential neighbourhoods, using 1991 Census data, found 4,000 neighbourhoods with postcodes in the four poorest categories – that is, 'council estate residents, better-off homes', 'council estate residents, high unemployment', 'council estate residents', 'greatest hardship', and 'multi-ethnic, low-income areas', and 1,600 in the poorest three categories. Working from these estimates, the government's Social Exclusion Unit reported that there were up to 4,000 neighbourhoods that were "pockets of deprivation where the problems of unemployment and crime are acute and hopelessly tangled up with poor health, housing and education. They have become no-go areas for some and no-exit zones for others" (SEU, 1998, p 9). These were neighbourhoods where the economic and social problems confronting many residents contributed to what the New Labour government has called a "poverty of aspiration and opportunity … to learn, to work, to look after your family, to lead a fully active life, and to make the most of what society has to offer" (DfEE, 1999). They were areas of concentrated social exclusion[3].

Moreover, there was evidence that the gap between these neighbourhoods and others was growing. While the divisions between declining cities and industrial areas and small towns and cities and rural areas had been gradually widening for several decades, the 1980s saw a particular increase in intra-urban polarisation, with increasing contrasts between poorer and more affluent electoral wards *within* cities (Hills, 1995). It appeared that poverty was becoming more concentrated in certain neighbourhoods.

The scale and escalation of the problem meant that by the time I visited Bridgefields in 1999, dealing with the problems of these neighbourhoods had become a political priority. The New Labour government elected in 1997 argued that tackling them effectively was a vital element in its mission to bring Britain together as a nation, reducing social exclusion. Neighbourhoods of concentrated poverty were socially unjust, economically wasteful and a major burden on the public purse. It was, said the Prime Minister:

> … simply not acceptable that so many children go to school hungry, or not at all, that so many teenagers grow up with no real prospect of a job and that so many pensioners are afraid to go out of their homes. It shames us as a nation, it wastes lives and we all have to pay the costs of dependency and social division. (Tony Blair, in SEU, 1998, Foreword)

In September 1998, the government produced a report on the problems of poor neighbourhoods, *Bringing Britain together* (SEU, 1998) and established 18 policy action teams (PATs), across Whitehall, to develop a National Strategy for Neighbourhood Renewal. It announced new funding for poor areas in England:

action zones for health and education, an early years programme, Sure Start, and the New Deal for Communities, a locally managed, comprehensive 10-year renewal programme for some of the poorest neighbourhoods, costing £50 million of government money per neighbourhood. In Wales, 1998 saw the launch of a new programme known as 'People in Communities', aimed at tackling social disadvantage by involving local communities and coordinating the work of agencies at neighbourhood level. In Scotland, Social Inclusion Partnerships were established for 48 disadvantaged areas, with extra funding from a new Social Inclusion Partnership Fund but with the principal aim of bending mainstream programmes to better serve the needs of the poorest neighbourhoods. There was, it seemed, a new determination to bring an end to the problems that had beset Bridgefields and other neighbourhoods like it.

Ideology and policy

An effective policy response, however, has to be built on an understanding of the problem to be tackled. So why was Bridgefields in the state that it was? Why were poverty concentrations deepening? What was driving neighbourhood decline and what would reverse it? Could public policy make any difference and what would it have to do?

These are the questions that this book sets out to answer, drawing on the experience of Bridgefields and 11 other areas with similar levels of deprivation. But they are not new questions. As Glennerster et al (1999) have pointed out, industrial Britain has always had poor neighbourhoods, and there have been numerous explanations of their origins and the causes of their problems. These explanations provide lenses through which the experiences of the areas in this book can be viewed.

One perspective is that area problems are merely a symptom of the wider structures of society, economic and social. Poor areas exist because the poor exist. Those who can will always choose to live in 'better' neighbourhoods with high quality housing, better amenities, a greener, more spacious environment, and good transport links, leaving the poor in the least advantaged neighbourhoods. Mass housebuilding programmes, whether the original urban expansion of the Industrial Revolution or the slum clearance programmes of the 20th century, have promoted residential segregation by building neighbourhoods of similar type and tenure, swathes of poor quality terraced housing, council housing estates or high-rise blocks. But the real problem is the division between rich and poor. If that gap grows, poor neighbourhoods will be correspondingly poorer. If it closes, the problems of poor neighbourhoods will be less marked in comparison with those of others. For this reason, Peter Townsend famously argued that area-based policies, in themselves, could not solve the problems of poor areas, because "The pattern of inequality within them is set nationally" (Townsend, 1979, p 560).

This 'macro' explanation of area problems has been popular both on the Right and the Left. From a free market perspective, poor areas can be seen as essential to the operation of markets for housing and labour. Poor residential areas, cheap to enter, provide a foothold for newcomers, an opportunity for immigrants to establish themselves with low housing costs (Park, 1952; Burgess, 1967), as well a chance for 'urban pioneers' or gentrifiers to buy and renovate properties, forcing up values. They also provide homes for the 'reserve army of labour', low-paid and low-skilled workers who are needed in times of economic expansion and redundant in times of decline. These areas will suffer periods of decline, but will also be pulled up by the rising tide of a growing economy. State intervention is helpful only to support private investment, not to interfere with the operation of the market. From a left wing perspective, poor areas are the inevitable consequence of an economic system that distributes wealth unevenly. Economic growth is unlikely to rescue poor areas, because its benefits will largely accrue to the rich, not to the poor. Growth tends to promote, not diminish, inequality, and therefore to perpetuate the divisions between areas as well as between individuals. The only way to transform the fortunes of poor areas is to transform the fortunes of the poor, by redistributing economic gains and not just by creating them.

However, there have also been 'micro' explanations of area problems, suggesting that part of the problem at least is caused at local level. One long-standing and controversial view, put forward most recently by the polemicist Charles Murray (1996), is what has been labelled the 'social pathology explanation' (Hill, 2000). Murray and others purport that the problems of poor neighbourhoods arise in part from the moral deficiencies of the poor. Residents of such neighbourhoods, they argue, develop a 'culture of poverty', with an expectation of welfare benefits, normalisation of illegal behaviour and a different set of values from those of 'mainstream' society. The answer, they suggest, is to withdraw state support, to break down the 'welfare culture' and to avoid throwing good money after bad.

This view has largely been rejected in Britain, certainly as a basis for policy. Those who have argued that local factors are important have focused not on individual pathologies but on the characteristics of poor areas themselves, and the way in which they can compound individual disadvantages. There are a variety of theories of 'area effects' (for useful reviews, see Jencks and Mayer, 1990; Ellen and Turner, 1997; Buck, 2001). Some concentrate on the physical or institutional characteristics of areas – isolated locations, poor quality housing, or worse services than in more advantaged areas where spending power is greater and residents have more 'clout' to demand effective public services. Others point to the relationships between poor areas and other areas, such as discrimination against residents, or losing out to other areas in competition for resources. Finally, qualitative studies (Wilson, 1997) have produced evidence of the effect of reduced social networks in low-income neighbourhoods, such that residents lack access to people who could help them to find jobs, training, or leisure opportunities outside the neighbourhood. Importantly, Jargowsky (1996) demonstrated that some of these effects disappear in times of economic upturn, showing that it is not the moral deficiency of those living in poverty that holds them back, but the opportunities available to them.

All of these theories of 'area effects' point to the conclusion that area problems cannot be solved simply by 'macro' policies, but need to be tackled by targeted programmes to address the compounding effects of neighbourhood. And, indeed, these kinds of programmes have had a long history in this country. The first area-based programmes had their origins in the 1960s. New Labour's policies represented a renewed interest but not an original approach. Reviewing this history puts current policy in context and tells us something about the way the problems of places like Bridgefields had been conceived, up to the point at which we began to study them in 1999.

Thirty years of area-based policy

In its first phase, in the 1960s, policies towards poor neighbourhoods appeared to be based on the idea that problems were both local and social. The policy response consisted of improved services and living conditions, along with the provision of compensatory services, such as extra educational help. The Urban Programme, launched in 1968, funded social and welfare projects in deprived areas; pre-school provision, advice centres and community facilities, and the Community Development Projects (CDPs), launched the following year, were designed to address the interlocking problems of poor areas by improving the coordination and management of local services. It seemed that the problems of the poorest neighbourhoods were to be sorted out by effective management and by ameliorative projects.

As one of the CDPs reported:

> When the community development projects were set up in the sixties, it was generally believed in official circles that widespread poverty and deprivation in Britain were things of the past. The age of affluence was upon us ... poverty could be seen as a problem of inadequate individuals in particular places; it could be tackled by special social programmes designed to bring these people and places into the mainstream of British society. Poverty was a marginal issue of conscience – the real problem was how to manage economic growth. (Benwell Community Development Project, 1978, p 5)[4]

In a sense, this could be seen as a 'social pathology' model, but the Urban Programme and CDP projects, improving services and coordinating management, also reflected an acknowledgement of the weakness of public institutions in providing for the needs of residents in the poorest neighbourhoods. They remedied some of the problems that Bridgefields later experienced: lack of transport, meeting places and other community facilities.

However, 10 years later, it was clear that far from entering a period of sustained prosperity in which every area could prosper with a little help from central government, Britain's economy was in decline, with its traditional industries of coal, steel and shipbuilding and its newer manufacturing industries all struggling to compete internationally. Competition and technological change were causing large-scale job losses, as firms closed or rationalised to stay in business. Unemployment in areas dependent on these industries was rising at an alarming rate. It was no longer possible to see the problem as anything other than economic. For the next 15 years, the question became how, not whether, to intervene to promote economic revitalisation.

In 1977 the Labour government's White Paper, *Policy for the inner cities* (DoE, 1977), and the 1978 Inner Urban Areas Act signalled a change in focus from social action to economic regeneration. As a start, the Urban Programme was recast, with more of the funding going to fewer (58) very deprived authorities (the Urban Programme Authorities), and with a greater emphasis on place-based schemes, such as industrial estate development, rather than the people-based schemes of the previous programme. But by 1979, Labour was out of office and the Conservatives were in. Under the Thatcher governments from 1979 to 1990, the emphasis was on restoring the economic viability of poor neighbourhoods by stimulating private enterprise, not by public investment in infrastructure. Policy efforts were concentrated on key flagship locations. From 1981 the government established 11 Urban Development Corporations (UDCs), each operating for 10 years, publicly funded but non-governmental organisations with planning gain and compulsory purchase powers, and a remit to create industrial and commercial space and an infrastructure that would stimulate private sector investment. It also experimented with Enterprise Zones, covering combinations of 22 local authority areas, to test the degree to which industrial and commercial regeneration could be promoted by rate exemptions and capital allowances for firms, and by the streamlining of planning and administrative procedures. In 1986, Inner City Task Forces were established in 22 areas within the Urban Programme Authorities, which had both high unemployment and industrial development potential, with the aim of boosting economic opportunities through job creation, business support and training. The idea was that economic revitalisation would bring 'trickle-down' benefits to the poor, such that these areas would be self-sustaining without the need for extensive public intervention.

This is not to say that the problems of day-to-day living in these areas were neglected. Declining residential environments were addressed through Estate Action (1985-94), an improvement programme for over 500 council housing estates, about three quarters of which were within the Urban Programme Authorities. But just as the economic development programmes were aimed at restoring economic viability, Estate Action was designed to "transform unpopular properties into decent homes" (DoE, 1996, quoted in Robson et al, 1994, p 65). It was supposed to restore their market position, not just to patch them up.

These programmes were not without their successes. But by the early 1990s it was clear that they would not resolve the problem. First, the experience of areas such as London's Docklands, transformed from industrial dereliction to global financial centre and high class housing area, demonstrated that economic benefits did not necessarily trickle down to the poor of their own accord. Long-term unemployment and high levels of economic inactivity did not leave people ready to take up the opportunities afforded by the new office blocks, hotels and restaurants. Local residents lost out in competition to those from further afield. Second, physical and economic regeneration was not necessarily bringing social benefits. Problems such as family breakdown, crime, disorder and substance misuse persisted. And third, it was evident that the number of poor areas was extensive, and not just confined to a few high profile locations.

In the 1990s, therefore, the basis of area programmes was changed again. They were to be comprehensive, combining economic revival with physical renewal and social welfare projects. Social welfare interventions were once given a higher profile. In 1991, the government launched City Challenge, covering 31 areas, each with a fixed budget of £37.5 million over five years. This was followed in 1994 by the SRB, made up of 'top-sliced' funds from other departments, including Estate Action, and delivering regeneration programmes through local multi-agency partnerships. Unlike City Challenge, which was limited to the Urban Programme Authorities, the SRB was allocated via a competitive bidding process into which any area could bid. Finally, there was New Labour's New Deal for Communities programme, which, while different in some ways, as I demonstrate in Chapter Seven, was very much an extension of the holistic area-based approach of the rest of the decade.

Critically, all these programmes were local – not explicitly linked to broader local authority or regional regeneration strategies, and not underpinned by any interventionist regional economic policy, which effectively finished in 1979 with the Conservative abolition of the regional economic planning boards. These were 'micro' policies. Of course, the existence of area-based policy per se does not necessarily imply, as some have suggested, a belief in 'micro' explanations as the whole reason for decline and recovery. Smith (1999), among others, has noted a number of reasons for area-based policies that do not rest on there being local reasons for local problems:

- there are equity grounds for levelling up services in the poorest areas;
- spatial concentration makes area-based programmes an efficient way of targeting resources;
- focusing activity can make more impact than dissipating it;
- area-targeted programmes can more easily adopt a 'bottom-up' approach which can result in more efficient identification of problems and delivery of solutions;
- area programmes may be a good way to pilot initiatives intended for wider roll-out;
- local programmes may lead to increased confidence and capacity to participate in the community.

Nevertheless, it is also the case that, for most of their history, area-based programmes in this country have been pursued in the absence of any 'macro' policy to address more fundamental causes of area problems. The rhetoric of 'regeneration', and the local basis of programmes, has given the impression that poor areas could be transformed, or at least significantly ameliorated, by local interventions.

Enduring problems and enduring questions

Whether or not this was true in principle, no one coming afresh to the story of Bridgefields could be convinced that it was working in practice. While facilities had improved and Estate Action had helped with physical improvements, the area had certainly not been transformed economically or socially. In fact, it was quite the opposite. Despite the efforts of urban policy makers, poverty appeared to have become more concentrated. Many of those who could leave the estate had done so and not been replaced. Although unemployment had fallen, labour market problems appeared still to be entrenched. The gap between this neighbourhood and others seemed to have become wider, even though absolute poverty had patently diminished. Despite considerable efforts to provide local services, neighbourhood conditions had declined, and residents were still excluded from provisions such as decent shops and financial services that others might take for granted. And, despite heavy council investment, trust in local democracy had all but broken down.

As the New Labour government launched its new programmes for neighbourhood regeneration, therefore, it was far from clear that another round of area-based programmes would do the trick. With areas like Bridgefields in just as bad a state as ever, there were still important questions to be answered about the reasons for area decline and the mechanisms by which real 'regeneration' could be effected.

First and most importantly, what was it that was causing apparently continuous decline and an increasing gap from more advantaged areas? Is it the case that neighbourhood decline is essentially an economic problem? Or has it been created by other forces: the slum clearance and mass social housing programmes that created estates like Bridgefields, for example; the failure of public management and local democracy; the impact of wider social changes such as the growth in car ownership or the availability of illegal drugs; or the resistance of British society to giving equal opportunities to people from minority ethnic groups? Are the problems that manifest themselves locally, such as joblessness or low housing demand, essentially local problems, such as a spatial mismatch between jobs and people, or a particularly unpopular type of housing or environment? If so, they might be capable of solution at neighbourhood level. Or do they reflect wider problems, at city-wide or regional level, necessitating wider strategic responses rather than neighbourhood interventions? Or, at a higher level still, are they simply the inevitable consequence of structural changes in housing and labour markets, rather than their spatial distribution? Can neighbourhood problems only be resolved by changes at national or international level? And whatever their fundamental causes, are local concentrations of poverty self-reinforcing, through inadequate services, weak social networks, learned behaviours or cultures of poverty? Are there 'area effects'? How much can these problems be tackled by area-based initiatives?

Second, does it make sense to consider 'worst neighbourhoods' as though their problems are common, or are there in fact major differences between poor neighbourhoods in the North and in the South, inner-urban neighbourhoods and small towns, ethnically mixed areas and ethnically homogenous ones, areas of public housing and areas of low-income private renting? What is the extent of difference, and what explains it? Are the trajectories of these neighbourhoods the same or are they beginning to diverge, as one might expect, if problems are essentially economic? Are there places where urban policy has worked, where private investment, government, local authorities or local people have been able to halt or reverse decline? What is it that has worked, and what do the experiences of different areas tell us about the extent to which policy needs to be differentiated rather than universal?

These are the issues that *Poverty Street* explores. It tells the stories of 12 disadvantaged areas: inner-city areas, outer estates, and small towns in all parts of England and Wales[5], from Newcastle in the North to the tip of Kent in the South, and draws on the experiences of these scattered and diverse neighbourhoods to build an understanding of the reasons for area decline, the current directions of change, and the bases for area regeneration policy.

The material for the study was gathered in two phases: one in 1999 and one in 2001-02, enabling a view of the areas before New Labour government's policies had begun to have an impact, and then again two years later when changes had begun to be made. Chapter One explains how the 12 areas were selected, to represent poor areas more generally, and how the data was collected. Chapters Two to Six then paint the picture up until the start of the study in 1999. Chapters Two and Three describe the history of the areas, telling the story of their decline during the 1970s, 1980s and 1990s. They concentrate on 'macro' explanations: economic changes, population trends and housing policy. Chapters Four and Five look at 'micro' explanations: the failure of public services to manage the areas effectively in the face of decline and the impact of decline and of management failure on social interaction and on neighbourhood reputations. Chapter Six examines policy responses, cataloguing attempts at regeneration, with a particular focus on the initiatives of the 1990s.

The second half of the book takes the story forward from 1999. Chapter Seven examines the new policies of the New Labour government, not just the area-based policies already mentioned here, but also the National Strategy for Neighbourhood Renewal, launched in 2001, and wider urban, regional and housing policies. Chapter Eight revisits Bridgefields, examining changes on that estate in close up, and Chapters Nine, Ten and Eleven take a broader view, looking at the impact of the new policy regime in the light of continuing trends in the economy, population movements and housing markets. They paint a picture of positive local changes, of serious underlying problems impeding recovery, and also of diverging area fortunes. Finally, Chapter Twelve reflects on the lessons learned from this journey around the country's 'poverty map', and draws conclusions about its enduring 'poverty gap'.

Notes

[1] All place names in this book have been changed. We decided that it was important to name the towns and cities in which the neighbourhoods were located, in order to locate them in their wider urban and regional context, but that it was not helpful to reveal the actual place names, since attracting attention to certain neighbourhoods as being 'deprived' might add to their notoriety and further disadvantage their residents. We acknowledge that those familiar with the towns and cities may be able to identify the neighbourhoods, and for this reason some quotations have not been attributed or have been loosely attributed (for example, youth worker rather than youth centre manager), where there is a risk that they might identify an individual.

[2] Further instalments in the protracted negotiations over the future of Bridgefields are reported in Chapter Eight. This chapter records the positions at the time of my initial visit in 1999.

[3] The term 'social exclusion' came into widespread use in British politics in the mid-1990s. Its use is contested (see Levitas, 1998; Byrne, 1999; Lee and Murie, 1999; Hills et al, 2002). While some have argued that the term is more useful than 'poverty' or 'multiple deprivation', because it captures notions of relativity and of agency, and of the process of exclusion as well as the state of exclusion, others have suggested that its use is a political convenience to avoid addressing issues of relative poverty directly and to focus on integration rather than on redistribution. The question of the causes of social exclusion is an important one for the debate about poor neighbourhoods and is discussed in later chapters. However, for simplicity, official definitions of social exclusion are used here, implying a broad use of the term incorporating the notions of multiple deprivation, lack of opportunity to participate, persistent problems and a sense of alienation or marginalisation.

[4] Benwell Community Development Project was one of the 12 experimental CDPs set up by the Home Office to examine the nature and causes of urban poverty. Benwell is not one of the areas reported on in this book.

[5] For practical reasons and because of problems of data comparability and different legislative contexts, it was decided to confine the scope of the study to England and Wales and not to include Scotland.

ONE

The 12 disadvantaged areas

The study and the areas

Work on this book began in 1998, with the selection of 12 areas to study. It was an unusual undertaking, as area studies in the past have tended to take one of two alternative approaches. Either they have drawn on statistics from a very large number of areas, such as the Social Exclusion Unit's *Bringing Britain together*, (1998), to map and quantify the national problem, or they have been based on detailed sociological investigation of just one neighbourhood. Examples include Young and Willmott's famous study of East End life (1962), Coates and Silburn's work on Nottingham (1970), and Rex and Moore's analysis of change in inner Birmingham (1967). Recent policy interest in the problems of poor neighbourhoods has spawned a number of projects based on small area case studies, such as the Joseph Rowntree Foundation's investigations of neighbourhood images and social cohesion (Forrest and Kearns, 1999) and housing abandonment (Power and Mumford, 1999). However, such studies have typically drawn on three or four cases, and not as many as 12, and funding determines that they are rarely longitudinal.

It was the Economic and Social Research Council's (ESRC) 10-year funding for the Centre for Analysis of Social Exclusion (CASE) that presented us with an opportunity to take a different approach[1]. CASE adopted the monitoring and understanding of neighbourhood change as one of its core longitudinal projects, under the direction of Professor Anne Power. The work drew directly on Power's two influential studies of change on social housing estates: *Swimming against the tide* (Power and Tunstall, 1995), which remains the most significant attempt to document neighbourhood conditions in the UK across a range of areas over time, and *Estates on the edge*, an account of the social consequences of mass housing in northern Europe (Power, 1997). Like these studies, the current research was premised on the belief that it is essential to build a picture from the bottom up, based on the detailed stories of particular areas and neighbourhoods, and that it is vital to follow the same places over time.

However, in order to draw wider lessons for policy, we needed to be able to talk about poor neighbourhoods in general, and not just about specific neighbourhoods. We needed to show the similarities and differences between different types of neighbourhoods, the different influences at work in the North and South, inner- and outer-city, predominantly white neighbourhoods and ethnically mixed ones, and neighbourhoods of owner-occupation and social housing. No fewer than 12 areas, it was decided, would be necessary to reflect this range of characteristics.

But what are 'areas', or 'neighbourhoods' as they are more commonly referred to in academic and policy circles? How big are they and on what basis should their boundaries be drawn? Objectively, their attributes clearly vary across different spatial scales. Housing types, for example, might vary across a few metres, whereas school quality might vary across school catchment areas or even across local authority areas (Galster, 2001). Subjectively, areas and neighbourhoods mean different things to different people at different times, as each individual's activities, networks and travel patterns shape their concept of their neighbourhood (Massey, 1994). Kearns and Parkinson (2001) have argued that neighbourhood exists at three different levels: home area, relevant for issues of familiarity and community; locality, for service provision and the housing market; and urban district or region, for employment connections, leisure or extended social interaction. But wherever the boundary is drawn, what happens to neighbourhoods and to people within neighbourhoods will be influenced both by in-neighbourhood and out-neighbourhood factors. Different spatial levels overlap and interlock. Glennerster et al (1999) suggest that influences within neighbourhoods, such as the family, home and peer group, can be described as similar to 'the layers of an onion'. Influences crossing more than one neighbourhood are like 'overlapping rings' and influences of wider areas and agencies that subsume neighbourhood can be thought of as a 'chain effect'. Thus the influence of labour markets, for example, is not entirely determined at district or regional level, but also through the effects of locality and home area employment and training opportunities, local histories and expectations of employment, job-finding networks and peer interactions (Wilson, 1987).

Once neighbourhoods are seen not just as physical spaces but as complex and overlapping webs of social relationships, each serving a different purpose, the impossibility of defining them by drawing fixed boundaries becomes clear. But the study of place demands a degree of boundedness, especially when places are being compared with one another. We decided to look at three main spatial levels, and within each to adopt broad definitions of place that made sense to local people and were also measurable in statistical terms. Our bottom layer consisted of 12 'neighbourhoods', defined as "made up of several thousand people" (SEU, 2001a) and identifiable in broad terms to people who lived there. Each had a population of between 1,000 and 7,000 at the 1991 Census. They were social housing estates, small towns, or groups of city streets delineated by natural or man-made boundaries, housing type or tenure, socioeconomic or ethnic mix, history, or a combination of all of these factors.

Each of the 'neighbourhoods' was contained within a larger 'area' of about a 20,000 population, which in turn was included in a city or local authority area. We compared the trajectories of neighbourhoods with those of the areas around them, and the trajectories of areas with their wider cities or boroughs. For statistical purposes, we matched them to electoral wards, the smallest unit of analysis for most social data. Wards vary in size from about 1,000 to over 30,000 in population, so some areas contained more wards than others. Neighbourhoods were usually smaller than electoral wards and entirely contained within one ward, except in one case, where the neighbourhood contained two small wards. The 12 neighbourhoods, therefore, related to 13 electoral wards. The areas contained anything between one and seven wards, and comprised, in total, all or part of 44 electoral wards as at 1991. In some cases, these ward boundaries have subsequently changed.

Our selection was made after a thorough analysis of disadvantaged areas in England and Wales, which explored their definition, regional distribution and characteristics. This was carried out by Philip Noden at CASE in 1997-98, and is fully documented in a discussion paper produced at the time (Glennerster et al, 1999). Using two broad measures of deprivation based on 1991 Census data, the Breadline Britain Index and the proportion of people not working, studying or on a government training scheme, Noden's analysis identified 284 electoral wards (3% of all wards) that could be described as the most disadvantaged in England and Wales. These wards, which we labelled 'poverty wards', came within the top 5% of wards on both measures. They fell into six main categories using the Office for National Statistics area classification (Wallace and Denham, 1996): Inner London (33 wards), Areas with inner-city characteristics (72), Coastal Industry (39), Coalfields (34), Manufacturing (67), and Others (39). For our study, we selected two areas from each category, reflecting their regional distribution. For example, poverty wards in manufacturing areas were mainly found in the North West and West Midlands, so we selected one area from each of these regions.

We based our selection on 1991 Census data showing the characteristics of each of the 284 wards. We decided that the final sample should broadly match the overall distribution and characteristics of the 284 wards, but should include at least two areas on each of a selection of key area characteristics:

- inner-city, outer-city and other areas;
- mainly white areas, and ethnically mixed areas;
- areas dominated by social housing, and areas of mixed tenure;
- areas with high proportions of street housing, and those with high proportions of flats.

This process brought us to a shortlist of eligible areas, which we refined by site visits to over 20 towns and cities, guided by local authority representatives. These officers helped us to make a final choice and define sensible boundaries for our areas and neighbourhoods. Each area contained at least one of the 284 poverty wards but was not necessarily defined by ward boundaries if others (such as regeneration scheme boundaries or local authority sub-areas) made more sense locally. The neighbourhoods were chosen to reflect the characteristics of the areas in which they were situated, but we also attempted to build up a sample that would enable us to observe and compare a range of circumstances. We chose not only areas in decline or showing signs of decline, but ones which were stable, recovering or showing signs of recovery. We included a range of government programmes and local authority interventions.

Our final selection was as follows. All place names have been changed.

West-City in Hackney, inner London, a densely populated inner-city area consisting mainly of council flats. West-City had been a white working-class community but its character had changed rapidly in the 1990s, with a growing minority ethnic population, including significant numbers of Turks and Kurds, Africans and Asians, as well as an increase in higher income households, because of its proximity to central London. Within West-City, our study neighbourhood was **The Grove**. It was typical of West-City, a large council estate with poor quality flats in desperate need of improvement.

A high-rise block in West-City (Hackney). There were similar blocks in East-Docks (Newham)

East-Docks in the Docklands area of Newham, inner London. Like West-City, East-Docks was formerly a white working-class area but was becoming much more ethnically diverse. Extensively bomb-damaged in the war, it had been rebuilt with a mix of family houses and high-rise flats, and was mainly council owned. It suffered steep economic decline with the collapse of the docks in the 1970s and 1980s, but by the late 1990s had begun to recover, with a major new exhibition centre, hotels and retail developments. The study neighbourhood, **Phoenix Rise**, was a dense flatted estate with particularly severe economic problems.

Modern council housing in Riverlands (Nottingham)

Riverlands in Nottingham, an inner-city area very close to Nottingham's commercial centre and new business parks and leisure developments. It had two distinct parts: an area of Victorian terraced housing with a sizeable Asian minority, and an area of 1970s and 1980s council housing, with a sizeable African Caribbean minority. When we first visited, the physical environment was pleasant and levels of empty housing were low, but the area had serious economic deprivation and a long-standing reputation for drug dealing and crime. **Rosehill** was a small modern council-owned estate, a mixture of family houses and flats and one of the least popular estates in the area. One large block of flats and bedsits was particularly unpopular and attracted a transient population.

Modern council flats in The Valley (Sheffield)

The Valley in Sheffield. The Valley was an inner-city area with a mix of housing types; large Edwardian houses, Victorian terraces and modern council houses and flats, and high numbers of empty properties in pockets. It was close to the city centre but also to Sheffield's steelworks, and had suffered serious economic decline in the 1970s and 1980s. At the start of the study, unemployment was high and the area had a reputation for crime and drug dealing. An extremely diverse area, it had a white majority, a long-established Caribbean population, significant and growing Pakistani and Bangladeshi groups, as well as smaller minority ethnic groups such as Somalis and Yemenis. **East Rise** was a neighbourhood of mixed housing stock and mixed ethnicity.

Terraced homes in Broadways (Birmingham)

Middle Row, an inner-city area in Birmingham. Middle Row consisted mainly of Victorian terraced homes, many of them in poor condition and occupied by owners on very low incomes. The area had a predominantly Pakistani and Bangladeshi population and was extremely deprived, with very high unemployment and benefit dependency, and poor health. It was, nevertheless, a popular area among the Asian community and a vibrant one, with plentiful shops, restaurants and other small businesses. **Broadways**, a neighbourhood of several streets known by the name of the housing trust that once owned them, was typical of the area in its design, housing stock and socioeconomic problems.

Council homes in Saints' Walk (Knowsley), with new walls, railings and pavements funded by Estate Action

Overtown in Knowsley, Merseyside, a white working-class area consisting mainly of council housing estates built in the 1930s and 1940s. Employment on the nearby industrial estates collapsed during the 1970s and 1980s and the area had exceptionally high levels of worklessness, benefit dependency, lone parenthood and teen pregnancy. Housing demand was falling and there were pockets of empty housing. **Saints' Walk** was a small council estate with among the highest levels of deprivation. It suffered acute decline in the mid-1990s when drug dealing and intimidation drove some residents away, but was successfully 'cleaned up' by intensive policing and investment in the housing and environment, and was one of the more popular estates in the area by the time we visited it.

Shipview, overlooking the River Tyne in Newcastle. Shipview developed to serve the shipyards and consisted mainly of interwar council estates of family houses. It had a predominantly white population with high levels of unemployment and welfare dependency following the decline in the area's industrial base. Demand for council housing in the area was falling and there were unpopular pockets where some streets were almost entirely empty. **Sunnybank** was one of these neighbourhoods, a small estate on the edge of the area.

Family housing in Kirkside East (Leeds). The homes in Sunnybank (Newcastle) were of similar design

Kirkside East in Leeds. Kirkside East was a very large council estate, mainly consisting of family houses, but with some high-rise blocks and maisonettes. It was a predominantly white area which had high unemployment and benefit dependency, but was well placed to benefit from the economic boom in Leeds generally and from local jobs in a large new supermarket and shopping centre. **Southmead** was a particular part of the estate, bounded by major roads, which had long suffered from a particularly bad reputation in the city and had a higher concentration of deprivation than the area as a whole. It had additional problems with empty housing and a poor neighbourhood environment.

The declining main street in Borough View (Redcar and Cleveland)

Southside, on the banks of the River Tees in the Borough of Redcar and Cleveland. Southside was made up of three small adjoining towns forming one urban area. It had a predominantly white working-class population and depended for its employment on the huge steelworks, shipyards and chemical plants that still dominated the landscape. Massive industrial decline in the 1970s and 1980s led to depopulation and long-term unemployment. In the early to mid-1990s, parts of the area began to suffer severe crime and disorder and extensive housing abandonment. **Borough View**, a small town consisting of a council estate and several streets of Victorian terraces, was one of those neighbourhoods. While some problems had been tackled, parts of it were still in rapid decline at the end of the 1990s.

High Moor in Blackburn, Lancashire, a mixed part of the town stretching from close to the town centre, where it consisted mainly of privately owned Victorian terraced properties, to the edge of the town, where it incorporated interwar and modern social housing estates. The inner part had a growing Asian population while the outer part was predominantly white. Demand for council housing was low, while some Asian families were overcrowded in poor quality private homes they could not afford to repair. **Bridgefields**, the neighbourhood described earlier, was on the edge of High Moor and was its most notorious estate.

Fairfields, the upper part of one of the South Wales valleys, in the County Borough of Caerphilly. Fairfields consisted of a number of small towns and villages. It was formerly dependent on mining employment and then on heavy industry, which had also gone. Job losses led to a long period of population depletion. Unemployment and economic inactivity were high and confidence

and skill levels were low. The population was almost exclusively white, with many long-established families. **Valley Top** was the town at the head of the Valley, with several modern council housing estates (for which demand was low) as well as privately owned terraced stock and a declining town centre.

A council estate in Valley Top (Caerphilly)

Former hotel properties in Beachville (Kent)

Beachville, a seaside town in Thanet in Kent, including the town centre, an area of large Edwardian and Victorian properties formerly trading as hotels but now mainly converted to bed and breakfast (B&B) or hostel accommodation, a council housing estate and areas of private housing. Beachville had suffered from the decline of its main industry, tourism, and had high unemployment and low wages and house prices, as well as high levels of social deprivation, such as high proportions of children in care. **Sandyton** was the hotel area and had been in continuous decline since the 1960s. It was known for a time in the 1980s as 'Dole on the Sea' because of the high numbers of migrants living on unemployment benefits in its B&B hotels and hostels, and at the end of the 1990s was home to large numbers of refugees and asylum seekers from around the world.

Brief details of the areas and neighbourhoods are shown in Figure 1.1 for reference throughout the book.

Area characteristics

The extensive selection procedure ensured that, overall, the 12 areas were a good reflection of the 'poverty map' of England and Wales, which shows a heavy skew towards London and the North (Glennerster et al, 1999; DETR, 2000a). Ten of them were in the North East, North West, Merseyside, London or Wales. They reflected the concentration of poverty in cities and in old industrial areas (Philo, 1995; Green, 1996). Nine were in major conurbations, some of them in the inner-urban core, on average about a mile from the central business district, some in the 'outer core' (within the city boundary but further from the city centre) or on the city edge, bordering a major city. Of the three remaining areas, one was in a manufacturing town, one a former coalmining area and one a seaside resort (Table 1.1).

Our sample also reflected the characteristics of the poorest areas in 1991. Our initial analysis had shown that nearly two thirds (62.6%) of 'poverty wards' had 50% or more public housing. Nine of our 12 areas (75%) had more than 50% public housing in 1991, but there were also areas with a majority of owner-occupation, and ones with mixed tenure, including higher than average levels of private renting. The areas in the inner-urban core had a higher proportion of flats and three had some of the original Victorian red-brick terraces. As a result, they all contained high density neighbourhoods with dwellings close to one another and a lack of open space. The outer core and city edge areas typically had lower density housing, in spacious 1930s and 1940s estates (Table 1.2).

Figure 1.1: Brief description of areas and neighbourhoods

Local authority	Area (not real names)	Neighbourhood (not real names)
HACKNEY	*West-City* Adjacent to city. High proportion council housing. Business/market area. Some gentrification.	*The Grove* Large council estate. Poor quality housing stock. Higher proportion of older tenants and white people than rest of Hackney.
NEWHAM	*East-Docks* Formerly white working-class area, becoming more diverse. Council housing and industrial sites. Close to new business and transport. Potential for growth.	*Phoenix Rise* Council estate, mainly flats and maisonettes. Highest unemployment in area. Demand among lowest in borough. Higher turnover than other estates.
NOTTINGHAM	*Riverlands* Inner-city area adjacent to city centre. Sizable black and Asian population. High lone parenthood. Close to major redevelopments.	*Rosehill* Small 1970s council estate with shopping precinct and poor design. Bedsit/flat block attracts transient population.
SHEFFIELD	*The Valley* Adjacent to inner-city. Mixed area. Council flats (high voids) and other tenures. Some light industry. Mixed ethnicity.	*East Rise* Mixed tenure area. Poor quality private housing stock. Council flats – low demand. Mixed ethnicity. Pockets of drug/crime problems.
BIRMINGHAM	*Middle Row* Inner-city area. Mixed tenure. Large Asian minority. Exceptionally high unemployment. Poor health. Busy shopping/restaurant area.	*Broadways* Mixed tenure area of Victorian street property, much in poor condition. Asian majority (over 70%).
KNOWSLEY	*Overtown* Mainly council estates. Predominantly white. High unemployment, high lone parenthood. Low housing demand.	*Saints' Walk* Small council estate with severe socioeconomic problems. Successful action against drugs/intimidation. Recent estate improvements.

cont ...

Figure 1.1: contd.../

Local authority	Area (not real names)	Neighbourhood (not real names)
NEWCASTLE	*Shipview* Area close to river and docks. Mainly interwar council estates. Stable white working-class area. Low housing demand.	*Sunnybank* Small council estate in more affluent ward. Bad reputation. Starting to decline. Drugs problem and increasing voids.
LEEDS	*Kirkside East* Very large council estate. Predominantly white. Strong stable community. New shopping centre bringing employment.	*Southmead* Part of council estate. Higher proportion of large homes. Concentrated problems. Low housing demand. Environmental decay and voids.
REDCAR and CLEVELAND	*Southside* Three distinct communities built to serve industrial plants. Mixed tenure. Two had rapid major decline and were being regenerated. One starting to decline. High worklessness. Low housing demand.	*Borough View* Small town including council estate, housing association and private terraced housing. Major problems of crime, abandonment.
BLACKBURN	*High Moor* Area of mainly white council housing and some terraced streets with high Asian population.	*Bridgefields* 1970s council estate. Very bad reputation and severe voids problems. Much investment. Redevelopment plans.
CAERPHILLY	*Fairfields* Six towns/villages in upper valley. Former mining community. Poor transport links. Isolated. Mixed tenure.	*Valley Top* Strung-out town. Several council estates and private housing. Low attainment and high unemployment and economic activity.
THANET	*Beachville* Declining seaside town. Mixed tenures. Low-wage economy and high unemployment. Economic growth possibilities.	*Sandyton* Former hotel area. Many properties converted to houses in multiple occupation. Concentration of refugees, homeless.

Table 1.1: Location of the 12 areas

Location	Areas	Distance of area from city centre (miles)
Inner core areas	West-City (Hackney)[a]	2.5
	East-Docks (Newham)[a]	6.5
	Riverlands (Nottingham)	<1.0
	The Valley (Sheffield)	1.5
	Middle Row (Birmingham)	1.5
Outer core and city edge areas	Overtown (Knowsley, bordering Liverpool)	5.5
	Shipview (Newcastle)	2.5
	Kirkside East (Leeds)	4.0
	Southside (Redcar and Cleveland, bordering Middlesbrough)	2.5
Other areas (not in a city)	High Moor (Blackburn – manufacturing town)	
	Fairfields (Caerphilly – coalmining area)	
	Beachville (Thanet – seaside resort)	

Note: [a]Because London is so much bigger and has no defined 'city centre', inner core areas are further from the city centre (defined here as Trafalgar Square) than outer core areas in other cities.

Reflecting their location in the former industrial areas, most of the poverty wards (70%) were predominantly white areas in 1991, with less than the average proportion of people from minority ethnic backgrounds, although this is lower than the proportion of predominantly white wards in England and Wales overall (88%). Our sample of 12 over-represented ethnically mixed areas compared with poverty wards in general. Half of the 12 had above average minority ethnic populations in 1991.

The sample reflects the diversity of ethnic communities in England and Wales: Middle Row in Birmingham had a majority ethnic population, mainly Pakistani and Bangladeshi. The two London neighbourhoods had more African and Caribbean people, with West-City also having significant Turkish and Kurdish minorities. The Valley in Sheffield, and Riverlands in Nottingham, had long-established African Caribbean communities, as well as sizeable Asian populations and more recently arrived minority groups from countries such as the Yemen and Sierra Leone, and from Eastern Europe. These ethnically diverse areas were mainly in inner cities (the only exception being in the Lancashire town of Blackburn). All of the outer core and city edge areas were predominantly white.

Once we had selected our areas, we could begin to follow them in detail. We used two methods, one qualitative, one quantitative. The quantitative approach involved tracking social statistics through which the fortunes of the areas could be compared with areas around them, cities, regions and the country as a whole. We used Census data from 1971, 1981 and 1991 to give a historical picture of continuity and change until the beginning of the 1990s, and administrative data to track changes thereafter. Some of the data were drawn from publicly available national datasets such as labour market statistics, the annual scan of the Income

Table 1.2: Housing and ethnic mix in the 12 areas (1991)

	% purpose- built flats	% social housing	Main housing types	% Black or Asian population
Inner core areas				
West-City (Hackney)	83	74	1950s/1960s flatted estates	28
East-Docks (Newham)	53	68	1950s and 1960s houses and flats	19
Riverlands (Nottingham)	28	52	1970s flats and houses and older terraced stock	19
The Valley (Sheffield)	39	52	1970s flats and houses and older terraced stock	26
Middle Row (Birmingham)	29	55	1950s and 1960s flats and houses and older terraced stock	67
Outer core and city edge areas				
Overtown (Knowsley)	15	57	1930s and 1940s estates (houses)	1
Shipview (Newcastle)	28	61	1930s and 1940s estates (houses)	1
Kirkside East (Leeds)	24	70	1930s and 1940s estates (houses)	2
Southside (Redcar and Cleveland)	8	45	1930s and 1940s estates (houses) and older terraced stock	2
Other areas				
High Moor (Blackburn)	21	53	1970s flats and houses and older terraced stock	18
Fairfields (Caerphilly)	11	38	1970s flats and houses and older terraced stock	0
Beachville (Thanet)	16	18	Large Victorian/Edwardian properties. Some older terraces and post-1950s council estates	2

Source: 1991 Census and site visits

Support computer system, school performance tables from the Department for Education and Skills (DfES) and the Index of Multiple Deprivation (IMD) compiled by the then Department of the Environment, Transport and the Regions (DETR). Other information was collected directly from local authorities and other agencies: information such as numbers of empty properties, crime statistics and numbers of children on the Child Protection Register.

Our initial round of data collection produced shocking evidence of deep spatial inequalities across many dimensions. Just as they had in 1991, in 1998 all the areas had severe concentrations of poverty, much worse than the national average. According to the IMD (DETR, 2000a), which is based mainly on social and economic statistics from 1998, wards in the 12 areas, excepting Wales which was not included in the Index, had a median deprivation score of 65.4, compared with the English average of 21.7[2]. Although three areas, Southside (Redcar and Cleveland), Shipview (Newcastle) and Beachville (Thanet) all contained slightly more advantaged wards as well as severe pockets of deprivation, the others were highly deprived throughout (Figure 1.2). All but one of the 13 wards in which the neighbourhoods were located had scores in the top 5% of the Index.

We looked more specifically at levels of benefit claims, unemployment, health

Figure 1.2: IMD scores

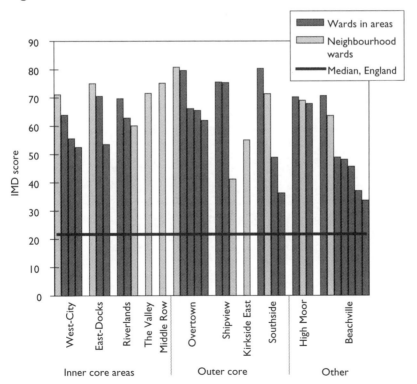

Source: DETR

and educational attainment. On every indicator of deprivation, the difference between these areas and the national norm was stark.

On average across the areas, an estimated 20% of adults (aged 16+) were claiming Income Support, the welfare state's principal means-tested benefit (Figure 1.3), compared with 9% nationally, consistent with the Social Exclusion Unit's finding that benefit claim rates were twice as high in the top 10% most deprived wards than the national average (SEU, 1998). On average nearly half of the children (45%) were in Income Support households. Inevitably there was even more variation at neighbourhood level. We found that a third of adults (33%) in Saints' Walk ward (Knowsley) were claiming Income Support, and approximately one quarter in each of the wards containing the two London neighbourhoods, the Grove (Hackney) and Phoenix Rise (Newham).

Income Support claimants are mainly pensioners, lone parents or people who are disabled. The study areas typically had a fewer than average number of pensioners[3], but the concentration of lone parents was very marked – 27% of households in 1991 compared with 12% nationally. In eight of the 12 areas, the proportion of lone-parent claimants was higher than the national average of 25%: in one case (East-Docks in London) it was as high as 41%. Claim rates

Figure 1.3: Income Support claims for area wards (1998)

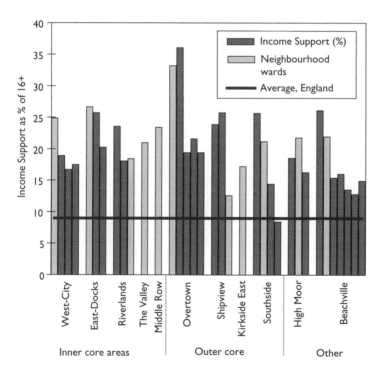

Note: Fairfields, the Welsh area, is not included in Figures 1.3 or 1.4 because no up-to-date population estimates were available.

Source: DSS

were high not just because there were more lone parents but because they were younger than average and less likely to be in work[4]. In 11 of the areas, young lone parents, aged 16-24, were a higher proportion of all lone parents than they were nationally, ranging from 24% in East-Docks (Newham) to 34% in Fairfields (Caerphilly) and in High Moor (Blackburn), compared with a national average of 18%. No more than 26% of all lone parents in any of the areas were in work in 1991 compared with 35% nationally.

Unemployment was even more concentrated than low income. On average, the areas had 13% of economically active adults claiming Jobseeker's Allowance, three times the national average (4%), again with greater variation at neighbourhood level (Figure 1.4).

All areas, particularly those in inner cities, had significantly worse health than the national average, as measured by standard mortality ratios (Figure 1.5), as well as lower levels of skills and attainment. While the Basic Skills Agency found 15% of the population, nationally, with low or very low literacy in 1995[5], the areas had much higher proportions, in one case, Middle Row in Birmingham, twice as high. In nearly half of them, more than 25% of the population had low or very low literacy (Figure 1.6). And low levels of basic skills went hand in

Figure 1.4: Jobseeker's Allowance claims for area wards (1998)

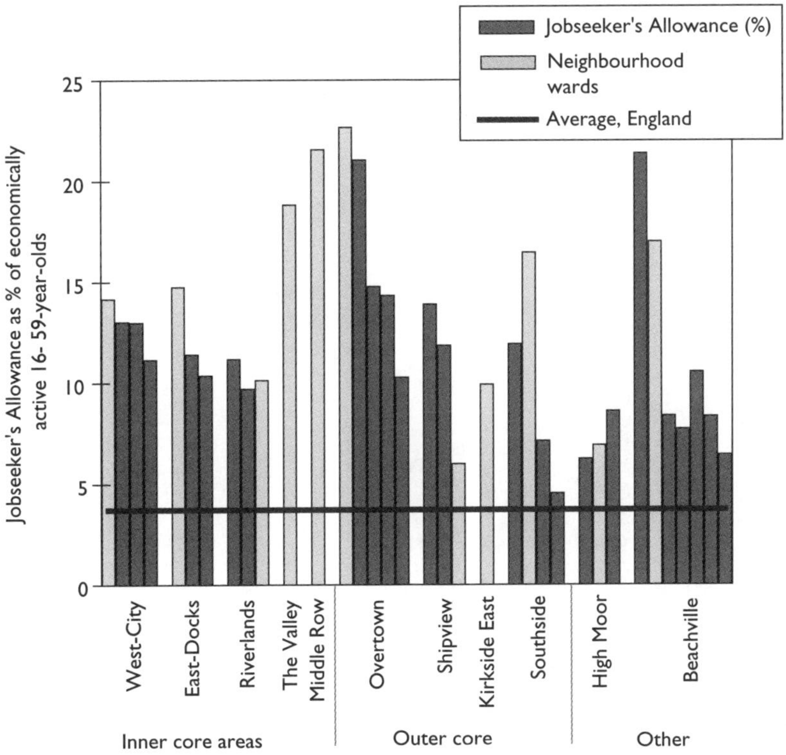

Source: DSS

hand with low levels of attainment at schools. None of the secondary schools serving the areas[6] achieved the national average GCSE pass rate in 1999 (Figure 1.7). On average, the rate for these schools was that 21% of pupils passed five GCSEs at grades A★-C compared with 47.9% nationally. In total, 11% of pupils left with no GCSEs, double the national average[7].

Figure 1.5: Standard Mortality Ratios (U65) for constituencies in which areas are located

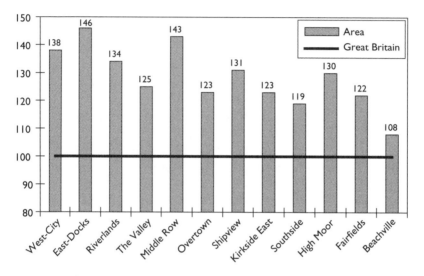

Source: Shaw et al (1999)

Figure 1.6: Proportion of adults with low or very low literacy (1995)

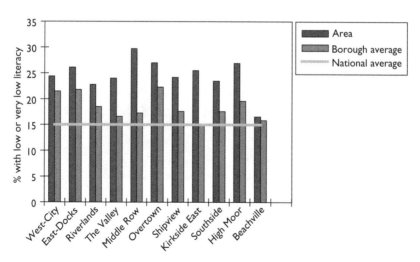

Note: The survey from which this data is drawn did not cover Wales.
Source: Basic Skills Agency

Figure 1.7: Higher grade GCSE performance in area schools (1999)

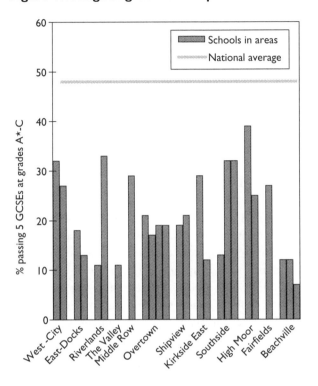

Source: DfES

Investigating area trajectories

The quantitative work could help us to track the problem but not to explain it. To develop a fuller understanding, we also undertook qualitative fieldwork, all of it carried out by the author so that a single consistent perspective could be maintained over time. This began with a one- or two-day familiarisation visit to each area, between October 1998 and March 1999, in which I spent time walking about the area, establishing a firm picture of the geography, topography, major physical features and transport links; this was essential if I was to make sense of the later interviews, where informants would refer to these aspects. I made an initial photographic record and, importantly, spent time with one or two key local actors to find out about local history and sources of historical accounts, and about organisations and individuals that were active in the area, and to identify people to interview. I collected background reports, research studies and Census data, and produced a basic 'thumbnail sketch' of each area, setting out a brief description and history. I started to track the stories of the areas through press cuttings.

The first main phase of qualitative fieldwork began in April 1999, and continued until December 1999. This was a period of rapid policy implementation in the most deprived neighbourhoods. New regeneration programmes and action zones had been announced, and national policies such as the New Deal for the Unemployed and the Working Families' Tax Credit were beginning to come on stream. To capture a moment in time, I decided to compress the fieldwork into as short a time as possible. In each area I spent between seven and ten days, within a one-month period. I had two purposes. One was to add to, confirm or clarify the factual picture provided by statistics and documentary evidence, and to understand how to interpret it. Some vital facts about small areas simply do not exist in statistics or reports, such as the number of empty homes on a particular estate, the amount of litter, the number of police officers, or the extent of the shopping facilities. Other statistics are best understood alongside an informed opinion. For instance, police officers could explain how well-resourced policing operations had led to short-term increases in crime because more offences were reported. Employment advisers could point to the way that welfare-to-work programmes reduced unemployment not just because some claimants found work but because the more stringent regime caused others to cease claiming.

To gain this factual knowledge and understanding, I interviewed a range of frontline and senior staff and residents: community activists, housing managers, social workers, headteachers, police officers, health visitors, religious leaders and others, nearly 300 in all. I identified them initially through contact with a local authority liaison officer with good knowledge of the area and later through 'snowballing' as one interviewee would refer me on to colleagues or organisations with useful knowledge. Table 1.3 lists the respondents in each area. Different patterns of public service provision and voluntary sector activity, and different organisational structures meant that the number of interviews varied from area to area, between 17 and 32. The interviews were semi-structured, lasting about one hour. I asked for facts and opinions about each interviewee's specific area of work. For example, I asked housing managers about housing demand, stock condition and management problems; and community workers about the types of community groups and their development and impact. In addition to the interviews, I also recorded field observations and took photographs of the housing and environment. I observed the provision of facilities and services, the distance people had to go to the bank, shops or post office, and the cost and convenience of the public transport.

My other purpose was to gain a perspective on area conditions and change through the eyes of participants. Area change is a social process, its reality created by its participants and only fully understandable through their eyes. The objective measures I collected could only be part of the picture. I could count, for example, empty houses, but could only fully understand their importance when I knew what they symbolised to different people in the area. I could record community facilities, but also needed to know who used them, how often and why. Thus, in addition to the factual information, all respondents were asked about, and encouraged to elaborate on, their impressions of the area, its strengths and weaknesses, how it compared with other areas, and how and why it had changed

Table 1.3: Interviews in each area (1999)

Areas of enquiry	Hackney	Newham	Knowsley	Nottingham	Newcastle	Sheffield	Blackburn	Birmingham	Caerphilly	Redcar and Cleveland	Leeds	Thanet	Total
Residents	3	–	–	–	–	1	2	3	2	3	2	0	20
Local authority policy/regeneration	1	0	0	2	0	3	1	0	3	2	1	2	15
Local Regeneration Programme	1	–	2	1	2	1	–	1	–	1	–	–	10
Housing	2	–	1	2	2	2	4	2	–	2	1	–	21
Schools/education	3	3	3	2	2	3	3	2	2	2	3	3	31
Police	–	–	–	–	–	–	–	–	–	–	–	–	12
Social services	0	0	–	2	2	0	–	–	–	–	2	–	12
Employment/economic development	1	3	2	2	3	3	2	5	3	1	1	–	27
Health workers and GPs	2	1	2	0	1	6	2	0	0	–	4	1	20
Community and youth workers	2	3	4	3	2	3	3	4	3	3	4	2	36
Community and voluntary groups	2	1	1	4	3	4	3	4	0	–	2	2	27
Religious leader	–	–	–	–	–	–	–	–	–	–	–	0	11
Ward councillor	1	1	1	0	–	1	1	–	2	2	1	2	14
Area coordinator	–	–	–	–	–	–	–	1	–	–	–	–	5
Business representative	1	0	0	1	–	0	2	–	–	2	2	0	11
Estate agent	0	0	0	–	–	0	–	0	0	0	–	–	6
Other	2	0	2	2	1	2	0	1	1	1	0	1	13
Total	**23**	**17**	**23**	**26**	**25**	**32**	**28**	**28**	**22**	**24**	**25**	**18**	**291**

Note: Table records interviews, not interviewees. The number of interviews was smaller than the number of interviewees, because more than one person was present at some of the interviews.

over time. I learned something about social relations in the area, community interaction and participation, and the 'feel' of the area to its inhabitants. I heard accounts of why social changes occurred, for example, why certain neighbourhoods developed drug dealing problems while others did not, and similarly, gained an understanding of the dynamics of public policy implementation. Respondents explained how and why national and local government policies hit the ground, why some triggered change and others did not. They told how, in practice, new initiatives boosted or jeopardised services and with what effect, and how attempts to involve communities sometimes empowered people and at other times divided and disillusioned them. Unsurprisingly, they did not agree on all issues. There were contrasting impressions of area change from individuals or subgroups within each community who experienced their neighbourhood differently. Particularly, the views of professionals and residents were sometimes at odds, with different perceptions of the area and different perspectives on the reasons for the success or failure of interventions by public agencies. It was hearing this wide range of different perspectives, and understanding the positions from which they were formed, that illuminated the processes of area change. As well as the formal interviews, I attended over 20 youth groups, tenants' meetings and local conferences to observe and to talk informally to participants. In four areas, I was also able to draw on CASE's parallel 'neighbourhood study', conducted by Helen Bowman, Bani Makkar and Katharine Mumford, who were interviewing local families at nine-month intervals (Bowman, 2001; Mumford, 2001; Mumford and Power, 2003).

In late 2000, I re-visited each area to discuss initial findings, and to update on major developments since the fieldwork a year previously, and in late 2001/early 2002 I carried out a second wave of interviews and field observations. These focused on changes since our baseline position in 1999. Again, all interviewees were asked about area change in general and about their own specific area of expertise. This was a smaller-scale exercise, since baseline and historical information about the area did not have to be collected. I focused on a smaller number of topic areas that had arisen from the initial analysis; local economies, housing, crime and disorder and area regeneration policies, and conducted 120 interviews, ranging from five in one area to 16 in another. The list of informants is shown in Table 1.4. Where possible, I interviewed the same respondent as in 1999, or their replacement if they were no longer available.

The combination of statistical data and intensive local fieldwork provided a rich picture of the changing area scenes, looking back in time, taking a snapshot of the present and hinting at prospects for the future.

Table 1.4: Interviews in each area (2001)

Areas of enquiry	Hackney	Newham	Knowsley	Nottingham	Newcastle	Sheffield	Blackburn	Birmingham	Caerphilly	Redcar and Cleveland	Leeds	Thanet	Total
Residents	2	1	1	0	1	0	2	1	1	1	1	0	11
Frontline staff/religious/councillor etc	2	2	1	2	1	1	3	0	2	2	2	3	21
Local authority policy/regeneration	2	1	0	1	0	2	1	1	1	2	1	1	13
Local regeneration programme	0	1	2	1	1	3	0	0	2	1	1	0	12
Housing	1	1	1	2	2	2	0	0	0	2	1	1	13
Police	1	1	2	0	1	1	2	1	1	1	1	1	13
Employment/economic development	0	1	1	2	2	0	3	2	3	1	2	3	20
Other	2	0	2	0	0	0	2	0	3	0	1	7	17
Total	**10**	**8**	**10**	**8**	**8**	**9**	**13**	**5**	**13**	**10**	**10**	**16**	**120**

Note: Table records interviews, not interviewees. The number of interviewees was smaller than the number of interviews, because more than one person was present at some of the interviews.

Summary

- The book is based on 12 areas and neighbourhoods selected to be representative of the most disadvantaged areas and neighbourhoods in England and Wales. They are urban and industrial areas, in six different regions and with diverse locations, housing types and tenures and ethnic composition.
- CASE is following the fortunes of these areas over a 10-year period. This book covers the first four years of the study. It aims to describe and explain the problems of the areas as we found them in 1998, to document changes since then and to explain the impact of wider economic and social changes, and of national and local policy interventions. We aim to show how the poorest areas are changing, relative to others, and why.
- The areas were selected on the basis of 1991 Census data. Historical data has been collected from the 1971 and 1981 Censuses. Administrative data has been collected to track change during the 1990s.
- These data show that by 1998, the baseline year for the study, the gap between these areas and the national average was very wide. Unemployment was three times the national average; levels of Income Support claims twice as high. Health and educational attainment were well below average.
- The book is based not just on evidence from statistical data, but on qualitative material. We conducted two sets of field visits to each area, one in 1999 and one in 2001-02. We interviewed frontline and senior staff and resident representatives, collected local strategy documents and reports, statistics and newspaper cuttings, took photographs and made observation notes on community facilities and the physical environment. The combination of quantitative and qualitative data provides a unique insight into neighbourhood change.

Notes

[1] The ESRC also funded the 'Changing Urban and Regional System' (CURS) research in the late 1980s, which, in looking at the impact of economic restructuring through studies of seven diverse localities, offers perhaps the closest parallel to our own approach (Cooke, 1989).

[2] The overall deprivation score in the IMD is the combined sum of scores on six domains of deprivation: Income; Employment; Health Deprivation and Disability; Education, Skills and Training; Geographical Access to Services; and Housing. Prior to summing, the domain scores were standardised (by ranking), exponentially transformed to a common distribution, and weighted, with income and employment having the most weight. Thus the score in itself does not represent a percentage of deprived households, or any other such measure. It is a tool for ranking and comparing wards.

[3] The populations of the areas were younger than average. Nationally 20% of people were aged under 16 in 1998. All of the areas had a higher proportion of children than this, ranging from just above the average in West–City (Hackney) and Beachville (Thanet) to 32% in Middle Row (Birmingham). Nine of them also had a greater than average number of large families, with four or more children. In all of the areas with large Asian families, the proportion of large families was very much higher than the national average – 10% in The Valley (Sheffield), 14% in High Moor (Blackburn) and 25% in Middle Row (Birmingham), compared with a national average of 5%.

[4] Other studies have found that young lone parents are most likely to be on low incomes (Kiernan, 2002).

[5] Further research in 1997 estimated the figure at 19% (6% with very low skills and 13% with low skills), but ward-level comparisons are not available for this data.

[6] Because school places are not allocated according to geographical catchment areas, there is not an exact fit between schools and areas. In determining which secondary schools could be identified as the main ones serving the areas, I took advice from local authority officers and primary school headteachers.

[7] There was wide variation between schools. In some schools in the sample, one in five pupils left with no GCSEs. Most of the higher attaining schools were girls' schools or Roman Catholic schools, which tend to draw pupils from further afield as well as from the local area.

TWO

Historical poverty and the roots of decline

"The Valley became a poor area because poor people moved there. Now it's poor because it's poor because it's poor. It can't get out of that cycle." (economic development worker, Sheffield)

Long histories of concentrated poverty

Our initial data showed that at the end of the 1990s, the poverty gap between these disadvantaged areas and the national average was wide. But what was equally evident was that none of this was new. Relative poverty was long established. With the exception of parts of Beachville in Kent, which had been largely non-residential until the 1980s, all of the 12 areas had been poor for many years.

The historical poverty of the areas had two interlinked causes: their industrial structure and position in the housing market. It was a function of the fit between their 'intrinsic' or hard-to-change characteristics – location, topography, housing stock and economic structure – and the demand for labour or accommodation. Some of the areas were poor because they were built to house industrial workers. They were, from their inception, home to people with little choice over their jobs, homes or consumption. Such areas, of which there were nine in the study, can be described as areas of primary deprivation (DoE, 1977). Often their location was unattractive. They were close to mines, factories or warehouses, so there was no incentive for the better-off to move there, and the housing was low cost and rarely a first choice for people with more options. Concentrations of poverty became quickly embedded and hard to change.

In the other three areas, deprivation was a secondary phase. These were central areas of towns and cities that had once housed the middle classes, but lost their relative advantage in the housing market as the better-off moved to the suburbs. They had been colonised by people with less housing choice, often immigrants who could not get access to newer housing. By the time we visited them, these areas had seen several waves of disadvantaged communities passing through. Their poverty was long term but changing and, unlike most of the areas of primary deprivation, they had intrinsic advantages of location and housing stock, with a potentially higher value than they could currently command.

We examined the trajectories of each of these groups in more detail, using historical sources.

Areas of primary deprivation

The nine areas of primary deprivation were themselves of two types. First there were the inner-city or industrial areas that had grown up in the mid to late 1800s to house workers in rapidly expanding industries (Table 2.1). Southside, in Redcar and Cleveland, for example, consisted of several separate settlements, each built to serve separate workplaces, in the steel and shipbuilding industries. Valley Top (Caerphilly) consisted of strings of miners' cottages. East-Docks' residents worked in East London's docks and gasworks. In Riverlands (Nottingham), where the edges of the area contained large houses occupied by the city's professional classes and factory owners, the majority of homes, over 10,000 of them, were densely packed back-to-back terraced houses "intended for the lower paid working classes" (Fleckney, 1997, p 10)[1].

These industries gave rise to different forms of industrial organisation. Mining and shipbuilding areas, for example, were dominated by large firms which, in boom periods at least, provided steady work, some skilled trades and a social infrastructure geared around male employment. Nottingham's Riverlands, by contrast, had a diverse economy with a tradition of female work: lace, hosiery, manufacturing and light engineering. Wages were depressed and many workers were paid on a piecework basis. Nevertheless, all of these were low-income neighbourhoods, constructed for the relatively poor, and the quality of the housing reflected the incomes of the workforce. East-Docks developed rapidly in the mid-19th century when the city of London banned 'obnoxious industries' such as chemical factories, forcing them to locate just outside its border. At the same time, the building of the new docks and the railway brought a massive increase in labour opportunities and a flood of workers to the capital. But much of the work was low-paid, seasonal or casual. Workers could only afford the cheapest houses and builders took advantage of weak planning controls not to install adequate sewage, water supplies or pavements. Dickens (1857) reported how the poor quickly became concentrated there:"The condition of the place prevents the steadier class of mechanics from residing in it. They go from their work to [other areas]. Many select such a dwelling place because they are already debased below the point of enmity to filth; poorer labourers live there because they cannot afford to go further, and there become debased". The description is dramatic, but illustrates how the social status of areas was quickly shaped by their industrial base and their housing stock.

All of these older areas of primary deprivation underwent redevelopment on some scale during the 20th century. Age, poor quality building, and lack of investment over time had turned the original workers' homes into slums deemed to be unacceptable by modern standards. In Hackney, where the first phase of mass housebuilding had been early, between 1820 and 1860, redevelopment

Table 2.1: Areas of primary deprivation built in the 1800s and redeveloped

	First phase of major urban development	Reason/ type of development	Redevelopment
West-City (Hackney)	Early to mid-1800s	Industrial development alongside canal: gasworks, electricity, furniture and shoe manufacture, tobacco	Slums replaced by flats in long programme of redevelopment starting in 1920s. Mostly complete by early 1960s
East-Docks (Newham)	Mid-1800s	Industrial development. Cheap housing built for workers in noxious industries	Late 1940s/1950s/1960s. Rebuilding after bomb damage
Riverlands (Nottingham)	Mid to late 1800s	Cheap housing for low-paid working classes	1970s. Slums replaced by council estates
High Moor (Blackburn)	Mid to late 1800s	Housing for mill-workers	1950s/1960/1970s. Building of new estates on greenfield land and to replace slum areas. Many original streets remain
Fairfields (Caerphilly)	Mid-1800s	Mineworkers' homes	Some redevelopment in 1970s. Slums replaced by council estates
Southside (Redcar and Cleveland)	Late 1800s	Housing for workers in shipbuilding and steelworks	Two council estates built in 1940s and 1950s and slum housing demolished. Many original streets remain

Source: Interviews and historical documents from study areas

began in the 1920s, with the replacement of terraced houses by council flats, and continued until the 1960s (Mander, 1996). By contrast, in Blackburn, where industrial development had been later, in the mill building boom of the 1850s to 1870s, the housing was still in relatively good condition by the time of the Second World War. Slum clearance and redevelopment did not start until the late 1950s and was still underway in the 1970s (Beattie, 1992).

The condition of the homes and the land available for new building determined the scale of the redevelopment. In West-City (Hackney), East-Docks (Newham) and Riverlands (Nottingham), redevelopment was almost complete, with very few, if any, of the original homes left standing. Wartime bombing had destroyed 85% of the houses in East-Docks (Newham), and it was completely rebuilt after the Second World War. Elsewhere, slum clearance was the main reason for redevelopment. Riverlands, in the late 1960s, was described by a group of social scientists as "a large, deteriorated district ... an area of manifest environmental

*Terraced homes in West-City (Hackney)
c.1920*

A new estate in West-City, built in 1927

and social deprivation" (Coates and Silburn, 1970, p 13). Living conditions, according to these observers, were poor:

> ... general amenities are at the most rudimentary level; there are almost no trees; until recently there were no adequate play facilities ... the schools are old and decrepit; with dingy buildings and bleak factories and warehouses, functionally austere chapels, a host of second-hand shops stacked out with shabby, cast off goods; overhung throughout the winter by a damp pall of smoke. (Coates and Silburn, 1970, p 13)

The area had, according to the Nottingham Corporation, "come to the end of its life span" (Fleckney, 1997). The slum clearance and redevelopment programme involved the building of over 5,000 new homes in 11 sequential phases from 1971 to 1978.

Other areas saw more limited redevelopment, leaving some of the original homes intact. In Blackburn, about 5,000 homes were built on new estates (including Bridgefields) to ease overcrowding and to house people from slum clearance areas, but the scale and pace of the proposed redevelopment provoked a huge public outcry, forcing the council to leave much of the terraced stock in place and to instigate improvement programmes rather than undertake further demolition (Beattie, 1992). High Moor was left with a mixture of small privately owned street houses, in increasingly poor condition, and post–war council estates further from the centre of the town. Similarly in Southside (Redcar and Cleveland) and Fairfields (Caerphilly), redevelopment was partial. Southside's new estates were mainly built in the 1940s and 1950s; Fairfields' in the 1970s. A council report from Fairfields in 1969 noted that 29% of homes in Valley Top were in such poor condition that they needed replacing. By 1980 two new council estates stood in their place, although other streets in the town and further down the valley were left with their original homes.

Redevelopment transformed the areas physically. New housing estates replaced old street layouts. Streets of small shops were bulldozed over to be replaced by new shopping centres. In Riverlands, about 650 shops were demolished in the main street and replaced by just 50 in neighbourhood centres. But physical change was not accompanied by sociooeconomic transformation. The new homes were provided by local authorities. They were subsidised housing for people on low incomes who could not afford market rents. Although neighbourhood-based networks of family and friends were destroyed, the new estates essentially housed the same people as before, or people moved from slum clearance areas elsewhere. In the 1870s, Engels had described how a clearance programme in Manchester to make room for the new railway station had simply moved the slum area of Little Ireland from one side of Oxford Road to the other: "the same economic necessity which produced them [slums] in the first place produces them in the next place also" (quoted in Coates and Silburn, 1970, p 83). A hundred years later, a similar process was repeating itself. The economies of the areas were still dominated by low-skill, low-wage jobs. High proportions of workers were in low socioeconomic groups, and few had higher qualifications. Even in the more diverse economies, households in these areas could not command high incomes. A social survey in Riverlands in 1967 found that the main cause of poverty was not unemployment but low wages, even though the town's economy was booming. Some areas still depended on their traditional industries, which were now beginning to decline. So while housing and living conditions were improved, industrial structure and single tenure housing programmes ensured that clusters of relative poverty remained. In some areas, they were exacerbated by slum clearance, since areas awaiting clearance were effectively blighted, and many of those who moved into them were those who had no choice of accommodation elsewhere.

The second type of primary deprivation area (Table 2.2) was created by the housing boom of the inter-war and immediate post-war years. Beginning in the 1920s, new swathes of housing were developed to rehouse the urban working class from congested inner-city areas. Previously undeveloped land on the edge of cities was swallowed up by new public housing estates. Kirkside East on the edge of Leeds was transformed from farmland into one of Britain's largest council estates. In Newcastle, much of Shipview was still undeveloped at the time of the First World War, despite the opening of the shipyards at the turn of the century,

Table 2.2: Areas of primary deprivation: inter-war developments

	First major phase of urban development	Reason/type of development
Overtown (Knowsley)	1930s and 1940s	New homes created as expansion/ slum clearance for nearby city
Kirkside East (Leeds)	1930s and 1940s	New homes created as expansion/ slum clearance
Shipview (Newcastle)	1920s/1930s/1940s	New homes created as expansion/ slum clearance

Source: Interviews and historical documents from study areas

and the provision of workers' housing close to the riverside. The first council estates were built in the 1920s to provide accommodation for the city's growing population, and development accelerated from the 1930s to house people from cleared areas of slum housing (Michael, 1992)[1]. Overtown, on the edge of Liverpool, was created as part of a massive decentralisation of jobs and people after the Second World War. The scale of the development was huge. Merseyside's outer estates, built on greenfield land, mainly from 1945 onwards, housed nearly 200,000 people by the late 1960s. Like the new housing estates in the inner-city areas, these were new homes for people from areas that were themselves relatively disadvantaged. Richard Meegan, writing about the post-war Liverpool overspill housing programme, described the inevitability of the creation of new areas of relative poverty:

> ... given the emphasis in the population dispersal on those in 'housing need' in the old working class areas of the inner-city, the new 'communities' had very distinct class profiles. They were predominantly 'one class townships': working class, with a marked bias towards semi-skilled and unskilled manual workers. (Meegan, 1989, p 202)

Even so, the extent of disadvantage varied, between and within neighbourhoods. Long-standing residents of Kirkside East remembered that the new estate, built in 1937, had new residents from all over the country who came for work in the city's thriving industries, as well as those rehoused from other parts of Leeds. People who moved into one part of the area were better-off, skilled tradespeople,

Inter-war housing and a modern tower block in Shipview (Newcastle). Both being improved when we visited in 1999

whereas those moving into Southmead and the neighbourhoods around it were mainly unskilled or semi-skilled workers moved from a particular back-to-back housing area. These low-skilled workers were not only more poorly paid but more vulnerable to recession, so a geographical pattern of poverty became established, even within the area, from its inception.

In all of these areas, development continued, in pockets, until the 1960s and 1970s, with high-rise blocks and low-rise maisonettes being interspersed with the original council estates.

Areas of secondary deprivation

While the nine areas of primary deprivation were relatively poor from the start, the three other areas had once enjoyed greater prosperity (Table 2.3).

Beachville in Kent had its heyday as an Edwardian seaside resort, and was still popular for holiday makers and day trippers until the 1950s, when it began to decline under competition from the foreign holiday market. Large up-market hotels closed and were turned over to benefit-subsidised B&B accommodation, and later to temporary housing for asylum seekers and refugees. The Valley in Sheffield and Middle Row in Birmingham, each only about a mile from the centre of big industrial cities, were home to the professional and merchant classes of the late 19th century. Their big Victorian houses still remain, as well as streets of artisans' cottages, along with council flats built in the 1960s and 1970s as part of city slum clearance programmes.

An account of Middle Row in the late 1960s described how in one part "the houses are large, three storey brick buildings, at one time richly ornamented and porched. The residents included headmistresses, doctors, businessmen and, at one time, the Town Clerk of Birmingham" (Rex and Moore, 1967, p 43). Another neighbourhood consisted of red-brick cottages for the "working class but not rough labourers" (p 44). The neighbourhood of Broadways itself was owned by a housing trust which selected its tenants from "the better working class, those with higher, more secure incomes, better job status" (p 45).

Table 2.3: Areas of secondary deprivation

	First major phase of urban development	**Reason/type of development**
The Valley (Sheffield)	Mid-1800s	Large homes for professional and merchant classes, and cottages for better working classes
Middle Row (Birmingham)	Mid-1800s	Large homes for professional and merchant classes, and cottages for better working classes
Beachville (Thanet)	Mid to late 1800s	Hotels

Source: Interviews and historical documents from study areas

Large houses in Middle Row (Birmingham) and cottages in the Broadways neighbourhood

However, the status of the area began to decline in the 1930s and this decline accelerated after the war, as the middle classes moved out to the suburbs. Their large homes were converted to lodging houses. With a shortage of housing in the city and a residence qualification for new council housing, these were the only available homes for the new waves of immigrants who arrived in the 1950s and 1960s, first Irish then West Indians and Pakistanis. The working-class neighbourhoods began to change character as parts of them were earmarked for slum clearance and allocated only to people who were considered unsuitable for new tenancies. By the 1970s a once well-off area had become a relatively poor one. And while this inner-city area had previously had the advantage of plentiful work, its manufacturing industries were already declining or moving. New jobs were mainly to be found in industrial sites on the edge of the city, or in city centre service industries that required different skills.

Decline 1971-91

Although the areas had always been relatively poor, the people we spoke to in every one of them told a story of decline starting in the 1960s. They talked about increasing crime and antisocial behaviour, declining sense of community, and the loss of shops and services. Underlying these changes were three consistent themes: economic restructuring, resulting in every case in enormous job losses; widening inequality (driven in large part by economic changes); and changes in the size and composition of the population. All of these increased the concentration of poverty in the poorest areas and neighbourhoods.

The disappearance of work

For most of the areas, the 1970s and 1980s were periods of catastrophic employment decline. Two distinct processes were underway: the ongoing decline of traditional industries and the collapse of the manufacturing sector. Some areas were affected by both these processes, others by only one. Their varying industrial composition determined the timing and scale of decline and its social impact.

For Britain's traditional industries, such as coal, shipbuilding, and port-related activities, decline was nothing new. Facing competition from abroad and burdened by old equipment and plant and low productivity rates, their problems were evident in the depression of the 1930s and only masked by wartime demand. Attempts to modernise production by the introduction of new technology further reduced labour demand. For areas dependent on these industries, the 1960s was a period of dramatic collapse, continuing in most cases into the 1970s and 1980s. Firms that had been the major local employers for several decades either closed or rationalised drastically, followed by associated suppliers and producers. All of the 29 coalpits in Fairfields (Caerphilly) closed in the 1960s and 1970s. In London's East-Docks, work in the docks and sea transport declined in the 1960s and collapsed in the 1970s. Between 1971 and 1978, East London lost 20,000 dock jobs, with the final dock closures coming in 1980-81.

Less predictable but equally devastating was the collapse of manufacturing. Employment in manufacturing went into a protracted decline in the major cities in the 1960s, initially due to spatial shifts rather than structural change. As Massey (1994) has pointed out, the main trigger for the decline of manufacturing in inner-city areas was not that there were too many jobs in declining sectors, but that within industries, it was the cities, with their outmoded production techniques and old factory buildings, that were the first to lose out to rationalisation or to modernisation. Public policy contributed, as city authorities deliberately orchestrated the decentralisation of jobs and people to alleviate inner-city congestion and pollution. In Birmingham, for example, much of the new industrial development in the city was in outer areas, a deliberate policy to prevent unemployment in overspill housing areas. Existing firms relocated from cramped inner-city areas to more modern premises in the outskirts, creating a spatial dislocation between jobs and people and a particular problem of minority ethnic unemployment. As the number of immigrants into Middle Row and other inner-city areas was growing, the labour market into which they were moving was shrinking. The Birmingham Inner Area Study (DoE, 1977) showed that three quarters of immigrants worked in manufacturing. They were twice as likely as white people to be unemployed. But decentralisation was only a contributor to inner-city employment decline, not its main cause. More than half the manufacturing job losses in the inner areas of major cities involved no locational shift. They were straightforward closures rather than moves to the outskirts (Massey, 1994).

However, while manufacturing in the cities was already on the wane in the 1960s, the sector as a whole was still seen as the answer to Britain's industrial problems, not the source of them. Post-war consumer growth provided direct employment in product manufacture and prolonged life for some of Britain's heavy industries. On Merseyside, the major expansion of employment on Knowsley's industrial estates came in the early 1960s, with the arrival of major multinational firms such as Ford and Vauxhall. While Liverpool's port-related activities were running down, the manufacturing sector was building up. On Teesside, planners were still predicting expansion in the mid-1960s, seeing the area as a sub-regional growth centre capable of compensating not only for its own shipbuilding job losses but for the loss of jobs on the Durham coalfield. Substantial public sector investment underpinned the expansion of capacity for steel and chemical production, industries that were dependent on demand for metal, plastic and man-made fibre products.

It was a short-lived boom. The expected demand for British manufacturing output failed to materialise, in part because of the rise in world oil prices in the early 1970s, leaving firms with problems of significant overcapacity. Competitive pressures to enhance productivity and reduce labour costs through technological change increased the pace of job losses. Industry was increasingly becoming globalised. The large firms whose presence had been the engine of growth for places like Knowsley and Teesside were increasingly likely to source production in countries where labour costs were cheaper. From the mid-1970s onwards, manufacturing employment contracted dramatically. Overall, three million British manufacturing jobs were lost between 1971 and the mid-1990s, as the sector dwindled from a third of all jobs to only 17% (Green and Owen, 1998).

The decline in manufacturing had nowhere near the spatial concentration of the loss of traditional industries. Its impact was felt much more widely. Nevertheless, job losses were inevitably greater in areas where manufacturing was concentrated: the cities, where decline continued; the old industrial areas, where manufacturing had complemented or replaced older industries; and the new outer-city industrial estates, where new post-war housing and new industrial development had been so closely linked. Meanwhile, growth in the British economy was located elsewhere. A total of 70% of the growth in private sector services between 1981 and 1996 was in towns and rural areas (Breheny, 1999).

Overall, 9 of our 12 areas were affected by these major structural changes, with over 70% of their total employment in traditional industries or newer manufacturing or both (Table 2.4). Table 2.5 demonstrates that despite service sector growth, net job losses were substantial, and full-time male job losses even more so. Only Fairfields, in Caerphilly, which saw the redevelopment of former mining sites as industrial estates in this period, saw job growth in excess of its losses.

Among the cities, Hackney, with a tradition of manufacturing employment for men and women, particularly in shoes, clothing and furniture, lost more than a half of its manufacturing jobs between 1971 and 1991. By the early 1990s, it had no remaining manufacturing firm employing over 200 people. In nearby Newham, the number of jobs nearly halved between 1971 and 1991 as dock closures were followed by losses in engineering, printing, chemicals, and food and drink industries. The collapse of steel had disastrous consequences for Sheffield, where one quarter of the city's jobs were lost in the 1970s and 1980s. The steel workforce was decimated, from 45,000 in 1971 to 7,000 in 1991 as the bulk of the industry closed down. Here, the impact of jobs losses in coal were still being felt too, and another 10,000 jobs were lost as all 24 pits in South Yorkshire closed. Similarly, Shipview in Newcastle saw continuing losses in shipbuilding as well as closures of major engineering firms. On Teesside, plans

Table 2.4: Industrial structure: areas dependent on traditional industries and/or manufacturing (1971)

	Traditional industries in area	Main employment sectors (1971) (any with more than 15% of workforce) (%)	
West-City (Hackney)	Manufacturing, particularly shoes and furniture	Manufacturing Transport, communication Distribution	44 26 17
East-Docks (Newham)	Docks and gasworks	Transport, communication Manufacturing	46 37
The Valley[a] (Sheffield)	Steel	Manufacturing Transport, communication	49 22
Middle Row (Birmingham)	Engineering, particularly motor industry	Manufacturing	61
Overtown (Knowsley)	Manufacturing	Manufacturing Transport, communication	48 20
Shipview[a] (Newcastle)	Shipbuilding and heavy engineering	Manufacturing Transport, communication	30 27
Southside (Redcar and Cleveland)	Steel, chemicals and shipbuilding	Manufacturing	90
High Moor[a] (Blackburn)	Manufacturing	Manufacturing Transport, communication	52 20
Fairfields (Caerphilly)	Mining and heavy engineering	Manufacturing Transport, communication	57 21

Notes: [a] Figures based on amalgamated job centre areas. Where [a], these refer to a substantially bigger area than the study area, including the town/city centres in each case.

The table includes areas with 70% of more of their employment in these sectors. Shipview is included because the area covered by the data is substantially larger than the area itself and because qualitative evidence suggests that the profile of the area itself was much less diverse than these figures suggest.

Source: Census of Employment data from NOMIS. Interviews in 12 areas

to expand steel production were abandoned in 1978. Southside's steel plant, with its main strength in semi-finished products, faced increasing competition from lower-cost producers in 'developing' countries. Its other major employer, ICI, was also facing stiff competition, and between 1970 and the late 1980s, increasingly located its production overseas. Its business was also changing, with less demand for bulk chemicals and a higher proportion of work in speciality products: high technology, low volume and high-risk operations (Beynon et al, 1989). Eighteen thousand jobs were lost in Redcar and Cleveland in the late 1970s and 1980s. In Knowsley, over half of male manufacturing employment was lost between 1971 and 1984 (Meegan, 1989).

The impact of these rapid and profound changes varied from place to place according to the history and structure of employment and the organisation of

Table 2.5: Industrial decline: areas dependent on traditional industries and/ or manufacturing (1971-91)

| | | Employment change 1971-99 (%) | | |
	Manufacturing jobs	Service sector jobs	All jobs	Male full-time jobs
West-City (Hackney)	−75	+48	−11	−24
East-Docks (Newham)	−75	−59	−65	−74
The Valley[a] (Sheffield)	−64	+22	−25	−41
Middle Row (Birmingham)	−75	+43	−37	−55
Overtown (Knowsley)	−48	+23	−13	−24
Shipview[a] (Newcastle)	−72	+14	−18	−45
Southside (Redcar and Cleveland)	−76	+181	−53	−64
High Moor[a] (Blackburn)	−44	+34	−12	−28
Fairfields (Caerphilly)	+13	+116	+46	+42

Note: Figures based on amalgamated job centre areas. Where [a], these refer to a substantially bigger area than the study area.

Source: Census of Employment data from NOMIS

work and social life. The psychological effect of the loss of the major employer in a one-company town, where the firm had a major part in local social organisation, running transport, sports and social clubs and even owning housing, differed from that where large numbers of jobs were lost across numerous small companies. The impact on family life of the shift from male to female work was different in communities organised around full-time male labour and female domestic roles (such as South Wales or the North East) than in manufacturing areas such as Hackney or Leeds which had a tradition of female work. Even the psychological impact could be different. Knowsley's new communities, for example, were experiencing the boom/bust cycle for the first time, while those in Newcastle had a collective memory of the high unemployment of the 1930s. Decline in the East End of London had the same structural causes as that of Newcastle, but took place in the context of nearby business and service sector prosperity, rather than wholesale regional downturn (Massey, 1994).

Yet, although the local experiences were different, the scale of the physical and social change was consistently huge. Taylor et al (1996) describe how the industrial area in Sheffield, close to The Valley, was literally "razed to the ground. By 1986 the same thoroughfares which had previously wound past the high frontages of massive steel plants ... now cut across vast open stretches of wasteland" (p 65). A long-standing resident of East-Docks said:"It's been amazing to see the difference since the docks closed from the thriving 60s and 70s to the dead 80s and 90s. It was bustling – shops and cafes on every corner. People could hold their head up here and work every day from when they left school to when they retired", and in Overtown on Merseyside a resident pointed out the "dead" bus stops where scores of people used to queue in the mornings to go to work. In Newcastle, a local priest described the enormous change since his arrival in 1972:

> "Everyone went from school to the shipyards. Jobs were automatic. You didn't have to have an interview. Sons followed their fathers. Even at the best of times there was unemployment. There were families that never worked. But the big change was in the early 1980s. It was a horrific experience for families here. There were men who brought their tools home and just never went out of the house. It put a huge stress on families which broke down at an alarming rate."

The changes were also enormous in smaller settlements. In Valley Top in South Wales, the loss within several years of an engineering firm which employed 500 people, mainly men, and 1,000 female jobs in a clothing company, was devastating in a town with a population of only 6,000:"When Hymac closed, that had a lot to do with it [the decline of the town]. And Smith's. Every woman in Valley Top worked there at one time" (resident).

Only three of the study areas suffered less through industrial restructuring. All had more diverse economies, with employment spread across a greater number of sectors and firms. Manufacturing made up a smaller proportion of the economy and its job losses had correspondingly less impact and, indeed, were outstripped by service sector growth (Table 2.6), reflecting a wider trend for areas with a lower degree of employment specialisation to respond more readily to structural economic change (Begg et al, 2002).

However, these changes did not necessarily represent a substantial improvement in labour market conditions or incomes. In these areas and the others, sectoral changes were also causing structural adjustments in the labour market. Manufacturing and traditional industries had demanded large-scale workforces, utilising both skilled and unskilled manual labour. While some industries (such as the docks) had a tradition of casual work, others offered stable employment and relatively good wages for unqualified workers. The new economy brought different demands. Increasingly complex technology and the demands of global communication and decision making created a demand for high-level technological, professional and managerial skills, commanding high rewards. The top end and the bottom end of the labour market became more highly differentiated and the premium on educational attainment increased. Few manual workers whose jobs were made redundant by cuts in capacity or by the

Table 2.6: Industrial structure and decline: areas with more diverse economies (1971-91)

	Main employment sectors (1971) (with more than 15% of workforce)	Employment change 1971-91 (%)			
		Manufact-uring jobs	Service sector jobs	All jobs	Male full-time jobs
Riverlands[a] (Nottingham)	Manufacturing (37) Transport, communication (27)	−35	+39	+6	−11
Kirkside East[a] (Leeds)	Manufacturing (35) Distribution (22) Transport, communication (22)	+33	+107	+85	+54
Beachville (Thanet)	Miscellaneous services (25) Manufacturing (24) Transport (22) Distribution (17)	−21	+36	+19	−7

Note: Figures based on amalgamated job centre areas. Where [a], these refer to a substantially bigger area than the study area, including the city centre. Kirkside East job centre area includes a more prosperous area in addition to Kirkside East.

Source: Census of Employment data from NOMIS

introduction of new technology had the skills to make the transition into the growing tier of managerial and professional positions (Elias and Bynner, 1997). Their prospects more realistically lay within the remains of the manufacturing sector or in new service industries. In both cases, the middle ground of the labour market was shrinking, with particular consequences for men. Within manufacturing, fewer workers were needed, but with higher skills and more modern skills, while service industries required large numbers of low-skilled workers, often part-time, who could only command relatively low wages. These jobs were not a replacement for full-time jobs and were often taken by women, supplementing the earnings or benefits of other family members. Across all sectors, the number of people in temporary work grew as companies attempted to retain flexibility to respond to competitive pressures, and moved to leaner structures with a small core and with more functions contracted out (Howarth et al, 1998). Thus, in working-class areas, increasing numbers of jobs could obscure a picture of increasing differentiation in wages, loss of full-time employment and opportunities for progression, and more limited security.

Changes in Beachville are a good example of restructuring in an overall situation of growth. The town's tourist industry was in serious decline throughout this period. The number of hotel rooms declined from 407 in 1971 to 124 in 1985, by far its most rapid decline since the start of the mass market foreign holidays in the 1950s. Manufacturing, which had been seen as the replacement for tourist jobs, also declined. The growth sector was private welfare provision: residential care homes for older people and disabled people, offering primarily part-time and low-skilled work and employment instability, which had long been a feature of the area's economy (Buck et al, 1989).

Thus the picture of employment change in the 12 areas in the two decades up to 1991 was one of substantial local difference in timing and impact, underpinned by the same broad structural changes, and resulting in rising unemployment, increasing proportions of part-time work, an increasing distinction between 'core' employees with stable employment and those in a series of temporary and casual jobs, and increasing pay differentials between skilled and unskilled workers.

Rising inequality

The result of these labour market changes was widening income inequality. First, the policy of successive governments to link benefit payments to prices rather than to earnings meant that the incomes of those who were not working fell further adrift from the average. Second, there was a widening gap in pay. Earnings in low-skilled work fell significantly in relative terms. Wages for the lowest paid male workers were lower in real terms in 1992 than in 1975, while median wages rose by 35% and high wages by 50% (Hills, 1995). Low-skilled workers thus moved down the income distribution, closer to those with no work and further adrift from the incomes of the higher skilled. And third, there was a polarisation of prospects, as both employment chances and earnings became more closely linked to educational attainment. The earnings premium on qualifications increased. For younger workers especially, the difference in pay between those with qualifications and those without increased, as did the difference in future pay prospects (Hills, 1995).

These were national trends, affecting whole classes in society, individuals and families, not areas per se. Even within disadvantaged areas, some people benefited while others lost out. Writing in 1989, Richard Meegan described widening social divisions within residential estates in Knowsley, between employed and unemployed, and between those in stable employment with large firms and those in low-paid or insecure employment. Those with stable employment tended to be able to buy their council houses, own a car, and shop and socialise further afield, broadening their social networks and weakening the economic base for local shops and leisure facilities. The unemployed, or those in low-paid work, were on another trajectory with a different lifestyle; state dependent, in lower quality housing, dependent on public transport and on declining local shops and services (Meegan, 1989). Nevertheless, the very fact that industrial decline was unevenly spatially distributed meant that differences between areas would be more marked than those within. Inequality between areas populated mainly by 'haves' and those populated by 'have nots' was bound to grow, even if nothing else happened. Unemployment figures show this process at work. Census data indicates that male unemployment nationally, as a proportion of economically active males, nearly trebled between 1971 and 1991, from 4% to 11%. In the study areas, it typically increased four- or five-fold, except in Shipview and

Fairfields, where substantial job losses had already occurred by 1971. By 1991, male unemployment in most of the areas was between one quarter and one third of the economically active male population, compared with 11% nationally (Table 2.7).

Meanwhile, something else was happening to compound these changes. As jobs were disappearing, the populations of the areas were also changing, increasing the concentration of poverty even further.

Population change

As jobs disappeared from disadvantaged urban and industrial areas, so did people. Cities were the earliest and biggest losers. In most cases, population drain preceded job loss, as slum clearance and suburbanisation pulled people away from urban areas (Rogers and Power, 2000). Housing redevelopments reduced overcrowding and improved standards of living, but also reduced the everyday hustle and bustle of the areas and the economic base for shops and services. The population of most cities was already declining, in relative terms, in the 1950s, while employment continued to grow in the urban cores. By the 1960s most cities were experiencing actual population decline and relative employment decline, as deindustrialisation began to impact (LSE, 1976; Spence et al, 1982; Champion et al, 1998).

The loss of jobs from cities ensured that the decline of their populations continued during the 1970s and 1980s. While nationally the population grew

Table 2.7: Change in unemployment rates (1971-91)

	Male unemployment as % of economically active males		
	1971	1991	% point change
West-City (Hackney)	5	26	+21
East-Docks (Newham)	8	27	+19
Riverlands (Nottingham)	8	29	+21
The Valley (Sheffield)	6	30	+24
Middle Row (Birmingham)	8	36	+28
Shipview (Newcastle)	10	28	+18
Kirkside East (Leeds)	6	22	+16
Valley Top (Fairfields, Caerphilly)*	14	27	+13
England and Wales	4	11	+7

Notes:

1. Because of boundary changes we can only look at this data for eight of our areas.

*2. Because of boundary changes, we are only able to compare Valley Top, not Fairfields as a whole.

3. There are some definitional changes between 1971 and 1991. In 1971, there was no 'unemployed' category. Economically active people were classified as either working or 'seeking work' (which is used here for comparison with unemployment in 1991). Students were not classified separately in 1971 and could be included in the economically active total, thus increasing the size of the denominator compared with 1991. However, these differences would not account for the significant changes recorded here.

Source: 1971 and 1991 Censuses of Population

by 1% between 1971 and 1991, most of the cities in the study lost more than 10% of their population. Populations in the city study areas fell even more dramatically, with the exception of Middle Row in Birmingham (Figure 2.1).

Outside the cities, population losses for the local authorities in the study were smaller, with some settlements within them benefiting from urban to rural population shifts and inter-regional shifts. Thanet, in Kent, gained population over this period, mainly in the 35-54 and 55+ age groups, older workers and retirees attracted by the seaside environment (Beatty and Fothergill, 2003a). However, both historical accounts and Census data for the eight areas where ward boundaries permit comparison over time suggest large declines in most of the study areas themselves, which were industrial communities located within semi-rural local authorities. When work declined, these communities declined. Deindustrialisation was the direct driver of change.

Accounts from the areas of population decline illustrate its impact. Long-standing residents in Southside, Redcar and Cleveland, recalled how the population began to ebb away in the late 1970s when jobs were lost, and particularly after the closure of the major employer, a shipyard, in 1986. There was what one local authority officer described as a "drift westwards" to areas of

Figure 2.1: Population change (1971-91)

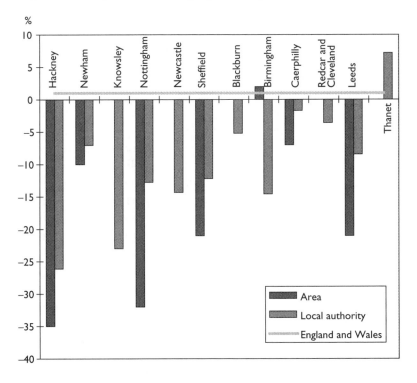

Sources: Local authority data from OPCS (1994). Ward-level data calculated from 1971 and 1991 Census data where wards have remained comparable over time

55

higher employment. The thriving shopping centre in Borough View started to struggle: "You used to be able to get anything you wanted but it all went very quickly when the jobs went" (resident). We were told that five schools shut because pupil numbers were falling so quickly, and by the early 1990s, private landlords had bought up homes from owner-occupiers who had moved away, and empty homes had begun to appear on the once popular council estate. There was a sense of depletion: "The place got torn to shreds – everything's gone, the houses, the shops, everything" (resident). In Fairfields, a resident said it was "unbelievable how it's degenerated from a town into absolutely nothing" after the houses were redeveloped and jobs and people went. West-City pensioners described their thriving market, now struggling, and a gradual decline, since the Second World War, of shops and services. In East-Docks and in The Valley, stories of decline were similar:

"… the shops have declined. There used to be Woolworths and some good little shops. There's nothing now – just food and £1 shops." (resident, East-Docks)

"… in the 1960s you could get anything you wanted here – a co-op, fruit and veg, furniture, anything. Now there's nothing except a few ethnic shops." (resident, The Valley)

People who were economically active were more able to move in search of work. At the same time, older workers, having lost their lifelong employment, were dropping out of the labour market. These trends, in combination, led to an enormous drop in the numbers of economically active men, and a fall in economic activity well in excess of the national average, which was in any case declining partly as a result of expanding opportunities in further and higher education.

Women's economic activity rates, which increased nationally, typically remained the same in these areas or even fell. The loss of male employment in a family meant that it was often more beneficial for a female part-time worker to give up work and depend entirely on benefits than to try to support a family on a low wage. High rates of single parenthood also kept women of working age out of the labour market. Thus, by 1991, there were fewer people in the areas, fewer of them were active in the labour market, and fewer of those were employed (Table 2.8).

Moreover, apart from the fact that economic changes were putting pressure on the incomes of existing residents, the position of the areas in the housing market ensured that new residents were also likely to be poor. The hotels in Beachville were beginning to be used as B&B hostels as they became redundant for tourism. Areas of private ownership and renting such as Middle Row in Birmingham and parts of The Valley (Sheffield) and Riverlands (Nottingham) had become established as low-status areas and were becoming home to growing Asian populations, predominantly from impoverished rural areas of Pakistan. Middle

Table 2.8: Changes in population and economic activity (1971-91)

	Change in economically active male population	Economically active males as % of population 1971	1991	Male economic activity rates 1971	1991	Female economic activity rates 1971	1991
West-City (Hackney)	−33	30	28	84	71	52	48
East-Docks (Newham)	−20	32	26	86	73	48	45
Riverlands (Nottingham)	−50	29	26	81	68	46	45
The Valley (Sheffield)	−34	26	25	84	66	47	43
Middle Row (Birmingham)	−23	30	24	87	69	45	37
Shipview (Newcastle)	−40	25	25	80	67	43	42
Kirkside East (Leeds)	−36	28	23	84	67	49	41
Fairfields* (Caerphilly)	−20	29	23	78	62	34	38
England and Wales	−14	29	28	81	73	43	50

Notes:

1. Because of boundary changes we can only look at this data for eight of our areas.

*2. Because of boundary changes, we are only able to compare Valley Top, not Fairfields as a whole.

3. Students were not classified separately in 1971 and could be included in the economically active total. This, and the rising number of students generally, partly accounts for falling economic activity over the period.

Source: 1971 and 1991 Censuses of Population

Row's minority ethnic population grew from 35% in 1971 to 67% in 1991 (driving its population growth overall), Riverlands' from 7% to 19% and The Valley's from 9% to 26%. This growing ethnic group was the poorest in the country. Government statistics show that people of Pakistani or Bangladeshi origin are more likely than others to have long-term illness, to live in overcrowded households and to be unemployed (SEU, 2000b). They are less well paid than other ethnic groups, are least likely to have formal savings, and draw the largest proportion of their income from state benefits (ONS, 1996). Because of the disadvantage and discrimination faced by minority ethnic groups, the changing ethnic composition of these areas contributed to their aggregate poverty rather than alleviating it.

But the most stubborn problems were building up in the areas of council housing. Overall in England and Wales, the proportion of households in social housing remained constant during the 1970s, with a trend towards owner-occupation offsetting new council housebuilding. However, as redevelopment of slum clearance areas continued, most of the areas saw significant increases in social housing. By 1981, the two inner London areas, East Docks and West-City, as well as Kirkside East and much of Shipview, had well over 80% council housing. Similarly concentrated neighbourhoods existed in most of the other areas (Table 2.9).

The development of single tenure social housing neighbourhoods ensured that new residents would be predominantly from lower-income groups. Social

Table 2.9: Tenure change (1971-91)

	% households in social housing		
	1971	1981	1991
West-City (Hackney)			
Ward A	78	93	83
Ward B	26	70	59
Ward C	15	86	73
Ward D	75	96	86
East-Docks (Newham)			
Ward A	48	92	81
Ward B	89	80	77
Ward C	58	80	58
Riverlands (Nottingham)			
Ward A	29	60	54
Ward B	29	75	61
Ward C	37	43	38
Shipview (Newcastle)			
Ward A	89	90	80
Ward B	52	75	74
Ward C	32	36	33
The Valley (Sheffield)	30	56	52
Middle Row (Birmingham)	23	44	56
Kirkside East (Leeds)	87	82	70

Notes:

1. Data only presented for areas where wards are comparable over whole period.

2. Individual wards shown rather than areas because 1971 data presented as rate per 1,000 households not as absolute numbers.

3. Social housing includes council-owned property in 1971 and 1981, and council-owned and housing association property in 1991.

Source: 1971, 1981, 1991 Censuses of Population

changes meant that demand from certain disadvantaged groups was growing, while changes to housing legislation during the 1970s altered the basis of council house allocations more in favour of the most needy, giving these groups greater access to social housing than they had previously enjoyed. The biggest group was lone parents, many of them being allocated homes as homeless families (because their own families could no longer accommodate them) and in priority need. The number of lone-parent households nationally trebled between 1971 and 1991, the majority of them on low incomes. In 1991, 63% were inactive or unemployed and a further 10% worked less than 16 hours per week; 68% were on Income Support. Moreover, the 1977 Housing Act, which gave priority to households with children, increased the numbers of lone parents in social housing. In 1971, 40% of lone parents lived in social housing, rising to 56% in 1991, compared with only 23% of households overall (Marsh et al, 1997).

These changes were referred to by many respondents in the study areas. In most areas, they commented on the high proportions of single mothers, many of them young and struggling to cope. The changing composition of the areas had been gradual. As one respondent put it: "The demographics have changed. There aren't enough stable families. It's not that single parents are to blame, it's that the balance is wrong" (priest, Shipview). On the Sunnybank estate in Shipview, the change had been marked, because a number of long-standing elderly residents all moved at once into a newly built sheltered housing scheme, replaced mainly by young mothers. Residents complained about "families moving in and dragging the estate down", and family workers about the high number of vulnerable and isolated young parents, with low incomes, needing support.

Lone parents were not the only disadvantaged group whose access to social housing improved during this period. Race relations legislation was also instrumental in opening up social housing to people from minority ethnic groups. Whereas in 1971, black and Asian households were substantially less likely than white households to be in public housing, by 1991 their access to this tenure had improved considerably. Black and Bangladeshi households were more than twice as likely as white households to be in public housing, although Indian and Pakistani households remained more likely to be in the private sector (Dale et al, 1996). This change had no impact in the industrial and outer-city areas in the North and Wales where minority ethnic immigration, if present, was confined to central areas, but it had a major effect on the two East London areas, which had historically been white working-class neighbourhoods, apart from a small but long-established African Caribbean population in East-Docks. Table 2.10 shows that in 1971, fewer than one in 20 was from a minority ethnic group, except in one particular ward with a lot of private rented accommodation, while by 1991 this had risen to more than one in four in West-City and one in five in East-Docks.

Table 2.10: Change in ethnic composition of London areas (1971-91)

Area		1971 estimated black or Asian population (%)	1991 black or Asian population (%)
West-City	Ward A	5	38
	Ward B	27	27
	Ward C	6	26
	Ward D (The Grove)	5	22
East-Docks	Ward A (Phoenix Rise)	12	23
	Ward B	1	15
	Ward C	4	19

Note: Census definitions have changed over time. The 1971 Census only collected information on country of birth. The category of people born in the New Commonwealth is the closest to the black or Asian classification used in the 1991 Census. However, Field et al (1981) estimated that in 1975 people born in the New Commonwealth accounted for only about 65% of the New Commonwealth population in the UK. The estimated figure thus grosses up the Census count by a multiplier of 100/65.

Source: 1971 and 1991 Censuses of Population

Increasing concentrations of poverty in social housing were exacerbated by Conservative housing policy during the 1980s. By this time, aspirations to home ownership were already increasing, making some of the least popular social rented homes 'difficult to let'. The introduction of the 'Right to Buy' in 1981 enabled tenants to buy their council houses at discounted prices, causing a significant reduction in the council stock overall, while new building was for owner-occupation. In 1980, council housing accounted for 33% of the total housing stock, reducing to 20% by 1991. This change had a geographical pattern, simply because the most popular stock tended to be clustered on certain estates, which had high rates of council house sales, while fewer people wanted to buy on the least popular estates. For example, one estate in Overtown (Knowsley) had Right to Buy sales of about 60-70%, while for most estates the average was 10%. In Shipview (Newcastle), only "a handful" of homes on the Sunnybank estate were sold, according to the housing manager, but bungalows on the estate across the road were popular. Local authorities were thus left with the less desirable stock, which probably in turn fuelled aspirations to home ownership.

By 1991, the relationship between social housing and area deprivation had become very strong. Incomes of council house tenants were falling relative to others, so areas of concentrated council housing were becoming relatively poorer. At the beginning of the 1980s, the income of the average council house tenant was 73% of the national average. By the beginning of the 1990s it had fallen to 48% (Bradshaw and Sainsbury, 2000). Figure 2.2 demonstrates that areas with high concentrations of social housing were very likely to be among the most deprived wards in the country, those we had defined as 'poverty wards' from the 1991 Census data.

Figure 2.2: Relationship between concentration of social housing and poverty

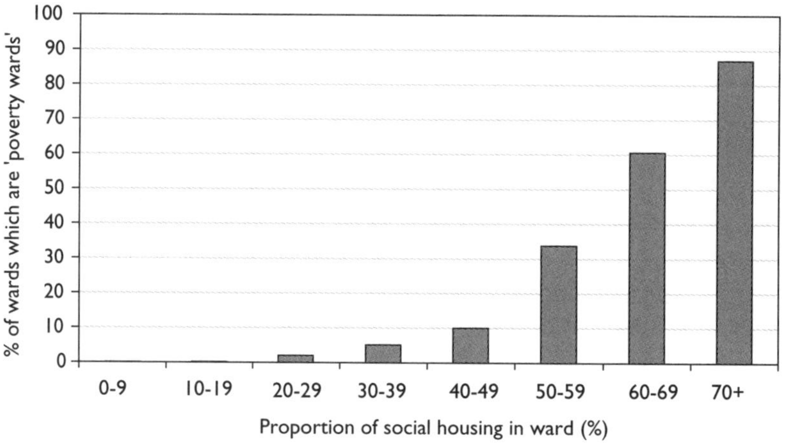

Source: 1991 Census of Population

The poverty map and the poverty gap

These changes, combined, meant that although with rising living standards, levels of absolute poverty diminished between 1971 and 1991, relative poverty did not. While housing conditions and the availability of material goods improved, poor areas stayed relatively poor.

Data on car ownership over time illustrates the point. 'Access to a car' was the only poverty indicator consistently used in the 1971, 1981 and 1991 Censuses, usefully so, since in a world of increasing car dependence, lack of access to a car is increasingly a causal mechanism in social exclusion as well as just a proxy for poverty (Rogers and Power, 2000). Data for those of our 12 areas where comparisons are possible show a striking picture. All experienced significant aggregate increases in car access, but smaller increases than the cities or boroughs in which they were located (Figure 2.3). The Valley, for example, saw an increase of 11 percentage points (from 25% to 36%), compared with 21 percentage points for Sheffield as a whole (34% to 55%), and a national increase of 20 percentage points (48% to 68%). So, while The Valley became increasingly 'car rich' in absolute terms, it became relatively more 'car poor'.

Figure 2.3: Access to a car (1971 and 1991)

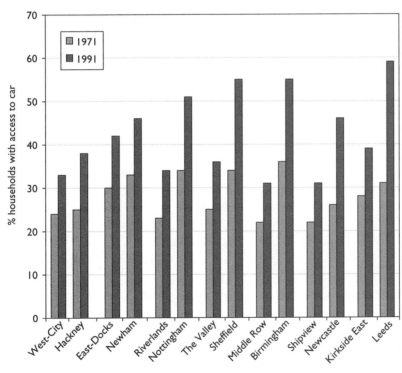

Note: Areas are only included where wards are comparable between 1971 and 1991. Bars indicating change in each area are shown alongside bars indicating change for the local authority in which the area is situated.
Source: 1971 and 1991 Censuses of Population

In Sheffield and Newham, where we can compare ward for ward between the 1971 and 1991 Censuses, this pattern was also replicated in other poor neighbourhoods. 'Car rich' areas in 1971 made greater gains in their rate of car ownership than 'car poor' areas, thus widening the gap. In Newham, the average percentage point gain among the bottom fifth of wards was 5%, compared with 10% in the top fifth of wards. Similarly in Sheffield, car poor areas gained 8% while car rich areas gained 13%. Thus the overall poverty map remained substantially unchanged. In both boroughs, nine of the bottom 10 wards in 1991 had been in the bottom 10 in 1971.

These findings are consistent with other studies using different indicators. Green (1996), comparing 1991 and 1981 Census data, found that there was essential continuity in the geography of poverty and wealth but that some poor areas, such as inner London, other large cities and coalmining areas even saw an increase in poverty. Noble and Smith (1996), using benefit claim data, also reported poor areas within towns and cities getting relatively poorer during the 1980s. And this was also the overwhelming impression from the people we interviewed in 1999, who reported persistent decline over at least two or three decades, sometimes more, and of the areas having become stuck in a poverty trap, despite some improvements in material conditions.

> "The area's been deteriorating for at least 20 years. The council hasn't invested in it … materially we're better off, but in many ways things in those days were less desperate." (resident, West-City, Hackney)

> "People seem more stuck in the city. There's more despair." (resident, East-Docks, Newham)

> "The problem built up over time. Some people had already lost their jobs in the 1970s so by the late 1990s you had third-generation unemployment. Problems just got more ingrained. Perhaps the population drain was allowed to go on for too long before there was any intervention." (youth worker, Southside, Redcar and Cleveland)

Thus, when we selected our 12 areas on the basis of 1991 Census data, we were selecting places that had long been poor and which, over the previous two decades, had experienced rapid and severe economic decline. Economic and welfare changes had meant that inequality between areas had widened, while changes in the housing system meant that the poor were increasingly funnelled into them, while the better-off moved away. And social changes were altering the composition of the areas, with new kinds of disadvantaged groups often lacking the support they needed. At the start of the decade, area problems were already entrenched and the poverty gap was widening.

The 1990s brought both change and continuity. There were broad patterns that were evident in all areas. Following a steep economic recession until 1993, the rest of the decade was characterised by sustained economic recovery, the benefits of which were felt even in the poorest areas (Evans et al, 2002), with falling rates of unemployment and means-tested benefit claims. The major job losses of the 1970s and 1980s were not replicated on the same scale, while service sectors grew consistently. However, while worklessness and poverty declined, skills and pay continued to diverge, with the problems of in-work poverty and exclusion being increasingly recognised as a problem for those at the bottom of the labour market. Technological and social change continued, and the most vulnerable and marginalised members of society continued to be funnelled into unpopular social housing or areas of low-income private sector housing. Urban to rural population shifts continued for most of the decade, with some evidence of an urban revival towards the end, and preferences for social housing continued to decline.

These were broad patterns that were evident in all the areas. But their impact was not the same everywhere. In particular, we began to see a divergence between inner-city areas in places of population growth, which were coming under increasing housing pressure and increasingly populated by disadvantaged immigrant communities, and areas of population decline, which were literally emptying out, with swathes of empty housing and increasingly derelict environments. Economically, there were areas that kept up with (or exceeded) national rates of job growth, while others fell further behind. It began to be clear that certain areas were well placed for economic recovery while others might have no long-term viability. During the 1990s, the trajectories of these disadvantaged areas began to pull apart as their location and characteristics proved a better or worse 'fit' with continuing social and economic change. It is to this story that I turn in Chapter Three.

Summary

- Poverty was a long-established feature of all the areas, with the exception of parts of one of them, Beachville in Kent, which had been largely non-residential until the 1980s.
- Nine of the areas (Box 2.1) were areas of primary deprivation; that is to say, that they had been poor since their inception. These included six inner-city or industrial neighbourhoods that had grown up in the Industrial Revolution. Some of the original workers' cottages remained but others had been cleared from the 1940s through to the 1970s, replacing slums with council flats and houses. Three of the primary deprivation areas had been built more recently, in the 1920s, 1930s and 1940s. They were estates of council housing built to accommodate city population growth and to rehouse people from slum clearance areas.

Box 2.1: Areas of primary and secondary deprivation

Areas of primary deprivation

Built in the 1800s:

- East-Docks (Newham)
- Riverlands (Nottingham)
- Fairfields (Caerphilly)
- Southside (Redcar and Cleveland)
- High Moor (Blackburn)
- West-City (Hackney)

Built in the 1930s/1940s

- Overtown (Knowsley)
- Shipview (Newcastle)
- Kirkside East (Leeds)

Areas of secondary deprivation

- The Valley (Sheffield)
- Middle Row (Birmingham)
- Beachville (Thanet)

- The other three areas, in inner cities, had once been better off, populated by middle-class households, who subsequently moved out to the suburbs. These areas had become home to successive waves of immigrant populations and to transient households in short-term rented accommodation. They can be referred to as areas of secondary deprivation (Box 2.1).
- However, it was the period from the 1970s to the early 1990s in which the areas suffered the most serious decline, as a result of three forces: economic restructuring, widening inequality in society generally, and population shifts.
- The 1970s and 1980s were a period of catastrophic employment loss, with the continuing decline of traditional industries (coal, shipbuilding and ports) and the collapse of manufacturing. Over 50% of male full-time jobs were lost in some areas between 1971 and 1991. Areas dependent on one or a small number of employers were hit much harder than those dependent on a larger number of industries.
- Structural economic change resulted in widening inequality. Earnings levels became more differentiated and benefits, linked to prices not earnings, failed to keep up.
- Population was inevitably lost as people moved in search of work. For the cities this exacerbated an urban to rural shift that was already happening. As the better off moved away, poverty became more concentrated in the remaining population.
- Council housing areas were developing the most entrenched poverty concentrations. Slum clearance programmes increased the number of council homes in the area significantly between 1971 and 1991, while the basis for allocations was changed so that a higher proportion of these homes went to the most needy. Increasing preferences for owner-occupation and the

---

introduction of the Right to Buy led to further residualisation of council housing as more advantaged tenants moved away.

- The result of these changes was that the map of poverty remained substantially unchanged, while the gap between poor areas and others grew. By the beginning of the 1990s, poverty concentrations were acute and inequality was wide.

Note

[1] The title of this publication includes the real name of the neighbourhood concerned. In the Bibliography, the name has been changed to protect the identity of the neighbourhood.

THREE

The 1990s: decline and divergence

Area fortunes pull apart: Southside and West-City

There is no better illustration of the contrasts of the 1990s than the stories of Southside, the cluster of small towns in heavily industrialised Teesside, and West-City, the densely flatted inner London neighbourhood close to the City.

Southside had traditionally been poor, but in the 1950s and 1960s it was enjoying a post-war boom. We were told that Borough View's main shopping street had about 360 shops, including branches of national retailers, and that jobs were readily available in the steel and chemical industries. One former resident described how people could expect to finish one job and walk into another on the same day, such was the demand for labour. All of this collapsed in the next two decades. Half the total jobs, and nearly two thirds of male full-time jobs, disappeared. People moved away, undermining the basis for shops and services, while the building of a new bypass cut off Borough View's town centre and effectively killed it off as a commercial area.

But it was in the 1990s that the area reached a critical point. Jobs continued to be lost throughout the decade, as ICI and British Steel underwent further rationalisation. The location of the area and its heavily industrialised past and contaminated land gave it no relative advantages for inward investors. Although incentives were offered for inward investment, similar opportunities were also available throughout the sub-region. New developments tended to locate in the North Tees rather than the South Tees area. The entire sub-region was doing badly compared to the national picture, but Southside was even worse off than its local neighbours.

The calamitous population losses also continued. Southside's population diminished by an estimated 12% between 1991 and 1998, Borough View's by 23%. By the mid-1990s it was estimated that the town had only about 7,000 people, about a third of its post-war population. Empty homes were appearing in large numbers on the main council estate, which initially had about 550 homes, and to a lesser extent in an area of pre-1919 terraced properties (about 1,200 homes), which were mostly privately owned. The nearby town, Furnace Walk, also had large numbers of empty homes.

As people moved away, poverty concentrations increased. Homes were mainly let to people who had little other choice of housing. In the private sector area, privately owned houses were turned over to renting, bringing more transient residents. The impact of long-term unemployment began to be felt in rising crime and drug misuse. Swathes of empty housing provided opportunities for theft and vandalism. Between 1994 and 1996, crime and disorder problems flared up on the main council estate, with large numbers of unoccupied properties on the outer edge of the estate being vandalised and fire damaged.

As conditions on the estate worsened, some residents took advantage of the availability of private sector or housing association homes and left, sometimes with no notice. The housing manager reported how tenants would simply leave over the weekend and move into a new tenancy with another landlord, leaving their home unsecured and vulnerable to theft and vandalism before its owner discovered that the inhabitants had gone. The empty property problem spread into the heart of the estate "like a cancer" (housing manager).

Empty properties on Borough View's council estate await demolition

Between 1997 and 1999, 160 council homes in Borough View were demolished to restore the estate environment and bring supply in line with demand. With funding from the SRB, the remaining homes were improved internally, with new kitchens and bathrooms, and externally, with new boundary walls, parking areas and security lights. The estate stabilised and by 1999 only 13 properties were empty.

However, the supply of homes in the area still exceeded the underlying demand and as the council estate improved, the number of empty homes in the private sector housing area increased. Again, empty homes became the target of crime, rubbish dumping and antisocial behaviour and brought a sense of decline and dereliction. Property prices plummeted, so that by 1999 a two-bedroomed house could be bought for £5,000. Unwilling or unable to sell, some residents let their homes and moved away, or even abandoned their properties. By 1999, about 370 of the 1,200 homes were empty, and many others had been bought up at very low prices by private landlords, of which there were now over 100 in the area. With little capital outlay and Housing Benefit of approximately £55 per week for rent, many such landlords had no interest in the area or in enforcing tenancy conditions. As long-standing residents left, a higher proportion of the new tenants were young, transient, vulnerable or disruptive. Living conditions deteriorated further, fuelling the exodus of people and the area's unpopularity, and thus undermining the demand base for local shops and services. By 1999, there were no more than a handful of shops in Borough View's main street, and the long-term viability of the neighbourhood began to be questioned.

West-City, meanwhile, was on a different trajectory. It had also suffered population and job losses during the 1970s and 1980s, but by the 1990s this process was beginning to go into reverse. There was economic growth, significantly in excess of the national average, with a 30% increase in jobs over the period. As the City of London boomed, West-City was close by, offering affordable business rents and a stock of warehouses and factories ripe for conversion. The neighbourhood closest to the City was the first to benefit. During the second half of the 1990s, as property prices elsewhere rocketed, this neighbourhood was colonised by artists, film studios and other media industries, by cafes and night clubs for City workers, and later by bigger firms as rising rents pushed the smaller concerns into other, cheaper, areas. A local property developer described the area as "the next Covent Garden", such was the speed of its transformation.

Job growth and the 'trendification' of the area had a knock-on impact on the

A new canalside office development in West-City (Hackney) contrasts with the run-down market

housing market as West-City began to be popularised as a residential location for highly paid City workers. This process began to be very noticeable in 1997/98. Very rapid rises in house prices in the more popular areas of inner London forced buyers to look for affordable homes in previously downmarket areas. West-City was one such area. House prices rose by 86% between 1996 and 1999, reaching an average price of £163,000 in 1999, well beyond the reach of anyone on a low or middle income. Tenant representatives commented on a sense that the area was "up and coming" but also that existing residents, or their children who might want to stay in the area, were being "squeezed out by gentrification", too advantaged to gain access to social housing, and too disadvantaged to enter the private market.

While the middle was squeezed out of the housing market, there was growing demand at the bottom as well as at the top. Like most areas of inner London, West-City was facing increasing demand for its housing, mainly from the homeless and from refugees. A local priest observed that the international crises seen on television almost inevitably had local consequences as small groups of displaced people arrived several months later to begin a new life in West-City. The influx of these very disadvantaged households meant that the concentration of the poor continued, even though the number of higher income residents increased.

It also meant that the area underwent rapid ethnic change. A survey in 1999 showed that the minority ethnic population had risen from 28% in 1991 to 37%, with 20% of households speaking a language other than English at home. White residents were concentrated in the older age groups, with minority ethnic communities having a much younger profile. A total of 77% of children in the local primary schools were from minority ethnic groups (Mumford and Power, 2003). The biggest change in both cases was the growth in the African communities, particularly from Somalia and from West African countries such as Nigeria, Ghana and Sierra Leone. Eastern European refugees, particularly Serbs, Bosnians and Kosovans, also started to arrive in the late 1990s.

Immigration, gentrification and the higher birth/death ratio of minority ethnic communities meant that, in sharp contrast to that of Southside, West-City's population actually grew during the 1990s, by 3.4%, keeping pace with the national rate. Council flats were in poor condition and not necessarily a location of choice, but there was no difficulty finding tenants. In 1999, the housing manager reported that about 3% of the homes were empty, roughly the national average, and none of these long term. While Southside was semi-abandoned and increasingly derelict, West-City was full. It looked and felt busy.

However, because of the circumstances of the incomers, the growth in the population was adding to the poverty problem and not taking it away. In 1998, West-City was one of the most deprived areas in the study, with high levels of benefit claims, poor health, high unemployment and low literacy. There was increasing polarisation within the area and the problems of those at the bottom of the economic pile remained as acute as ever.

These two areas represent the extremes of the contrasts between poor neighbourhoods in the 1990s: the abandoned industrial North compared with crowded, polarised inner London. Others were less stark examples, but they demonstrate the same forces at work. Structural changes were continuing, but they were impacting unevenly, causing the fortunes of the disadvantaged neighbourhoods to diverge.

Uneven economic recovery

In England and Wales as a whole, the economic story of the 1990s was one of employment growth and of a continuing shift from manufacturing to service jobs. Following a slight dip at the beginning of the decade, the number of people in employment grew steadily to 1998, the year in which we selected the study areas. Overall job growth in this period was 9%. The number of part-time jobs grew faster (by 13%) than the number of full-time jobs (7%). However, full-time jobs made up a larger proportion of the total and therefore accounted for a larger proportion of the overall growth (6%) than part-time jobs (3%) (Figure 3.1). The service sector was the main growth engine. Manufacturing declined by 1% while there was a 30% increase in banking, finance and insurance and 20% in other services.

This was, then, a national economic context that was certainly more positive than it had been for most of the previous two decades. However, as previously, growth was not evenly distributed. The main growth areas were New Towns and cities in the South of England (including inner London), while northern cities had slower growth and coastal cities actually lost jobs (Robson et al, 2000).

Figure 3.1: Job growth in England and Wales (1991-98)

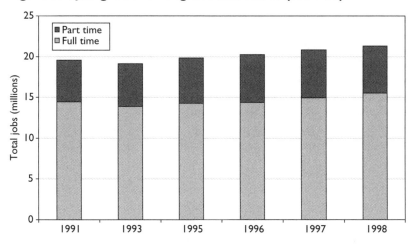

Source: Annual Employment Survey data from NOMIS

Because of sectoral shifts, cities that were heavily dependent on manufacturing suffered heavy losses that could not be offset by service sector growth. Manchester, for example, lost 9% of its total employment between 1991 and 1996, Liverpool 12%, Sheffield 6% and Birmingham 5% (Turok and Edge, 1999). On this basis, Breheny (1999) asserted that "those who have argued that cities have stemmed their decline and 'turned themselves round' on the basis of the information economy and knowledge-based services are flying in the face of the evidence" (p 17). There was, he claims, little evidence that the factors causing the decline of manufacturing in cities, such as the availability of industrial land and premises, had significantly changed, and nor had most of the factors that accounted for private sector service growth outside cities: urban depopulation, corporate reorganisation, availability of premises, changing working practices and the locational preferences of the self-employed.

There were, of course, exceptions. Cities with more diverse economies, such as London, Leeds and Nottingham, were in a better position. Although they lost manufacturing jobs in considerable number (Turok and Edge, 1999, reported that 22% of manufacturing jobs in London were lost between 1991 and 1996), service sector jobs more than made up for these losses. The number of jobs in Leeds grew by 7% and in Nottingham by 12% during this early to mid-1990s period. But these were star performers in a cast of cities that was generally performing poorly in economic terms. Outside the cities, in industrial areas, prospects of significant service sector growth were even more limited and depended on location and specific local features of the business infrastructure as well as on the wider regional economic context.

Most of the 12 study areas were, as described in Chapter Two, in the wrong place to benefit from this pattern of uneven growth. In northern cities, outlying industrial areas and coastal towns, they were located in precisely the places that were the losers in economic restructuring. In 1998, after five years of national economic recovery, the majority were absolutely worse off in employment terms than they had been at the start of the decade, and even those that gained jobs were struggling to keep up with national job growth. However, there were marked differences. West-City was the major gainer but two of the other city areas, The Valley (Sheffield) and Kirkside East (Leeds) also gained jobs, although their growth was slower than the national average. On the other hand, three of the northern city areas were actual job losers as was the coastal town (Beachville in Kent), which had seen job growth in the 1980s, and two of the industrial areas outside cities (Figure 3.2). Shipview in Newcastle lost over half its jobs, with key large employers undergoing restructuring between 1996 and 1998.

The stories of these areas demonstrate the relationship between local factors and wider economic trends in determining economic trajectories. To prosper, areas needed to be both located within a well-performing regional economy and to have beneficial characteristics that would ensure job growth in their locality rather than others. West-City was a good example. The other areas that saw job growth also had locational or infrastructure advantages. High Moor, in Blackburn, benefited from the extension of the M65 motorway and the development and modernisation of nearby business parks. Its location meant that its economic performance was actually better than that of the town as a whole. The Valley, close to Sheffield's Don Valley redevelopment, Kirkside East in Leeds, and Fairfields in Caerphilly, also gained jobs, although they all

Figure 3.2: Overall job change for study areas (1991-98)

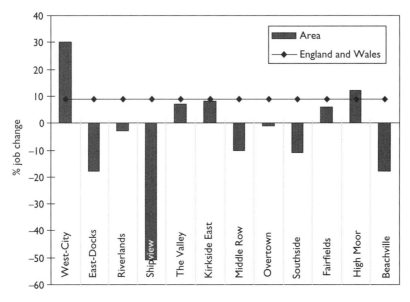

Note: London areas to far left of figure, followed by Northern cities, then other areas outside major cities.

Source: Annual Employment Survey data from NOMIS

experienced losses in male full-time jobs within a picture of overall growth. Fairfields and Kirkside East had very small local labour markets, of about 3,000–4,000 jobs, which were influenced considerably in percentage terms by the activities of one or two large firms.

By contrast, the job losers were located in weaker economies and/or lacked specific local advantages. Overtown in Knowsley was an example of an area with certain locational benefits in the context of a struggling regional economy. It had long suffered from 'branch plant syndrome', and continued to lose out through rationalisations and the decisions of multinational companies to source supply overseas. The area suffered significant job losses in the early 1990s. When the regional economy started to recover, it was positioned relatively well, with good transport links and available business park space, to capitalise on call centre and distribution work, and it made a small recovery up to 1998, but not sufficient to make up for earlier losses. Southside in Redcar and Cleveland, as described earlier, was relatively disadvantaged even within an underperforming region and sub-region.

The nature of work

Apart from changes in numbers of jobs, there was another important structural change taking place during the 1990s. Employment advisers and regeneration staff in Southside reported that many of the new jobs that the area was able to attract were in low-skilled, low-paid occupations, notably food processing. This was a familiar account. The main growth sectors mentioned by employment workers in most of the 12 areas were telework, retail or low-skilled factory work. In Fairfields in South Wales, firms on the industrial estates mainly employed people in low-paid packing or warehousing jobs. In Birmingham's Middle Row, there was an abundance of small businesses, shops, restaurants and taxi firms, all paying low wages, some as little as £2 per hour. In London's East-Docks, young adults reported working for £2.50 per hour in packing factories. Although in many cases the introduction of the national minimum wage in 1999 had raised workers' pay, it was not always applied and in some cases actually led to wage reductions. In Beachville, the seaside town where there were vacancies in cleaning and catering, and seasonal vacancies in agriculture and tourism, employment advisers reported that some small firms had actually reduced wages to the minimum wage level.

The other area of growth was at the top end of the job market. A major pharmaceuticals company was expanding close to Beachville and a marine and offshore technology centre had opened on the site of the former shipyards in Shipview, Newcastle. These jobs were beyond the skills of most local jobseekers. Even in existing firms like the steel and chemical industries in Southside, production jobs were becoming more skilled and technical. It was the middle ground in the job market that was continuing to erode.

This polarisation in skills applied in job growth as well as job loss areas. 'More jobs' often meant more part-time jobs, and/or low-paid or temporary work. Data from the Annual Employment Survey shows that, although there were exceptions, job losses in the areas were largely accounted for by losses in full-time jobs and job increases by gains in part-time jobs. Male full-time jobs were particularly vulnerable. Even in areas that made overall job gains, there were usually male full-time job losses. In seven areas, part-time jobs made up a bigger proportion of the total in 1998 than in 1991. These were large percentage point changes, compared with relatively small changes in the other direction in the other five areas (Table 3.1).

Table 3.1: Employment change (1991-98)

	Employment change (as % of all jobs in 1991)				
	Full-time jobs (male full-time jobs)	Part-time jobs	All jobs	Part-time jobs as % of total (1991)	Part-time jobs as % of total (1998)
West-City (Hackney)	+28 (+32)	+2	+30	19	16
High Moor (Blackburn)	+8 (+4)	+4	+12	17	29
Kirkside East (Leeds)	−5 (−10)	+14	+8	35	45
The Valley (Sheffield)	+3 (−3)	+4	+7	14	17
Fairfields (Caerphilly)	−3 (−11)	+9	+6	20	27
Overtown (Knowsley)	−1 (0)	0	−1	24	24
Riverlands (Nottingham)	−14 (−15)	11	−3	17	29
Middle Row (Birmingham)	−8 (−9)	-3	−10	20	19
Southside (Redcar and Cleveland)	−3 (−10)	-8	−11	29	24
East-Docks (Newham)	−18 (−27)	0	−18	12	14
Beachville (Thanet)	−10 (−20)	-8	−18	36	34
Shipview (Newcastle)	−48 (−64)	−3	−51	16	27
England and Wales	+6 (+5)	+3	+9	26	27

Source: Census of Employment/Annual Employment Survey data from NOMIS

Unemployment and worklessness

Net job losses, particularly in male full-time jobs, might have been expected to result in rising unemployment. They did not. In all the 12 local authority areas in the study, the numbers of people claiming unemployment benefit fell, in absolute terms, between 1991 and 1998 (Table 3.2). Most had falls similar to the national average.

These absolute falls were, in every area, reflected in falls in the unemployment rate (Figure 3.3). The data shown here expresses unemployment as a percentage of the working-age population, rather than as a percentage of the estimated workforce which is the method used in published data. This is to ensure a calculation method consistent with that used for ward-level data, rates for which are not published for this period. It is worth noting that this is a method that

Table 3.2: Local authority-level unemployment (1991-98)

	Number of claimant unemployed April 1991	Number of claimant unemployed April 1998	Change as % of 1991
Hackney	16,100	13,300	−17
Newham	14,400	11,100	−23
Knowsley	12,400	7,000	−44
Nottingham	17,100	11,400	−34
Newcastle	16,400	11,000	−33
Sheffield	26,900	18,000	−33
Blackburn	5,800	3,300	−43
Birmingham	56,400	38,400	−32
Caerphilly	7,300	4,200	−42
Redcar and Cleveland	9,600	5,300	−44
Leeds	27,800	19,200	−31
Thanet	5,400	4,400	−18
England and Wales	1,882,500	1,189,400	−37

Source: Claimant count data from NOMIS

tends to underestimate unemployment because it includes in the denominator people who are of working age but who are not in the labour market.

Data at the area level is only available from 1996, but shows that in all of the study areas there was a fall in unemployment from 1996 to 1998, both in absolute numbers (Table 3.3) and rates per working-age population (Figure 3.4). In most

Figure 3.3: Falls in claimant unemployment (April 1991-April 1998)

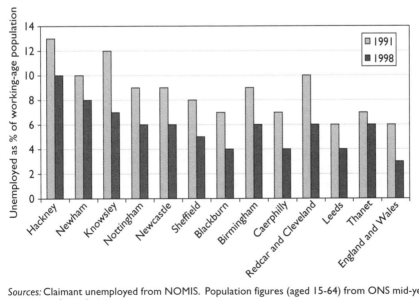

Sources: Claimant unemployed from NOMIS. Population figures (aged 15-64) from ONS mid-year estimates of population

Table 3.3: Area-level unemployment (1996-98)

	Numbers of claimant unemployed April 1996	Numbers of claimant unemployed April 1998	Change as % of 1996
West-City (Hackney)	2,660	1,830	−31.1
East-Docks (Newham)	1,610	1,270	−33.7
Overtown (Knowsley)	2,600	2,070	−20.3
Riverlands (Nottingham)	2,760	1,710	−38.0
Shipview (Newcastle)	2,300	1,700	−26.1
The Valley (Sheffield)	1,400	1,100	−22.4
High Moor (Blackburn)	930	590	−36.6
Middle Row (Birmingham)	2,800	2,120	−24.0
Fairfields (Caerphilly)	840	580	−31.9
Southside (Redcar and Cleveland)	1,510	1,110	−26.5
Kirkside East (Leeds)	1,220	830	−31.9
Beachville (Thanet)	2,220	1,490	−33.8
England and Wales	**1,937,100**	**1,189,400**	**−39.6**

Sources: Claimant count data from NOMIS

cases, the rate reduction in percentage point terms was greater than the national average, as might be expected given that the areas had a lot further to fall (Figure 3.4). However, in relation to their starting point (Table 3.3), all the areas performed worse than the national average, reflecting lower levels of job readiness. Evans et

Figure 3.4: Falls in claimant unemployment at area level (April 1996- April 1998)

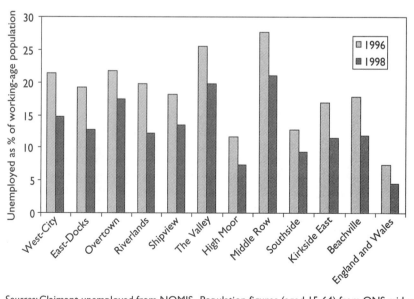

Sources: Claimant unemployed from NOMIS. Population figures (aged 15-64) from ONS mid-year estimates of population

al (2002), looking at the period 1995-2000, also found that the decline in benefit claims, in their case Income Support as well as Jobseeker's Allowance, was lower in areas with high claim rates than in those with low claim rates, thus increasing polarisation. Unemployment remained relatively high in all the areas at the end of the period.

Moreover, trends in claimant unemployment can only be treated as one indicator of economic performance. First, rates of claiming are heavily influenced by the rules of the benefit system. Beatty et al (2002) estimate that the claimant unemployed only make up about one third of all unemployed people, including those who are looking for work but not claiming[1], those on government schemes, people on sickness-related benefits and people who have retired early because there was no work available. Second, falls in unemployment, however measured, only reflect one aspect of a complicated process of labour market adjustment, as revealed by the use of labour market accounts (LMAs). LMAs add up changes in the working-age population, the inactive working-age population and the number of commuters, to demonstrate the impact of changes in the number of jobs in an area on the numbers of people unemployed. For example, an area can see falling unemployment even if the number of jobs falls, because the working-age population falls by a greater number. Conversely, unemployment can rise even if the number of jobs rises, because the new jobs and others are taken by in-commuters. Using LMAs, Beatty and Fothergill (1998) observed that in the UK coalfields, where there was a nine tenths loss of employment between 1981 and 1994, unemployment rates not only fell but converged with the national average, the consequence of job losses being seen not in registered unemployment but in out-migration or labour market withdrawal. The biggest single mechanism was the rise in economic inactivity, which included retirement, permanent sickness, full-time education or the informal labour market. Nationally, too, inactivity rose throughout the 1990s, while unemployment fell from 1993 onwards. The biggest rises in inactivity were among the unskilled, with a staggering increase over time from 4% in 1979 to 17% in 1990, rising to 30% in 2000 (*Economist*, 2001).

Drawing up LMAs is not possible at local area level, only for local authorities. Large local authorities, such as Birmingham, contain numerous local labour markets, some of them totally inaccessible from the study area, so using LMAs for the local authority would tell us little about the processes at work in our local areas. I have therefore looked here just at the four compact local authority areas in the study where the labour market for the local authority area corresponds reasonably well to the labour market for the study area – Blackburn, Knowsley, Redcar and Cleveland and Thanet. The data is only available from 1996.

Table 3.4 shows that all of these four districts lost resident jobs in the period from 1996 to the start of the study in 1998. In three cases, Blackburn, Redcar and Cleveland, and Thanet, they show exactly the same process that Beatty and Fothergill (1998) uncovered. The decline in resident jobs was entirely offset by the loss in working-age population and the growth in inactivity, causing

Table 3.4: Labour market accounts (1996-98)

	Blackburn	Redcar and Cleveland	Thanet	Knowsley
Change in local labour demand (number of resident employees) Accounted for by:	−5,000	−3,000	−4,000	−3,000
Change in number of employees	8,000	−2,400	1,700	1,200
Less change in net in-commuting	13,000	600	5,700	4,200
Change in local labour supply (economically active working-age population) Accounted for by:	−8,000	−6,000	−4,000	0
Change in working-age population	−3,000	−1,000	−4,000	1,000
Change in inactive population	5,000	5,000	0	1,000
Equals: Change in resident unemployment	−3,000	−3,000	0	3,000

Sources: Annual Employment Survey, Labour Force Survey

unemployment to fall or stay static. The number of resident jobs fell, but so too did the working-age population. At the same time, inactivity rose. Thus, although there were fewer jobs, there were also fewer unemployed people. Falling unemployment in these circumstances appears to reflect people moving or becoming inactive in response to a difficult labour market more than it reflects a transition from worklessness to work.

The changing profile of the labour market had its impact both for older workers and prospective labour market entrants – older people realising that their chances of satisfactory and secure employment might be slim, and younger people finding it hard to look forward to jobs with no identifiable trade, poor pay, little progression and possibly little security. Respondents made a direct connection between individual worklessness and the nature of jobs on offer:

> "People are getting work, but it's part-time or temporary work. Often it's low-paid. Some of these lead to permanent jobs but by no means all. It's a core and periphery situation. Lots of firms have reduced down to their core workers and those people are OK and stay in jobs, but people on the periphery have to pick up bits of work here and there but don't really get permanent or secure positions…. There's a genuine lack of well-paid employment." (employment adviser, High Moor, Blackburn)

> "There are jobs but there aren't necessarily the jobs that people want. For people who are used to claiming benefit, that's their automatic first option, then a job's second. If they're going to work they expect to get more from working than they can from benefit, and the service

sector jobs aren't offering the right salaries." (employment adviser, West-City, Hackney)

"… [the young people] hardly ever get decent jobs. The men do better. They seem to get warehouse work or labouring or the Post Office but the women mainly get packing or factory jobs. They're badly paid and there's no job security or health and safety. So there's a general apathy about work and low expectations." (youth worker, East-Docks, Newham)

While these respondents saw low expectations and apathy as a response to the kind of job opportunities on offer, in policy circles lack of incentive to work presented another problem – the danger of 'a benefit culture' and the development of an underclass cut off from the world of work. To stop people relying permanently on the security of benefits, and to connect them to employment opportunities as the economy recovered, successive governments in the 1990s attempted to tighten the unemployment benefit system, with greater requirements on claimants to demonstrate active jobseeking. This was especially the case after the introduction of the New Deal for the Unemployed in 1997. It became more difficult to claim benefit while not actively looking for work or while topping up income with informal cash-in-hand work. As a result, withdrawal from an unattractive labour market led increasingly to 'signing off' onto sickness benefits or into the informal labour market, rather than 'signing on' for unemployment benefit.

"Some of the fall in the register is due to older people, New Deal 25+, who are dropping off the register because they're working already. In this office we've been tightening up generally and that does account for people dropping off. One man even sent his card back with a note saying he couldn't be bothered with all the hassle." (employment adviser, Kirkside East, Leeds)

"… it's surprising that the register's gone down so much because there's been no real change in the number of jobs. The main reason is probably people dropping off the register." (employment adviser, Fairfields, Caerphilly)

'Dropping off' the register could mean switching to another benefit, typically Incapacity Benefit, which imposed fewer requirements. In six areas, the number of adults claiming Incapacity Benefit in 1998 was equal to or greater than the number of people claiming Jobseeker's Allowance. The highest proportion was in the Welsh former mining area, Fairfields, where 10% of adults were claiming Incapacity Benefit and just 3% claimed Jobseeker's Allowance. A recent survey of the non-employed in Thanet showed that while a third of non-employed men were claiming Incapacity Benefit, more than twice as many claimed Jobseeker's Allowance (Beatty and Fothergill, 2003a).

Moreover, for those staying in the labour market, changes in the structure of work meant that the prospect of 'churning' increased, with periods in work or on training schemes followed by periods on benefit. As an Employment Service worker in Sheffield commented:

> "There aren't enough quality jobs – lots of part-time service sector jobs that don't last. There's also a high turnover in manufacturing jobs, so you get people coming on and off the register." (employment adviser, Sheffield)

McKnight (2002) has described this as a 'low pay/no pay cycle' with low-paid employees more likely to become unemployed than those in higher-paid jobs and unemployed people most likely to enter low-paid jobs than to get anything better rewarded.

Thus the picture that emerged from the 12 areas was that falling unemployment masked changes in local labour markets which were generally to the detriment of low-skilled workers, causing an increasing divergence both between households and between neighbourhoods, exactly as suggested by Green in 1996:

> ... the decline in the number of non-precarious job opportunities for those at the lower end of the occupational spectrum, in many instances exacerbated by problems of spatial mismatch, would appear to be leading to a growth in no-earner households, neighbourhoods and labour markets, in conjunction with a growth in 'dual-career' neighbourhoods and labour markets in other locations within the urban and regional system. (Green, 1996, p 290)

Inequality, social change and social exclusion

Because economic restructuring continued in the 1990s, so too did its corollaries: inequality and labour market uncertainty.

While Hills (1995) has shown that, although earnings differentials did not widen much further in the early 1990s than they had done in the 1970s and 1980s, there was no evidence of a reversing trend. Earnings had become widely differentiated, as technological change and globalisation had both increased rewards for those with high-level skills and qualifications and created a large pool of low-skilled and low-paid jobs. While the real disposable incomes of the poorest 10% of households had remained virtually static since 1980, those of the richest 10% increased by one-and-a-half times (SEU, 2001b). Work had become relatively more rewarding to the highly skilled, and necessarily relatively less rewarding to the low-skilled. Agulnik et al (2002), for example, showed that in 1998, the difference in risk of unemployment between the unqualified and the average risk was twice what it was in 1979. Once unemployed, people remained so for three times as long as they did in the early 1970s. And benefit levels continued to fall behind levels of earnings. By 2002, Income Support levels were just 20% of average earnings, compared with 30% in the early 1980s, their lowest ever relative level (Rahman et al, 2001).

Differences in earnings and accumulated wealth meant that the spending power and lifestyles of the 'haves' and 'have nots' were poles apart. The aspirational world shaped by the marketing departments of global companies was increasingly affordable to the rich and increasingly unaffordable to the poor. For those born to low-income households, upward social mobility had become increasingly unlikely. McKnight (2002) found that young adults born in 1970 to low-income households faced greater disadvantages, in terms of both the probability of being in work and the earnings penalty, than those born in 1958. Although the expansion of middle-class occupations since the 1960s had meant that there was more 'room' for working-class children to be upwardly mobile, in reality the chances of them doing so had become smaller (Aldridge, 2001).

Economic change affected social and psychological outcomes as well as earnings and incomes. Sennett (1998) has plausibly argued that changes in economic structure and employment practices inevitably contributed to increasing uncertainty and to the weakening of other social institutions. The values of employment with a large, locally based firm – security in return for loyalty and mutual effort – were consistent with the values of long-term relationships and mutual associations. The values of employment in the new economy are different: the expectation of numerous short-term contracts, the building of portfolios of transferable skills, high rewards for individual contributions, and the essential disposability of the worker in the interests of large companies driven by short-term shareholder profit rather than long-term investment and growth. These are more consistent with a flexible and contingent approach to relationships and interest group memberships. Forrest and Kearns (2001) have referred to a change:

> ... from the stability of the post-war era based on universalism, organised trade unionism, rising real earnings, the patriarchal family and relatively secure employment ... to ... greater individuation in welfare rights and insurances against risk, a widening gap between those with and those without the necessary credentials for the new informational age and the rise of less secure and atypical forms of employment. As the role of the male breadwinner becomes increasingly compromised, so too does male identity. (p 2127)

Seen in these terms, the fact that economic change happened contemporaneously with the weakening of other social institutions, such as marriage, churches, and trades unions, cannot be seen as entirely coincidental.

Whatever the causal mechanisms, the 1990s saw the continuation of a trend towards greater labour market uncertainty alongside the fragmentation of other familiar structures of stability, and in the context of widening inequality. Those at the bottom of the income distribution were becoming increasingly distant from the opportunities afforded to those at the top, while social support structures that might have provided inclusion, in a social rather than an economic sense, were also being weakened by an increasingly individualistic and materialistic culture. As Castells (1997) has argued, these were ways of living that brought greater discontinuity and risk, and therefore a higher incidence of job loss, mental illness, drug dependency and general precariousness. While these were not new developments in the 1990s, they were certainly not things of the past. Their continued development ensured that, despite economic growth, social exclusion remained a problem and that, even in situations of job growth, areas of long-term relative poverty still faced linked problems of high unemployment, low skills, disaffection, low educational attainment, youth crime and disorder, poor health, drugs, teenage pregnancy, family breakdown and parenting problems. By the latter half of the decade, the UK was distinguished from other EU countries by its high levels of inequality and social exclusion. It topped the European league for children growing up in workless households, for teenage pregnancy rates and for drug use among young people. Adult illiteracy rates were among the highest in Europe (SEU, 2001b).

Meanwhile, changes in population and in housing policy combined to increase the concentration of the disadvantaged within the least advantaged areas. While social exclusion continued, its spatial concentration increased. There were two distinct forces at work. In northern urban areas, particularly outer-city areas and council estates, and in industrial areas, populations continued to decline, leaving areas that were seriously depleted and extremely unpopular. These areas concentrated the poor, because people with greater choice would almost invariably seek to avoid them. On the other hand, some inner-urban areas, particularly in London, were coming under increasing housing pressure, but mainly from large numbers of immigrants, many of them disadvantaged in the labour market and/ or on low incomes.

Population drain and unpopular housing

In half of the areas at least[2], the population decline of the 1970s and 1980s continued into the 1990s. While it was estimated that the national population grew by 3% between 1991 and 1998, population estimates for six of the areas suggest that their populations continued to decline, albeit typically more slowly than in the previous two decades, when major job losses and housing redevelopments had caused large-scale population movements. While birth to death ratios mostly compared favourably with the national average, more people were moving out than moving in (Table 3.5).

Area changes were a reflection of broader trends. In only one case, Riverlands in Nottingham, was the area losing population when the district in which it was

Table 3.5: Population losses (1971-98)

	Change 1971-91 (%)	Change 1991-98 (%)	Birth/death ratio 1998
Overtown (Knowsley)		−4	1.13
Riverlands (Nottingham)	−32	−2	1.35
Shipview (Newcastle)	−22	−7	0.95
The Valley (Sheffield)	−21	−7	0.92
Southside (Redcar and Cleveland)		−12	1.23
Kirkside East (Leeds)	−21	−9	1.17
England and Wales	**+4**	**+3**	**1.15**

Notes:

1. 1971-1991 change calculated using Census data (population present on Census night). Blanks indicate areas where boundary changes make comparison impossible for this period.

2. 1991-1998 data calculated using mid-year population estimates. 1998 data were taken directly from estimates produced for use with IMD. These are not directly comparable with Census data. However, there are no mid-year estimates at ward level for 1991. These were calculated by attributing 1991 Census ward population shares to 1991 mid-year estimates for districts.

Sources: 1971 and 1991 Census data. ONS mid-year estimates. University of Oxford ward-level population estimates calculated for use with IMD

located was more or less keeping up with the national trend. Nottingham's estimated population grew by 2.1% between 1991 and 1998. The pattern elsewhere was that the study areas seemed to be losing population faster than their local authority areas, which were also doing badly relative to the national average. Redcar and Cleveland (−5.2%), Knowsley (−1.5%) and Newcastle (−0.8%) all apparently lost population during the early part of the 1990s. Leeds (+1.4%) and Sheffield (+0.3%) made significantly smaller gains than the national average. The lack of demand was reflected in house prices, as shown by HM Land Registry data, available at postcode sector-level from 1996 onwards. In a time of booming house prices (1996-99), all of these local authority areas had lower house price rises than the national average, ranging between 8% and 20%, against a national average of 35%.

These changes reflected economic trends, changes in people's preferences about their living environments, and housing policies. They were changes that affected whole districts, not just particular areas. Research from the ESRC Cities programme (Begg et al, 2002) shows that major conurbations were continuing to decline in the 1990s, although at a slower rate than previously, as they lost people to small towns and rural areas. West Yorkshire and London were the best performers, each showing signs of recovery. Industrial districts outside the big cities, such as Knowsley and Redcar and Cleveland, had lost much of their raison d'être with the loss of their employment. Their loss of population was as a direct result of the spatial dislocation between jobs and people. House prices in these districts rose least of all, just 8% in Redcar and Cleveland and 13% in Knowsley, and house price changes in the study areas were typical of the districts as a whole.

There were also shifts in population within districts, as the economy recovered, population fell and tenure patterns shifted. As might be expected, economic recovery fuelled the housing market, enabling people to move and creating increasing divergence between prices in popular and less popular neighbourhoods. Falling populations also contributed, reducing pressure on the existing stock of housing. In general terms, it became easier for people to avoid the least popular areas and neighbourhoods, whether publicly or privately owned, council or housing association. The pattern of diverging demand was more evident in the large cities, with their greater variation in residential neighbourhoods, than it was in smaller districts. Prices in some parts of Leeds rose 40% in less than a year in 1998, while prices in other parts remained static (Leeds City Council, 1998). For the city as a whole, prices rose 20% between 1996 and 1999, whereas prices in Kirkside East rose by just 5%. In The Valley in Sheffield, prices actually fell 6% over this period, while in the city as a whole they rose by 18%. All of the local authority districts that were experiencing continued population loss began to see pockets of empty property in their least popular areas, even those in the private sector.

However, while population losses undermined housing demand generally, shifts in tenure patterns ensured that the impact was felt primarily in social housing. At the end of the 1990s, more people aspired to home ownership than at any time previously. A 1999 survey commissioned by the Institute of Public Policy Research showed that 89% of people hoped that their children or grandchildren would be homeowners in 20 years' time (Hills, 2000). This increasing preference for home ownership, combined with falling interest rates and increasing household incomes as the economy recovered, diminished the demand for housing in the social rented sector. As long-standing older tenants died or moved into residential care, there were far fewer younger households wanting to replace them as social renters. In Sheffield, for example, the number of applicants on the council's list nearly halved between 1991 and 1999. Whereas in 1991, an average of three people wanted every vacant property, by 1999 this had dropped to less than one (Sheffield City Council, 2001). According to the local housing manager in The Valley, people could wait a matter of weeks for a home in an area where, at the start of the decade, they might have expected to have to wait two or three years. There were more council homes than households wanting them and empty homes began to appear. This situation was replicated in most northern cities. In the North East and North West, more than a fifth of the council housing stock was categorised as 'low demand', compared with 10-15% in Yorkshire and the East and West Midlands, and less than 5% in the South (DETR, 1999).

Meanwhile, new private housebuilding was accelerating, encouraged in some cases by local authorities. In Knowsley, for example, the council's strategy during the mid to late 1990s was explicitly to diversify housing choice in order to stem population losses to other boroughs. Both private developers and housing associations built new homes while council homes were standing empty. The private rented sector also grew. Extracts from the Director of Housing's report to councillors in 1999 explained the consequences:

> ... most of Overtown has limited or in some cases no demand, and this is giving serious cause for concern, with voids starting to build up in certain areas ... the housing association new build has introduced new quality supply and reduced the size of the waiting list. The new build schemes have also led to an increase in expectations from some applicants. The prospect of new houses and bungalows has meant that some council stock is seen as unacceptable by comparison. This is particularly true of the elderly who in some cases are prepared to pass up the chance of moving to low-rise council flats.... The move into the private sector by some council tenants is still apparent, especially into ex-Right to Buy properties, which are often seen as more attractive than council-owned properties with central heating and fitted kitchens. Despite less security in the private sector many applicants believe they can return to the council sector with a relatively short waiting period, which in many parts of the District is of course a reality. (Knowsley Borough Council, 1999)

In Blackburn, council housing officials reported "a phenomenal number" of new private houses, with developers often offering exceptional deals, arranging 99% mortgages and throwing in carpets and curtains. People with moderate incomes could afford to buy, while renting out properties in lower-value areas. In one part of High Moor, consisting largely of Victorian terraced properties, the number of privately rented properties quadrupled between 1991 and 1998, enabling council tenants to "bounce in and out of the private sector" (local housing manager).

Council homes in Knowsley stand empty while new private dwellings are built a quarter of a mile away

The result of this overall fall in demand for council housing was that demand in the least popular neighbourhoods, which had been weak anyway, disappeared altogether and diverging popularity quickly became self-perpetuating, as poor impressions of areas were reinforced by the appearance of shutters and environmental neglect. Housing statistics for Overtown in 1999 show some estates with waiting lists of three to four years while others were literally emptying out, with no demand at all and empty houses appearing as existing tenants moved. In Leeds, the council's housing strategy in 1998 reported segmentation in the housing market generally as a result of economic recovery but also increasing polarisation within the council sector:

> Within social housing, patterns of use and demand have changed rapidly over recent years. A segmented market has developed between high demand areas either in outer or suburban areas or where particular housing sub-markets are evident; other areas are showing signs of either stagnation or decline and others rapidly becoming places where no-one wants to live. (Leeds City Council, 1998, p 6)

In those districts which experienced relative or absolute population loss between 1991 and 1998, the study areas suffered to some extent from this divergence of demand. Estimated population losses in the areas were greater than in the local authority as a whole, and in all cases but one, losses in the wards most closely corresponding to the study neighbourhoods were as great or greater (Figure 3.5).

By 1999, demand for homes in all the population loss neighbourhoods was low to non-existent (Table 3.6), although popularity varied between estates and between different types of stock. Estates in Borough View (Redcar and Cleveland), East Rise (Sheffield) and Saints' Walk (Knowsley) had recently been refurbished

Figure 3.5: Population losses (1991-98)

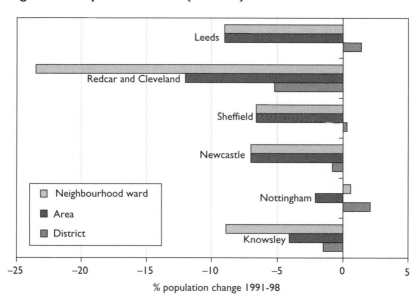

Sources: ONS mid-year population estimates. Oxford University population estimates for wards in England, mid-1998

Table 3.6: Demand for housing in population loss areas

	Description of level of demand by local housing manager	Level of empty properties in neighbourhood (1999)
Saints' Walk (Overtown, Knowsley)	Low – no waiting list	7% (worse in pockets)
Rosehill (Riverlands, Nottingham)	Low – no waiting list "... if there was a level playing field, no one would choose Rosehill at all."	2% (worse in pockets)
Sunnybank (Shipview, Newcastle)	"Nil."	10% for whole area. Considerably worse in study neighbourhood
East Rise (The Valley, Sheffield)	Low – no waiting list	Houses – few Flats – 25%
Borough View (Southside, Redcar and Cleveland)	Low – small waiting list for one estate "... hand on heart I can't say there's a demand."	31% street housing, of which 10% in clearance area. 3% council estate
Southmead (Kirkside East, Leeds)	"... low to non-existent." No waiting list	7% (worse in pockets)

Note: Figures usually refer to whole housing area, not just to the specific neighbourhood, as these breakdowns could not always be provided. Similar situations were described in Bridgefields and Valley Top.

Source: Interviews with housing managers (1999)

and were slightly more popular than neighbouring estates for this reason. Even so, flats were hard to let because prospective tenants could get access to larger homes instead. Sunnybank in Newcastle and Southmead in Leeds had historically bad reputations as low status, 'rough' areas and had not had the benefit of recent upgrading. By 1998 nearly a fifth of properties were empty. Large numbers of empty properties further fuelled the estates' poor reputations and even demolition of selected properties failed to restore the equilibrium between demand and supply.

Population losses in unpopular neighbourhoods contributed to increasing concentrations of poverty, as people who could exercise choice left or stayed away and only those with least choice moved in. Falling numbers of people and increasing poverty had an impact on private sector services. Shops struggled in most areas, with the number of units in decline and those that were trading carrying limited stock at high prices. The lack of banks and building societies was specifically mentioned as a problem in five areas.

There was also an impact on stability and social problems. On the one hand, new arrivals to these deeply unpopular neighbourhoods tended to be less likely to stay than existing residents who had already formed social and institutional ties, trusted friends and neighbours, voluntary work, a social life, or children at the local school. Housing managers and residents described new households who did not even unpack, or bother to get to know their neighbours. Housing managers and private landlords were under pressure to let homes and get a rental income rather than leaving them empty, at risk of crime and vandalism. In the absence of a waiting list, most lettings were to people on the homeless register. Larger flats and houses that would previously have only been available to families were let to single people, some of them at highly transient periods of their lives, for example ex-prisoners or young single unemployed men.

On the other hand, as population turnover and the concentration of vulnerable and difficult people increased, existing residents became more likely to leave. In private sector neighbourhoods, such departures often led to increases in private renting, either because householders could not sell their homes or because they were bought up at very low prices by speculators whose only interest was to secure rental returns, not to find responsible tenants who would want to stay and make a positive contribution to the neighbourhood.

Other authors have documented how this combination of empty properties and a higher proportion of vulnerable, transient or problematic individuals has a direct effect on neighbourhood conditions. People who have little commitment to the neighbourhood and who may additionally have social problems to deal with are less likely than others to take care of the communal environment, while population instability erodes the systems of support and control that encourage adherence to community norms and behaviours, and the collective efficacy of the population to organise against antisocial behaviour and lever in resources and support (Power, 1997; Power and Mumford, 1999; Sampson, 1999; Pitts, 2000). As neighbourhood conditions decline, population loss and instability increases, trapping neighbourhoods in a vicious spiral of decline (Figure 3.6). Thus, underlying population losses and housing market changes interact with very localised problems of vandalism, crime and antisocial behaviour, often with devastating consequences.

Bridgefields, the Blackburn estate described in the Introduction, fell victim to exactly this series of events, as did Borough View (Redcar and Cleveland), described at the beginning of this chapter. The same thing had happened, was happening or was beginning to happen in three of the other neighbourhoods where there were underlying population losses at area or district level.

In Saints' Walk (Knowsley), this cycle of events had occurred in the early 1990s, and by the time we visited in 1999, conditions had been restored by a combination of housing improvements, intensive policing and community action. Similar problems were occurring on neighbouring estates. In Southmead (Leeds) and in Sunnybank (Newcastle) they were happening on a smaller scale, with empty properties confined to certain parts of the neighbourhood. Only East Rise in Sheffield, Valley Top in Caerphilly and Rosehill in Nottingham had fewer problems, although even here there were signs of difficulty. East Rise had

Figure 3.6: The 'lettings spiral'

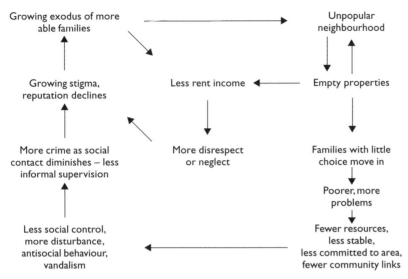

Source: Adapted from Power (1996)

a relatively popular housing stock for which demand was holding up, but estates on the other side of the road were undergoing exactly the problems described here. Valley Top had smaller pockets of problems rather than whole estates or groups of streets, and in Rosehill, severe instability and social problems affected one block, while housing demand in the area and city as a whole was sufficient to bolster the rest of the estate from similar problems.

As a result of these processes of decline, neighbourhood conditions were generally much worse in areas with high levels of empty property than they were in other areas. Table 3.7 shows problems with neighbourhood conditions first in population loss areas and then in areas of population gain.

The overall picture was that, in all the northern cities and outlying industrial areas, underlying trends of depopulation were deepening poverty concentrations in the least popular areas and neighbourhoods and, in some cases, literally beginning to empty them out. While not all had reached the point of collapse, all were caught in a cycle of deepening unpopularity that showed no sign of alleviating.

Population growth and ethnic concentration

A very different picture emerged from the other four areas. Although still regarded as low status relative to others (Table 3.8), their populations were growing, reversing the trend of the 1970s and 1980s. Each has a different story.

Both of the inner London areas were undergoing rapid change, of two kinds. The first was the arrival of new ethnic communities, and growth of those which

Table 3.7: Problems with neighbourhood conditions (1999)

	Derelict/ boarded-up houses or shops	Dumped household items/rubbish	Extensive litter	Poorly maintained common areas, kerbs, verges and fences	Extensive graffiti	Extensive vandalism	Total
Population loss areas							
Rosehill (Riverlands)	✓	✓					2
East Rise (The Valley)	✓						1
Saints' Walk (Overtown)	✓						1
Sunnybank (Shipview)	✓						1
Southmead (Kirkside East)	✓	✓	✓	✓	✓	✓	6
Borough View (Southside)	✓	✓	✓	✓	✓	✓	6
Bridgefields (High Moor)	✓	✓	✓	✓	✓	✓	6
Valley Top (Fairfields)	✓	✓		✓			3
Population gain areas							
The Grove (West-City)							0
Phoenix Rise (East-Docks)	✓						1
Broadways (Middle Row)		✓	✓				2
Sandyton (Beachville)	✓						1

Source: Observation and interviews with residents and frontline staff

Table 3.8: Population gains (1971-98)

	Change		
	1971-91[a] (%)	1991-98[b] (%)	Birth/death ratio 1998
West-City (Hackney)	−35	+3.4	1.47
East-Docks (Newham)	−10	+6	2.10
Middle Row (Birmingham)	+2	+8.8	3.24
Beachville (Thanet)		+3.3	0.83
England and Wales	**+4**	**+3**	**1.15**

Notes:

[a] 1971-91 change calculated using Census data (population present on Census night). Blanks indicate areas where boundary changes make comparison impossible for this period.

[b] 1991-98 data calculated using mid-year population estimates. 1998 data were taken directly from estimates produced for use with IMD. These are not directly comparable with Census data. However, there are no mid-year estimates at ward level for 1991. These were calculated by attributing 1991 Census ward population shares to 1991 mid-year estimates for districts.

Sources: 1971 and 1991 Census data. ONS mid-year estimates. University of Oxford ward-level population estimates calculated for use with IMD.

had settled in the 1970s and 1980s, and the second was the arrival of new higher-income residents, and a rise in property prices. Changes in West-City were described at the beginning of this chapter. East-Docks had been less ethnically mixed in 1991 and retained a larger indigenous community at the end of the decade. Nevertheless, it changed rapidly. A total of 39% of pupils at the local primary and secondary schools in 1999 were from minority ethnic backgrounds, compared with 24% of under-17s just eight years earlier. Similarly, property prices were much lower (an average of £84,000 in 1999) but had also, as in West-City, shot up (by 95% since 1996), as the extension of the Jubilee Line suddenly made for easy access to Docklands and Central London.

Middle Row in Birmingham was also experiencing a growth in its minority ethnic population. It already had a majority of minority ethnic residents in 1991 (66%), although compared with West-City and East-Docks it was more culturally homogenous, with the majority of households being Muslim families from Pakistan and, increasingly, Bangladesh. These communities were growing steadily through secondary immigration (family and spouses coming to join British citizens) and through natural increase. The birth/death ratio in the area was three times the national average in 1998. Smaller minority ethnic communities, particularly from Yemen and Somalia, were also establishing themselves, but were very much outnumbered. In 1999, 95% of pupils at Broadways' local primary school and 97% of pupils at the local secondary school were from a minority ethnic group, with 85% being Pakistani or Bangladeshi.

Beachville was a different case again. Since the 1970s, it had been experiencing population growth, largely in middle-aged and older age groups as people moved by choice to enjoy the seaside environment (Beatty and Fothergill, 2003a). In parts, it also experienced change of a different kind. Formerly a predominantly white community, it underwent dramatic ethnic change in the 1990s, but only in certain pockets, because its proximity to ports of entry to Britain and the availability of B&B accommodation made it a magnet for asylum seekers. The first arrivals, in the mid-1990s, were from East Africa, but from 1997 there were two main groups: Central and Eastern Europeans (Czechs, Slovaks and Kosovans) and Africans from Somalia, Sierra Leone and the Democratic Republic of Congo, among others. Official estimates suggested that there were about 300 refugee families in the town in 1999, but actual numbers were impossible to gauge. Support organisations suggested that there might be as many as 3,000.

Thus, although the populations of these areas were growing, much of their growth was accounted for by a growth in the numbers of people from some of the most disadvantaged groups in British society. There were two distinct phenomena. One was the growth in Pakistani/Bangladeshi populations to the extent where the neighbourhood became almost exclusively populated by people of that origin, an extremely disadvantaged population. Research by Birmingham City Council showed that 53% of the city's economically active Pakistani population had no qualifications, double the proportion of that of White, African, Caribbean or Indian ethnic groups. The unemployment rate for the city's Pakistani and Bangladeshi population was four times as high as for the population of white people. For those in work, low pay was more likely to be a problem. A total of 51% of Pakistani/Bangladeshi employees in the West Midlands earned less than £4.60 an hour in 1999 (the minimum wage), compared with 28% overall, and 28% of Pakistani/Bangladeshi workers earned less than the minimum wage (Birmingham City Council, 2001). These enormous discrepancies meant that areas such as Middle Row with increasing Pakistani and Bangladeshi populations, would inevitably have increasing concentrations of poverty.

The second phenomenon, in the other areas, was the growth in populations from diverse immigrant groups, recently arrived in the country, many of them refugees from war-torn countries. The prospects of these immigrants may be good, just as they were, on the whole, for Ugandan Asians who settled in Britain in the 1970s (Peach, 1996a). A number of respondents remarked on the determination and upward mobility of individuals in some of these immigrant groups, particularly Somalis, many of whom were professional or business people in their home country. Nevertheless, current disadvantage was evident in the high levels of Free School Meal eligibility in local schools (about 65% in each of the secondary schools compared with a national average of 18%) and the fact that they were able to access social housing, allocated on a needs basis. Professionals working with immigrant families reported difficulties such as lack of English fluency, low basic skills, poor health, low life expectancy and high infant mortality. Other research has demonstrated that progress may well be inhibited by 'structural racism'. Daley (1998), for example, has demonstrated how the qualifications of black Africans are devalued in British society, forcing them to take lower-paid jobs than they are capable of.

In sharp contrast to the swathes of empty housing in the population loss areas,

Table 3.9: Empty properties and housing demand: study neighbourhoods in population gain areas (1999)

	Description of level of demand by local housing manager	Level of empty properties in neighbourhood (1999)
The Grove (West-City, Hackney)	Good	3%
Phoenix Rise (East-Docks, Newham)	Lowest waiting list in borough but always possible to let properties	2%
Broadways (Middle Row, Birmingham)	High – long waiting lists	<2%
Sandyton (Beachville, Thanet)	N/A – mainly B&B accommodation	

Source: Interviews with housing managers (1999)

the population growth areas experienced pressure on their housing stock. In 1999, the study neighbourhoods in these areas had very few empty properties and hardly any that were vacant long term (Table 3.9). None of them had the severe environmental conditions caused by low demand in some of the northern neighbourhoods. The inner London neighbourhoods, predominantly made up of council flats and houses, were still regarded as relatively unpopular, but demand was such that it was always possible to find tenants. Middle Row, although regarded as a low-status neighbourhood in the city generally, was popular among the Pakistani and Bangladeshi communities, and there were long waiting lists for housing association properties. A cultural preference for large families meant that it was not unusual for families to have four or more children. In 1991, 25% of households with children in that area had four or more, and extended family households were also more common than average. With high pressure on housing in the area, newly forming households could not necessarily move out, nor large households move to bigger accommodation, so many families were living in overcrowded conditions.

Thus, both where population was declining and where it was increasing, these broad population movements tended to result in growing proportions of people from society's most disadvantaged groups within the least popular areas and neighbourhoods.

Home to the most marginalised and vulnerable

The increasing sorting of residential neighbourhoods reinforced another pressure on the poorest areas: their function as housing providers for society's most marginalised and most vulnerable members.

The disadvantaged inner-city areas in the study had, for many years, disproportionate levels of specialist accommodation for homeless people or people with mental health problems. Their central location made them accessible to city centre service provision and easy to reach by public transport, and they often had a supply of large old houses or industrial buildings suitable for conversion to communal living. A number of respondents also argued that hostels and residential or care homes could more easily be located in poor areas, with less resistance from organised groups of 'not in my back yard' campaigners. Riverlands, Nottingham, had nearly two thirds of the city's homeless hostel beds, and a bail hostel (about 350 hostel places in total), compared with only 10% of the city's population. Specialist mental health accommodation was also disproportionately concentrated here, but amounted to only about 30 bedspaces. Health professionals estimated that about 50% of people in the city diagnosed with schizophrenia lived in this one part of Riverlands where hostel accommodation was concentrated. The Valley had a quarter of the direct access hostel beds in Sheffield, but only 4% of the city's population.

Moreover, all the areas, because of their unpopularity, tended to have flats or houses available for people rehoused from the homeless register, recently released from prison or evicted from elsewhere because of their antisocial behaviour. The perception that the areas were 'a dumping ground' for people who found it hard to cope or who made life difficult for others was sharpened during the 1990s as neighbourhoods became more polarised and fewer homes were allocated to people with greater housing choice. Even a very small number of such individuals could create an impression of chaos and disorder. In West-City, a resident activist explained that:

> "… civil servants and politicians need to understand why living in an area like this makes people angry or frustrated or demoralised. Some of the people I live near are pitiful; they don't know how to clean their own flat; they dump rubbish in the stairwell; you can hear them shouting and screaming and climbing the walls all night. It's not their fault they're like that, but they haven't got the support they need and it's other residents who are left to deal with it."

On housing estates, vulnerable or problematic tenants tended to be dispersed throughout a neighbourhood. Blocks of single person's accommodation had a concentrating effect. Rosehill estate in Nottingham had one block of 130 small flats, including 55 bedsits, about half of the council's bedsit accommodation in the entire city. Because of the size of the accommodation, tenants were mainly single people. Most respondents in the area alluded to a high proportion of problematic drug users, ex-offenders, and people with mental health problems. As one respondent put it: "It's a bit of a dumping ground for people that can't get anywhere else. No one with any roots in the area would live there" (police officer). Turnover was reported to be extremely high. In Beachville in Thanet, social services and housing staff described how many of those released from prison or on the paedophile register in the area ended up in one high-rise block of 89 one-bedroom flats, which also contained people with severe mental health problems and drug and alcohol abusers. The housing department in Shipview (Newcastle) was considering the demolition of 10 clustered blocks of one-bedroom flats which had experienced similar problems, and similar blocks had recently been demolished in Overtown (Knowsley) and Fairfields (Caerphilly). In The Valley (Sheffield), tenancies in some blocks of flats typically lasted no more than three to six months because of the transient nature of the inhabitants. Other residents complained of antisocial behaviour: dumping of old furniture, rubbish and nappies thrown out of windows, and loud music and fireworks late at night.

Some of these blocks had been earmarked for demolition while others had been converted into bigger properties, for couples and families, or let as furnished accommodation. In Kirkside East (Leeds), the housing department had stopped letting properties to people aged under 25 in a block beset by antisocial behaviour, and drug and alcohol abuse. At the sharp end, the funnelling of society's most vulnerable, marginalised and problematic individuals into its least advantaged neighbourhoods was creating difficult living environments and management problems.

Continuing trends, new developments and diverging fortunes

The story of the 1990s, then, was essentially one of continuity with the trends of the 1970s and 1980s. Population continued to be lost from cities and from industrial areas, reducing the demand for housing and enabling greater polarisation between popular and unpopular neighbourhoods. Tenure preferences continued to shift. While new houses were built to satisfy demand for home ownership, demand for social housing fell further. Problems that had been emerging in the 1980s became more widespread in the 1990s, with more neighbourhoods acutely affected by empty homes and abandonment. While the huge job losses of the 1970s and 1980s were not replicated, the decline of manufacturing continued, causing most of the study areas to be no better off in terms of numbers of jobs at the end of the decade than they were at the beginning. Moreover, where there was job growth, it tended to be disproportionately in part-time work and in the service sector, which offered low-skilled and low-paid job opportunities. In all sectors, job security and wages continued to diverge.

These continuities are unsurprising. Decline was embedded in the areas through their long-term association with declining sectors of the economy and, correspondingly, with the low levels of skills and attainment in their workforces. Unpopular areas with very high proportions of social housing were trapped in a cycle of decline once demand for that tenure started to dwindle, fuelled by public policy. The fortunes of the areas were determined by these intrinsic or hard-to-change characteristics: location, economic structure and housing. Economic changes depressed the incomes and opportunities of current residents and, along with location and housing, gave shape to the process of residential sorting, determining that more advantaged residents would leave and be replaced only by those with little choice. Where the trajectories of the areas did diverge in the 1990s, it was because they were geographically well-positioned to take advantage of economic change and because their housing stock or transport infrastructure enabled them to do so. West-City began to attract jobs because of its proximity to the City, and to higher-income residents because of the attractiveness of some of its housing stock. High Moor in Blackburn saw job growth because of its proximity to a new motorway and the same thing was happening in East-Docks at the end of the decade following the extension of the Jubilee Line. To reverse the decline of previous decades, areas needed to have particular local advantages and/or be situated in bigger cities or regions that were themselves doing relatively well. In the majority of cases, neither of these pertained. With the exception of inner London, the spatial distribution of growth and decline in the 1990s mapped closely onto the existing pattern of wealth and poverty, so that poor areas continued to do relatively badly and better-off areas to do relatively well.

Moreover, the ethnic changes of the 1990s introduced a new dimension that threatened to reinforce the divisions between inner-city areas and others. Two important changes were underway. First, the arrival in significant numbers of displaced refugees from around the world meant that even in the London areas where higher-income residents were beginning to arrive, social housing was increasingly populated by people facing extreme disadvantage, at least in the short term. Second, areas that had large Pakistani/Bangladeshi populations in 1991 tended to become even more ethnically homogenous, through natural increase and immigration. People from these ethnic groups continued to be highly disadvantaged in many ways: in the labour market, income levels, housing and health. Their continuing spatial concentration reinforced the spatial divisions in wealth and poverty between neighbourhoods.

The causes of decline continued, therefore, to be structural, originating in the organisation of the economy and of society. The problems of the poorest neighbourhoods were the creation of wider societal changes, economic restructuring, rising inequality in income and wealth, population redistribution, housing markets and housing policies, the fragmentation of social institutions and the growth and concentration of disadvantaged immigrant groups. But both at national and local level, public policy decisions, such as those on housing policy or allocations or economic development, made a difference. And as neighbourhoods declined, it also mattered how quickly and how effectively local services could respond to the needs of their highly disadvantaged populations. Low levels of individual and household resources meant that public services had a disproportionate importance. Few people can afford to buy private healthcare, to send their children to private schools or nurseries or to protect themselves from crime by buying expensive security devices. Low rates of car ownership (between 31% and 57% of households in the 12 areas, compared with 68% nationally) rendered people more reliant on neighbourhood amenities and made public transport particularly vital for work, shopping and socialising. Many residents (over 50% on average in the 12 areas) relied on publicly provided housing and estate management. To check their decline, disadvantaged neighbourhoods needed good local services and effective local management as well as strategic policy interventions.

Summary

- The 1990s was a period of economic growth, but it was an uneven growth. As manufacturing declined, most urban and industrial areas had overall job losses, despite service sector growth. Seven of the 12 areas were net losers of jobs between 1991 and 1998. Three others gained jobs but less quickly than the national average (see Box 3.1).

Box 3.1: Job gainers and losers (1991-98)

Net job gainers

Greater gains than national average:
- West-City (Hackney)
- High Moor (Blackburn)

Smaller gains than national average:
- The Valley (Sheffield)
- Kirkside East (Leeds)
- Fairfields (Caerphilly)

Net job losers
- East-Docks (Newham)
- Riverlands (Nottingham)
- Shipview (Newcastle)
- Middle Row (Birmingham)
- Overtown (Knowsley)
- Southside (Redcar and Cleveland)
- Beachville (Thanet)

- Whether areas did well or badly in terms of job growth depended on the strength of the regional economy but also on their industrial structure and their specific locational or infrastructure characteristics – proximity to motorways and quality of business premises. The intrinsic features of some areas fitted better with the changing economy than others.
- Continuing the trend of the 1980s, the 1990s saw a further loss of male full-time jobs, and a shift from full-time to part-time jobs. Many of the new jobs in the 12 areas were in part-time or low-paid work. Unemployment fell in all the areas, but there was also evidence of rising economic activity as formal labour market opportunities became more unattractive. Falling unemployment masked continuing labour market exclusion. Economic change brought wider earnings inequality and greater uncertainty.
- Meanwhile, most of the cities and industrial areas continued to lose population (Box 3.2), enabling greater residential choice and greater polarisation in the housing market. Polarisation was accelerated by falling demand for social housing, as preferences for private ownership increased, and new homes were built. By 1999, demand for council housing in the areas that were losing population was low to non-existent. Most of the lettings were to homeless

people or others in very high need. Poverty concentrations and social problems increased. Certain blocks of flats and bedsits attracted intense concentrations of vulnerable and marginalised residents: people with mental health problems, ex-prisoners and problematic drug and alcohol users. The number of empty homes increased and neighbourhood conditions worsened.

Box 3.2: Population gainers and losers (1991-98)

Population gainers	Population losers
• West-City (Hackney)	• Riverlands (Nottingham)
• East-Docks (Newham)	• The Valley (Sheffield)
• Middle Row (Birmingham)	• Overtown (Knowsley)
• Beachville (Thanet)	• Shipview (Newcastle)
	• Kirkside East (Leeds)
	• Southside (Redcar and Cleveland)
	• High Moor (Blackburn)
	• Fairfields (Caerphilly)

• Four areas saw population growth (Box 3.2). Three were inner-city areas and one was a coastal town (Beachville). Population growth was mainly due to the growth of minority ethnic groups, either through natural increase, secondary immigration to join British citizens, or new primary immigration and asylum seekers. Many people from minority ethnic groups continued to be among the most disadvantaged in British society. Poverty concentrations were reinforced as new disadvantaged households arrived to replace those who were moving on and up. At the same time, all of the three inner-city areas were beginning to show signs of gentrification, enhancing the sense of polarisation within the areas.

• These uneven patterns of development meant that the fortunes of the areas started to diverge as they continued to be driven by the wider forces of the economic change, population movements and housing demand.

Notes

[1] This group (those looking for work but not claiming) is included in the International Labour Organization (ILO) definition of unemployment, which is recognised as being more reliable than official figures but is not published at ward level.

[2] For two areas, comparison of the population between 1991 and 1998 is not possible: High Moor because of boundary changes and Fairfields because of a lack of ward-level population estimates for 1998 in Wales. Qualitative data suggests that the population was declining in Fairfields. The direction of change could not be established in High Moor.

FOUR

Management failure

Problems with public services

The initial fieldwork in 1999 suggested that the interventions of some public services in the study neighbourhoods were far from effective. Most of the services we looked at had a neighbourhood focus, so we examined them at neighbourhood level, talking to ground-level staff and residents, rather than attempting to take an overview across the larger areas in the study. The problem was not that the services were absent. Only in primary healthcare, where GPs could exercise a choice about where to locate, was there a genuine absence of services[1]. More often, neighbourhood services were beset by two other problems. One was that they were insufficient to keep up with demand; the other that they struggled to provide the quality of services that was needed and that residents in other areas could expect to receive.

Inadequate levels of service provision

The most obvious gap in service provision was in frontline services to maintain social order. Areas that housed relatively high proportions of vulnerable, chaotic, and disaffected individuals had a potential for disorder, and needed a combination of responses. One was preventative work, engaging young people in constructive activities, with permanent, accessible staff with whom they could develop trusting relationships over a period of time. Another was a visible enforcement presence, to deter and deal with crime and antisocial behaviour, particularly in depopulated areas, or areas with a very transient population, where levels of informal surveillance and supervision were low (Power and Tunstall, 1995; Home Office, 2000).

All of the study neighbourhoods had these services in some form. Most had at least a basic level of youth provision, local housing management and frontline uniformed policing (Table 4.1). In 10 there were local youth clubs, and five also had some regular securely funded detached youth work, engaging with young people on the street. Most had patch-based housing management with local offices in the selected neighbourhoods, and half had estate-based caretaking staff doing odd jobs such as securing void properties, mending damage and removing rubbish. All except one of the neighbourhoods had police officers with specific neighbourhood responsibilities and a remit to carry out foot patrol at least some of the time. In 1999, at the time of the first fieldwork visits, none had neighbourhood wardens but such schemes were beginning to be considered[2].

Table 4.1: Frontline services within five-minute walk of neighbourhoods

	Housing office	Care-takers	Neigh-bour-hood wardens	Police foot patrols by dedicated officers	Youth club	Regular detached youth work
The Grove (Hackney)	✔	a		✔		
Phoenix Rise (Newham)	✔	✔		✔	✔	✔
Saints' Walk (Knowsley)				✔	✔	✔
Rosehill (Nottingham)	✔			✔		✔
Sunnybank (Newcastle)	✔			✔	✔	✔
East Rise (Sheffield)	✔	✔		✔	✔	a
Bridgefields (Blackburn)	✔[b]	✔		✔	✔	
Broadways (Birmingham)	✔	✔		✔	✔[c]	✔
Valley Top (Caerphilly)					✔	
Borough View (Redcar and Cleveland)	✔	✔		✔	✔	d
Southmead (Leeds)	✔	✔		✔	✔	✔
Sandyton (Thanet)	na	na	✔[e]	✔	✔	
Total	**9**	**6**	**1**	**11**	**10**	**6**

Notes:

[a] On other estates in area but not in our neighbourhood.
[b] About to be shut down due to small number of occupied homes on Bridgefields.
[c] Youth bus.
[d] Detached project funded by regeneration project.
[e] Limited warden service provided by housing department.

Source: Interviews with service managers and frontline staff (1999)

However, in the majority of cases, these services were failing to keep up with the job. When we asked residents about problems and concerns in their areas, their most frequent response was to talk about crime and social disorder, drugs and youth disturbance (Table 4.2). They were also critical of service responses, particularly the lack of recreational opportunities for young people and the lack of effective policing. In no fewer than eight neighbourhoods, residents spontaneously raised the issue of invisible or ineffective policing as one of the problems of the neighbourhood, reflecting a wider national trend of public disenchantment with police efforts at visible patrol and community engagement (HMIC, 2001).

> "The policing used to be good [in the mid-1980s]. There were two community policemen who used to come into the [community] centre and had a good relationship with the kids here. They used to have a police surgery in the centre. Now the kids wouldn't know who the community bobby was. People have lost respect for the police. The police station's only up the road but they don't come out 'til the next day if you report something. People don't bother any more." (resident, Kirkside East, Leeds)

Table 4.2: Neighbourhood problems most commonly identified by residents

Problem	Number of areas where problem mentioned
Drugs	11
Antisocial residents	10
Youth nuisance/nothing for young people	9
Crime/antisocial behaviour	8
Loss of community	7
Empty homes	6
Stigma/reputation	6

Source: Interviews in the 12 study areas

> "Policing, forget it! There's supposed to be a community police officer but you never see him, only now and again. Mainly they just speed about in their panda cars." (resident, The Valley, Sheffield)

Similar problems were noted with day-to-day environmental services such as housing management, cleansing and rubbish collection. The areas generated a high demand for these services. Vandalism needed to be repaired and graffiti removed, litter and dumped rubbish cleared, lighting maintained, bushes cut back, and parks, play areas and verges kept free of glass, metal and used needles. All of the services were present, and some neighbourhoods had a higher level of resources than their neighbours[3]. Borough View, in Redcar and Cleveland, for example, had an extra weekly refuse collection and additional litter pickers. But in general, they failed to keep control of the problems. Levels of environmental degradation and disrepair in some of the neighbourhoods (see Table 3.7) were visible evidence of the failure of the services, and in all the areas most of the residents we spoke to expressed dissatisfaction with environmental services, even those where neighbourhood environments were apparently in better condition. Their comments mirrored those reported in other local studies (Power and Tunstall, 1995; Lambert et al, 1999) and national surveys (Bramley, 1997; ONS, 1999; Duffy, 2000).

> "I reported a leaking ceiling and it took them a month to sort it out. I had water running into the flat! Then two months to sort out blocked drains. We've been complaining about the pigeon muck for three weeks and they've only just got round to it." (resident, Riverlands)

> "They don't bother with this end of the estate where there are so many empty houses. The street sweepers stop at the top." (resident, High Moor)

"The area's covered in litter. We've got two extra street cleaners but all they do is park up at the end of the road and drink tea all day." (resident, Southside)

"We're supposed to have environmental wardens and a special litter service, but look at the rubbish. That alleyway is covered in glass, slates and other rubbish. You can't get a response. Those slates have been there a month. There's been a dead ferret for three weeks." (youth worker, Southside)

The inadequacy of frontline services reflected a reduction in staffing levels at the same time as area problems had begun to escalate. Local authority budgets were under pressure during this period and demands in certain areas, such as personal social services, were increasing. Rate capping prevented authorities from raising money to pay for discretionary services such as youth provision, so it was these services that bore the brunt of the financial squeeze. At the same time, the nature of local authority service delivery was changing. The Conservative governments of the 1980s and early 1990s increasingly defined the local authority role in terms of service delivery, rather than democracy and civic governance. Public accountability was tightened with the introduction of performance indicators. Compulsory Competitive Tendering (CCT), which was introduced in the late 1980s, required services to be specified and provided by the cheapest contractor, and the wider influence of private sector management practice contributed to an emphasis on service effectiveness, value for money and performance measurement.

The net effect of these changes was what other writers have described as 'the new managerialism' (Keen and Scase, 1998), or 'the new public management' (Clarke et al, 2000), characterised by competition, management by contract, performance measurement, devolved management and customer orientation. Large, permanent staff teams gave way to chains of smaller organisations, joined by contracts and with more flexible employment structures that enabled them to form and reform according to demand. It was a transformation in the culture of public service provision and the prevailing models of service delivery. Even within organisations, targeted, time-limited inputs from specialist teams began to be favoured over generic provision and long-term funding commitments.

At ground level, three changes began to be noticed. First, the proportion of work carried out on a sessional basis increased substantially. Parks and open spaces, for example, were no longer maintained by site-based staff but by mobile teams who visited to conduct specific tasks. Youth workers were increasingly contracted only for specific sessions. In Knowsley, all three full-time youth work posts in Overtown were cut during the 1990s, leaving only part-time sessional staff by 1999. Second, core funding was whittled down while more money became available for specific projects. In Hackney, for example, we were told that cuts had been made in the core youth service while short life, geographically focused projects were on the increase, funded by regeneration programmes. While there was no core youth service provision for The Grove, the study neighbourhood in West-City, a nearby estate had three-year regeneration funding for a programme of detached work. Third, specialist groups of staff covering wide geographical areas replaced generic local teams. Housing repairs, for example, began to be dealt with by centralised call centres rather than at local housing offices.

The result of these changes was that regular frontline services tended to be thinly staffed. There were fewer people about to provide supervision, surveillance and reassurance, and to observe and hear what was going on, and they had less undirected time to build relationships and to provide ongoing, flexible support. Levels of neighbourhood policing illustrate the problem. Policing, by comparison with other public services, was relatively well funded during the 1980s and 1990s. However, there was also more legislation to enforce and more performance pressure, resulting in the development of more specialist teams, to deal with issues such as child protection, drugs, racial and homophobic attacks, domestic violence and Internet crime. The public reassurance role provided by uniformed patrol officers correspondingly diminished. Although nationally the number of police constables increased during the 1990s (Smith et al, 2002), the numbers of calls for assistance also increased, and the proportion of officers on patrol duties decreased. By 2001, only 56% of officers were engaged in uniformed patrol (HMIC, 2001).

Table 4.1 shows that 11 of the 12 study neighbourhoods had, on paper, groups of uniformed patrol officers with specific local responsibilities, in addition to the normal response police. However, closer examination of the detail of these arrangements shows a different picture (Table 4.3). It demonstrates that only two neighbourhoods, Sandyton in Thanet and Borough View in Redcar and Cleveland, actually had more than one dedicated officer. Sandyton, which was a hotspot for crime and disorder problems, had its own dedicated team of four patrolling officers, described by a senior officer as "in your face policing. Law enforcement, not being nice to old ladies". Borough View had a dedicated policing team, patrolling on foot, doing both enforcement and community liaison. All of the other neighbourhoods retained the traditional demarcation between response officers, who covered a wide geographical area and responded to immediate calls, and community officers, who dealt mainly with 'slow-time' response, problem solving and developing community networks[4]. Typically there was only one community officer covering an area larger than the study neighbourhood. This provided extremely limited coverage, since a full-time presence (even covering only daytime hours) requires a minimum of three officers per beat, one for each shift and one resting.

Moreover, community officers tended to be frequently abstracted to cover other duties, such as policing special events, and were also involved in time-consuming multiagency meetings and liaison. All of these activities limited the time spent on patrol in the neighbourhood.

Table 4.3: Community policing in study neighbourhoods

	Structure	Number of officers for neighbourhood (<I means officer covers larger area)
The Grove (Hackney)	Community team doing patrol and all non-urgent response. Each officer has dedicated beat	I
Phoenix Rise (Newham)	Two PCs based in local office. Can only commit to four hours' staffing per day	<I
Saints' Walk (Knowsley)	Dedicated officer for neighbourhood	I
Rosehill (Nottingham)	Beat managers undertake proactive, problem-solving role and crime analysis	<I
Sunnybank (Newcastle)	Community officer attached to each response team. Undertakes foot patrol Response teams also have geographical role	<I
East Rise (Sheffield)	Proactive 'beat manager role'. 2 officers per sector (similar to a ward)	<I
Bridgefields (Blackburn)	Dedicated community officer for neighbourhood. Response teams also have geographical role	I
Broadways (Birmingham)	Beat managers undertake proactive, problem-solving role and crime analysis	<I
Valley Top (Caerphilly)	All officers have geographical responsibility and do mixed community and response role. Each officer allocated a specific neighbourhood	0*
Borough View (Redcar and Cleveland)	Community policing team for neighbourhood. Patrol on foot 8am to 11pm. Community policing and enforcement	6
Southmead (Leeds)	Beat manager system: "... old style community policing but with a more proactive role" (police respondent)	I
Sandyton (Thanet)	Dedicated patrol team with emphasis on enforcement	4

Note: *None dedicated full time to community duties.

Source: Interviews with service managers and frontline staff (1999)

The impact of these broad changes at the neighbourhood level was explained by a senior officer in Fairfields:

"I've got 17 years' service. When I first joined, I'd parade with 17 other officers. Now, it'd probably be a sergeant and two PCs. There's been a progressive erosion of frontline capacity [in order] to deal with centralised or specialist functions – armed response, multipurpose vehicles, enlarged traffic function, drugs squads, call handling, you name it. It's just because the government's response to any problem is to legislate. Then what happens, you need officers to implement the legislation. I think it's got to a critical point. Look here, I've got 36 PCs, but between a third and half are long-term sick, light duties, or seconded to a force project. So each shift has four to five PCs, maximum. Today, at 6am, there was one officer on duty. The chief constable visited last week to 'see how the troops are getting on' and I said 'oh, they're both fine, sir'." (senior police officer, Fairfields, Caerphilly)

Thus, although policing was being done, and possibly in a more efficient fashion in terms of the number of crimes prevented or detected, there was a marked lack of low-level enforcement and deterrence. It had gradually dwindled at the same time as neighbourhoods had lost other site-based staff. Surveillance and reassurance functions had been lost, and community safety undermined:

"The problem is that core public services have just been allowed to dwindle. Ten years ago the City employed 30,000 people. Now it's 20,000, and we're trying to replicate it all with whizz bang projects. And for various reasons, the need for services has got greater because there are so many fewer people on the street generally. We don't even have milkmen any more. People in The Valley say that one thing they want to see is just more people on the street." (local authority officer, The Valley, Sheffield)

Operational problems and poorer quality

While some services were simply struggling with insufficient staff, others also appeared to be giving a poorer quality service than their counterparts in other areas. Quality differences between services in deprived areas and others have been highlighted in government reports (SEU, 1998, 2000a, 2001a), as well as by respondents in this study, but were almost impossible to quantify, because performance data for services at neighbourhood level are simply unavailable. The Office for Standards in Education (Ofsted) inspection data is the only exception. Three of the 23 secondary schools in the areas had been judged to be failing by Ofsted, slightly more than the 5% that would be expected if failing schools were evenly distributed.

It was evident that high-quality services were achievable in some circumstances. One of the schools had been awarded Beacon school status under the government's scheme to identify successful schools and promote good practice. However, the interview data indicated that service quality, in schools and other services, was often undermined by operational difficulties that were not sufficiently compensated for in service design and funding (Figure 4.1).

One difficulty was the additional pressure on service budgets. The local secondary school for the Saints' Walk estate in Knowsley, for example, had a £140,000 budget deficit because of persistent vandalism and arson. But this problem was less commonly mentioned by the respondents than difficulty with

Figure 4.1: Pressure on public services

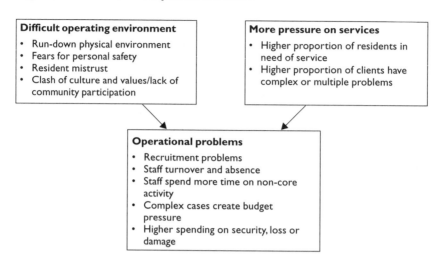

staffing. Because of the concentration of socioeconomic problems, workloads were higher than in more advantaged areas. In personal social services, caseloads tended to be bigger than average and in environmental services the general level of demand was higher than in other areas. There was more litter to clear up, more vandalism and more damage to mend. Emergency services had more call-outs, doctors had more minor infections, accidents and mental illness to deal with, although lower take-up of preventive health services. Professional staff in some services spent more time on what might be described as 'non-core' activities, for which there would be much less need in a more advantaged area, and had less time for their core functions. The housing manager in Sunnybank, Newcastle, for example, described how staff spent a lot of time on managing minor tenancy enforcement matters such as ensuring that tenants kept their gardens tidy. Headteachers reported that teaching staff more frequently had to spend time on non-teaching activities such as attendance, discipline or multiagency liaison.

Some of the work was also exceptionally stressful or demanding, because a higher proportion of cases were complicated or challenging, and because the working environment was potentially unsafe. Certain parts of The Valley in Sheffield were places that police officers preferred to patrol in vehicles or in pairs, while senior officers in Knowsley regarded the Saints' Walk estate as too dangerous for a community officer when crime and drug problems were at their worst. Housing managers in more than one area described how, because a higher proportion of interactions between staff and tenants involved accusations, complaints, ungrantable demands or aggression, staff responded by adopting a negative attitude towards tenants generally. In Kirkside East, the area was regarded as "a hard area to visit. There's more verbal aggression, more worry about things like your car being nicked. You might be invited into a house where who knows what goes on" (health visitor).

The result of these additional demands was extra difficulty in recruiting and retaining staff and in maintaining morale and preventing absence. In Beachville, recruitment problems in social services were acute, with 13 vacancies out of 60 staff at the time of the fieldwork. "I've got the budget" the manager said "but I can't get the staff to work here because the caseloads are so high". A police officer in West-City described the area as "one of those that no one really wants to work in ... we tended to think that you got sent here as a punishment".

It was evident that these difficulties could sometimes be wholly or partly overcome. The health visitor service in Kirkside East, for example, had had the same two core workers for nearly five years, but finding agency staff to cover absence was difficult. Such staff would rather take opportunities with fewer short-term challenges. Most secondary school heads described a core of committed staff who wanted to work in areas where many of the children faced barriers to learning, although recruiting specialist staff and supply teachers could also be difficult. Yet resolution of staffing problems rested on successful competition with other areas or on inspirational leadership. There was no evidence of systemic measures, in the form of additional resources, to enable job redesign, such as smaller classes or more non-contact time for teachers, nor additional incentives or career development for staff.

The barrier of mistrust

By the late 1990s, the standard of public service provision in disadvantaged areas had become a key political concern (SEU, 1998). It was evident that services needed to be at least as good, if not better, in these areas as others, but equally evident that they were often failing even to meet average standards.

The interviews with residents in the 12 neighbourhoods indicated that the persistent failure of public management had become almost an expectation. Levels of confidence in service providers, and in local politicians, were extremely low. It was frequently pointed out that services were designed and run by people who lived outside the areas, who had no personal experience of the problems faced and no personal stake in seeing them resolved. Services were perceived as being done to residents or, more often, not provided in response to residents' needs, and decisions as being made by faceless bureaucrats with little understanding of the reality of people's lives. Respondents frequently referred to an unidentified 'they' who had allowed the areas to become run down, alongside specific criticisms of councillors or service managers.

One resident in Shipview described the response of public service organisations as "empty promises. They come down here, write it all down and just walk out the door and take it all away with them. It's like nothing was ever said" (resident activist, Shipview, Newcastle). Similar comments were made in other areas:

> "Tenants weren't asked about what kind of services they needed –
> the things were provided rather than owned by us. It all adds to the

attitude that you can't do anything for yourself." (resident, High Moor, talking about the provision of facilities on the estate over the years)

"People have seen so many promises and seen nothing done. If someone from the council came round here and said they were giving out gold ingots, no one would bat an eyelid." (resident, Fairfields, Caerphilly)

In these circumstances, there seemed to be little incentive for residents to engage with services at frontline level. Nor did there seem to be much incentive to take part in local political processes. Voter turnout was consistently low (Table 4.4).

Low turnout can no doubt be attributed to general dissaffection with the political process, not just to opinions on local politicians. It may also have more practical origins, such as literacy problems, transport or childcare. Nevertheless, it indicates the failure of local democracy to engage people in the governance of their areas and neighbourhoods. Service failure and the persistence of problems had created a barrier to engagement in services and to political participation, contributing to neighbourhood decline and also to political exclusion. There was a barrier of mistrust that would be difficult to break down.

Table 4.4: Voter turnout: late 1990s local elections[a]

		% of voters turning out			
	Date of election	Neighbour-hood ward	Area (average for wards covering area)	Local authority	Great Britain
West-City (Hackney)	1998	33.0	36.5	34.7	30
East-Docks (Newham)	1998	30.4	26.3	28.4	30
Overtown (Knowsley)	1998	uncontested	17.9[b]	18.8	30
Riverlands (Nottingham)	2000	22.6	21.1	25.4	30
Shipview (Newcastle)	1998	25.0	20.1	22.5	30
The Valley (Sheffield)	1998	20.8	20.8	25.0	30
High Moor (Blackburn)	1999	18.5	21.6	29.9	39
Middle Row (Birmingham)	1998	23.2	23.2	26.2	30
Fairfields (Caerphilly)[c]					
Southside (Redcar and Cleveland)	1999	23.5	27.3	36.7	39
Kirkside East (Leeds)	1998	21.4	21.4	24.7	30
Beachville (Thanet)	1999	uncontested	24.5	28.6	39

Notes:

[a] 1998 data used if there was a local election in that year. Otherwise the nearest election to that date.
[b] Only one ward of five contested.
[c] Local authority unable to provide data.

Sources: Local authorities; Electoral Commission

Summary

- We looked at the provision of frontline services in the 12 small neighbourhoods on which the study was focused.
- All of the neighbourhoods had some frontline provision: local housing offices, dedicated police beat officers, youth clubs or detached youth workers. However, residents were critical of the standard of service provision, and there were problems in most neighbourhoods with drugs, crime and antisocial behaviour, and with youth nuisance and a perceived lack of recreational facilities for young people. Litter and environmental degradation were very bad in some areas and caused concern even where the neighbourhood was apparently in better condition.
- The main reason for service problems was that, although the services were present, the level of frontline staffing was actually very low. The numbers of permanent, full-time, site-based staff had dwindled since the late 1970s, as what can loosely be described as 'the contract culture' had transformed models of public service delivery. Part-time staff contracted for specific tasks or sessions replaced full-time workers. Specialist and centralised teams replaced generic local workers and core funding was cut while more money became available for short-life projects.
- There were also operational problems: bigger caseloads, more complex cases, pressure on budgets, and the stress of working in a run-down or high-crime area. These difficulties affected recruitment and retention of staff in some neighbourhoods. The additional challenges faced by services were not adequately recognised in their design and funding.
- Over the years, the failure of public services to deal effectively with neighbourhood problems had become an expectation among many residents. Cynicism and mistrust created a barrier to engagement with services and to political participation.

Notes

[1] Overtown in Knowsley had fewer multiple-GP health centres and a higher proportion of single-handed GP practices than was typical, because, according to the Director of Public Health, 'dynamic' GPs did not usually choose to work in the area. A vicious circle was created because these practices would not then attract ambitious partners or students. Low property prices were a disincentive to investment in surgery premises. Problems of GP recruitment in deprived areas, particularly outside the cities, have been acknowledged by the Department of Health and have continued despite additional payments to doctors in such areas (Hastings and Rao, 2001).

[2] Neighbourhood warden schemes were being discussed at this time by the Social Exclusion Unit (PAT 6). Their function is to provide a civilian enforcement presence and to be the 'eyes and ears' of the neighbourhood, identifying problems and referring them to the relevant organisation.

[3] Bramley et al (1998) demonstrated that public spending tends to be bent towards poor areas because of higher service demands.

[4] The distinction between geographic and response policing was not always clear. In some cases, senior officers had given response teams a geographical responsibility so that they could undertake preventive car patrols and low-level follow-up on a specific patch while not responding to calls. In four areas, the police had retained community policing but explicitly moved away from a foot patrol model. Their community officers were 'beat managers' whose role included intelligence gathering, crime analysis and multiagency problem solving, as well as a physical presence.

FIVE

Social interaction and neighbourhood stigma

Neighbourhood society

The failure of public services to manage neighbourhood decline made matters worse for people who were already socially and economically disadvantaged. But decline was not just an individual problem. The combined effects of economic collapse, social change and the increasing concentration of the poor also impacted on social relations within neighbourhoods and on relationships between poor neighbourhoods and others.

Strong but enclosed community

One of the most striking features of our interviews with residents, who were mainly active within their neighbourhoods, was their allusion to the strength of community ties. 'The community' and 'the people' were spontaneously cited as good points about the area in the majority of the 12 areas. Similarly, respondents in the CASE families study rated the importance of community spirit more highly than is the case generally across the country. A total of 90% of them said it mattered and two thirds felt that it existed in some form (Mumford and Power, 2003).

The existence of community was evidenced by supportive informal relationships: looking out for elderly neighbours, keeping an eye on neighbours' houses when they were away, helping with shopping or childcare, or meeting up for a coffee and a chat at a residents' coffee morning. Informal support for some people also included being linked into networks of illegal trading. In common with other studies, we found that the illegal economy was normal, rational and well established (Parker et al, 1988; Buchanan and Young, 2000; Elam et al, 2000). Buying stolen goods was commonplace and widely accepted even among households who would not consider criminal involvement, because they were cheap and made a meagre household budget go further. It was, as Buchanan and Young described, "a major source of income and exchange of goods ... the only way that many families are able to participate in the trappings of an affluent society" (2000, p 124). In Sunnybank (Newcastle), a number of respondents described door-to-door sales of stolen goods, mainly cosmetics, shampoos, household goods, and toys at Christmas. Similar markets were described in

Overtown, Borough View and Kirkside East, where one local worker described the alternative economy as one of "the survival techniques of living on benefit". In some areas, shoplifters would 'shoplift to order' to get items such as clothes, CDs and batteries for friends, neighbours and family.

We also observed a range of more formalised community networks. Every area had some voluntary activity run by residents, formal in the sense that there was usually a committee and some delineation of roles and responsibilities. The activities were of three main kinds: community events and entertainment, activities and support for young people or pensioners, and mutual aid organisations such as food cooperatives and credit unions. In West-City, a neighbourhood association organised coach trips to the seaside and a weekly playgroup. In Fairfields, volunteers ran a successful junior youth group for 11- to 13-year-olds. Residents in High Moor ran a credit union and in Fairfields a residents' group in one village organised parties for Christmas and Bonfire Night, as well as organising local people to tidy up 'eyesore' sites, and plant and maintain communal areas.

In many cases, residents had also taken on larger-scale projects, employing staff and managing buildings. The Fairfields group managed the local community centre and had secured funding to create a 'community house' as a base for health clinics, police surgeries, employment advice and other peripatetic services. In Overtown (Knowsley) a community partnership was formed with representatives from each estate, to run projects in response to local need and funded by regeneration programmes. By 1999, it employed eight staff, and had plans for another 14. Similar community-led initiatives were also present in six other neighbourhoods. Ten of the 12 areas had strong and active tenants' or residents' associations, and two had tenant management organisations to run the council housing stock. Three more had fledgling groups interested in pursuing this possibility (Table 5.1).

These findings are consistent with those of many other studies which have reported on strong communities in working-class areas (Young and Willmott, 1957; Gans, 1962; Forrest and Kearns, 1999). Poor neighbourhoods have been observed to have strong social networks for two reasons. One is that they typically have stronger kinship networks than middle-class areas where people are more geographically mobile (Bridge, 2002). Most of the 12 neighbourhoods exhibited this characteristic to some degree and in eight of them, respondents mentioned it unprompted as one of the characteristics of the area. It was particularly marked in the white working-class industrial areas. One woman in East-Docks in inner London, commenting on the close-knit community, identified 12 households from her immediate family within a few hundred yards. In Knowsley, some families had as many as five generations on the same estate. Shipview in Newcastle was described, by the chair of the local regeneration partnership, as an area with "a settledness" about it, with many long-standing families, a comment echoed by other respondents. In Middle Row, the predominantly Asian area of Birmingham, links across several generations were less common, but kinship and faith networks similarly provided shared values and social networks. These links

Table 5.1: Types of formal social organisation (1999)

	Strong and active tenants'/ residents' associations	Tenant manage-ment organisa-tions	Community-initiated or community-led regeneration projects
West-City (Hackney)	✔		
East-Docks (Newham)	✔	pursuing	Conversion of church for community cafe, primary healthcare, and office space to generate funds for community projects
Riverlands (Nottingham)	✔		Self-build community resource centre
The Valley (Sheffield)		pursuing	Community forum now established as trust
Middle Row (Birmingham)	✔		Highly developed neighbourhood forum
Overtown (Knowsley)	✔	pursuing	Resident-led organisation runs many regeneration projects
Shipview (Newcastle)	✔		
Kirkside East (Leeds)			
Southside (Redcar and Cleveland)	✔	✔	Community forum initiated regeneration bid and runs many projects
High Moor (Blackburn)	✔	✔	
Fairfields (Caerphilly)	✔		
Beachville (Thanet)	✔		Initiated local childcare/Sure Start partnership in one neighbourhood
Total	**10**	**2 (+3)**	**7**

provided a stable core even though some residents were transient, unsettled and isolated.

The second reason, which was also commented on in our study neighbourhoods, is that poverty tends to create greater dependence on local social networks. Since access to people and institutions outside the neighbourhood is limited by the availability and cost of transport, people on low incomes tend to spend more time in their home neighbourhood. As David Page (2000, p 2) reported in his study of housing estates: "estate life was important because it occupied a large part of their lives and provided most of their social contacts. Although poorly connected to wider society, most were well connected locally to supportive peer networks". They also need to rely on others more rather than buying solutions to domestic problems. Unpaid childcare, lifts to appointments and hospitals, borrowing tools, money or even food are all more likely than they are in communities where people can afford to buy these necessities. Respondents in our study made similar observations.

> "Poverty makes people dependent on one another as there's no one else to turn to. Because people don't have cars you do meet people round and about and there's a good sense of caring for one another. People watch out for one another – like the terraced street type of community. There are lots of families with different generations here – mum in one house and daughter next door." (resident, High Moor, Blackburn)

Some respondents suggested that mutual dependence enabled communities to thrive even without the bonds of kin or faith. People could "rub along together" (resident, West-City, Hackney) because they had to.

Myriad networks

Despite the evidence of strong community, it would be a mistake to portray the areas as single communities, socially cohesive and integrated. In practice, like any area, they contained numerous webs of overlapping social groupings. CASE's interviews with families in West-City, East-Docks, Kirkside East and The Valley (Bowman, 2001; Mumford, 2001; Mumford and Power, 2003) demonstrated that concepts of 'neighbourhood' and 'area', involvement in community networks, and use of local institutions and social space all depended on location, gender, family structure, ethnicity, and many other personal and household characteristics. Women with children found that social networks and institutional involvement were often built around their children, getting to know other parents through schools or playgroups and sometimes becoming involved as volunteers. On the other hand, some social spaces were mainly occupied by men, and there were male-based social networks, often based on contacts for work, crime or socialising. Long periods of residence in a neighbourhood could either put people in social positions where they frequently came into contact with new residents, or effectively contain them within tight-knit family or friendship groups, sometimes based around community organisations or community facilities.

> "I think it's nice [community spirit] but I don't need that sort of thing. Because I've got enough around me – my family and my friends – I don't need the outside." (resident, West-City, Hackney) (quoted in Mumford and Power, 2003, Chapter 3)

> "... there is [a sense of community] at the [community] centre and that's the only place I know." (resident, Kirkside East, Leeds) (quoted in Bowman, 2001, p 55)

> "... it's mostly the people from the Church that stick together." (resident, The Valley, Sheffield) (quoted in Bowman, 2001, p 55)

In ethnically diverse areas, community facilities and organisation were to some extent divided on ethnic lines, to provide support services to particular communities. In Middle Row, which had a long history of immigrant communities, an Islamic Centre based alongside the mosque offered adult and school-age education, youth activities and playschemes, advice and help with translation. A Bangladesh Centre provided advice, training, help with jobseeking, counselling and other activities for members of the Bangladeshi community, and there were similar smaller organisations for Irish and African Caribbean communities. Several respondents commented that there was no facility that catered for the whole community. Social networks built up around these facilities were divided on ethnic grounds. A community worker in Middle Row noted that "generally I'd say there's community spirit within the different ethnic groups, but not really across them. They're all looking after their own interests". Even public facilities that were not formally linked to particular groups had come to be associated with one group or another, determining who used them and the networks that were formed. The same worker commented that "mainly the users [of the community centre] are Bangladeshi or Pakistani, so people think it's an Asian centre but it's not". Similarly, in West-City, a resident interviewed as part of CASE's family study noted the presence of community within community:

"... there's definitely a community spirit in the Turkish-speaking community. But it doesn't matter does it, because living in England we should be mixing with the English! I wish we could be part of the English community – it's probably mainly due to language." (resident, West-City, Hackney) (quoted in Mumford and Power, 2003, Chapter 3)

Both on ethnic grounds and on others, such as family connections and length of residence, networks that could be inclusive and supportive to some could be exclusive to others. The existence of community did not prevent the possibility of exclusion or isolation. One person's safe and comfortable neighbourhood was another person's unwelcoming, unsafe and isolated environment, as these quotations from CASE's family study show (quoted in Bowman, 2001, pp 55, 22, 20 respectively):

"People have got their own communities. Certain cliques. I'm not in a clique. I know the [community centre] people but I don't sit in here.... I don't like cliques because it puts people off and people could make more of an effort. It's a community in itself up at the children's centre. I'll drop my son off, go upstairs and then go home. It's just a meeting thing, a kind of checking in, but some people hang around most of the day." (resident, Kirkside East, Leeds)

"The Valley East I don't mind, but I'm not keen on the Valley West. They just don't care. There's vandalism and the properties are derelict. But if you know people down there then they leave you alone." (resident, The Valley, Sheffield)

"… if you know people you're safe." (resident, Kirkside East, Leeds)

'Community' shrinking under pressure

Coleman (1988), writing on social capital, has argued that different kinds of social networks serve different purposes. While wide, loose networks can be valuable for job finding or information exchange, it is dense, closed networks that are most effective in terms of norm enforcement because all the actors in the network know each other and can mutually recognise and act against errant behaviour. As I have indicated, all of the study neighbourhoods did have these dense networks, based on kinship, residence or community organisation. In Saints' Walk (Knowsley), exactly the process of norm enforcement that Coleman describes was articulated by residents. A residents' action group had recently been established and was organising network-building community events such as an annual festival. Residents explained that getting to know other people on the estate, and feeling confident that they all wanted to keep the estate in good condition, gave them the confidence individually to challenge breaches of the acceptable behaviour code, such as dropping litter or causing noise nuisance.

However, networks like these were under pressure, especially in depopulating neighbourhoods. As existing residents struggled to come to terms with the decline of their neighbourhoods, the failure of public management, and the increasing concentration of vulnerable and chaotic households, social networks began to shrink.

In every area, a small number of chaotic households created problems disproportionate to their number: thefts, burglary, arson, criminal damage, joy-riding or drug dealing, and antisocial behaviour, which included excessive noise and 'comings and goings' late at night, aggressive attitudes towards neighbours, wrecking homes and common property, or dumping rubbish. Residents and service providers agreed that the numbers of such households were very small. In Nottingham, Rosehill's housing manager, for example, described "about 1% who are real trouble – violent and the like". In most of the study neighbourhoods, police attributed a large proportion of the crime to no more than 10 prolific individuals, or sometimes to a small number of extended criminal families, whose activities sometimes drew in others from outside the neighbourhood. The impact of such households was extremely localised, in certain streets or certain parts of streets, but could be very great, causing these micro-neighbourhoods to decline very quickly and with long-lasting effects. In The Valley (Sheffield), police observed several hundred visitors to the house of one active drug dealer in a 24-

hour period. In BoroughView (Redcar and Cleveland), the renewal team manager described how one street had only four residents remaining, two couples whose antisocial behaviour had "driven all the others out". Another was "notorious for its criminal element and drug-dealing problem" and was half empty. Residents complained of fire-setting, "young people wrecking the place" and intimidation. Streets like these found it difficult to shift their reputation, even after the culprits had moved away, and everybody in the street tended to be tarred with the same brush by residents and outsiders. The behaviour of the 'problem households' became magnified in local folklore, adding to the stigma (a similar example is described in Box 5.1).

The effect of developments like these was to make communities turn in on themselves. High levels of neighbourhood crime and disorder impacted on people's sense of control over their environment, their trust of their neighbours, and their confidence in the authorities to resolve neighbourhood problems[1]. Existing residents, whose quality of life was threatened by the behaviour of a minority of households, and who felt unprotected by public services, blamed newcomers for neighbourhood decline and agencies for allowing them in and not controlling their behaviour.

> "I like my house. I like the estate. I like the neighbours, and I don't want to move out because of the trash they've brought in." (resident, Shipview, Newcastle)

> "… it could be a brilliant area, but the question is, can we do it with all these same people here – the druggies, the people with mental illness etc, or do we need to get rid of them and start again?" (resident, Riverlands, Nottingham)

> "They're bringing in rough families. As soon as they come in it just deteriorates." (resident, Kirkside East, Leeds)

A 'them and us' situation could easily arise, with the 'us' (long-standing residents) gradually becoming a smaller group as people chose to move away or withdrew from social interaction because of fear of crime or intimidation. Newer residents sometimes commented regretfully on a lack of a sense of community and on how easy it was to become isolated, while older residents commented on the decline of a more extensive community spirit. In one interview, residents in the Southmead neighbourhood in Kirkside East in Leeds described their close-knit friendship group as one of the good things about the area but also said there was "no community spirit", only a handful of people who had pride in the estate and were prepared to do anything about it. A newer resident who entered the room while we were talking was made to feel unwelcome and subsequently described as "one of our so-called residents". Several respondents in CASE's family study who had grown up in Kirkside East described a broader sense of community in their youth, characterised by "pulling together" and adults enforcing norms of behaviour and being prepared to discipline other people's children. Social networks had not collapsed. Rather they had become smaller, tighter and narrower.

As communities shrank, residents found it increasingly difficult to exercise informal social control over neighbours' behaviour and neighbourhood conditions.

Box 5.1: Community under pressure, Sunnybank, Newcastle

In Sunnybank (Newcastle) resident activists described the changes in their community during the 1990s. The estate's reputation and the size of the houses made it relatively unpopular, and not a neighbourhood of choice in the light of the city's underlying housing demand problem. In the early 1990s, a small number of problematic tenants moved in and the estate became a focus for drug dealing, and entered a cycle of decline. Pockets of empty homes opened up, mostly in three streets, Leicester Avenue, Leyland Close and Marion Close (not their real names), and within these streets, they appeared in blocks. For example, numbers 3, 5, 7 and 9 were empty in Leyland Close, and 15 properties had been demolished in Leicester Avenue, of which 12 had been empty for many months. Blocks of empty properties were attributed to the fact that renowned 'trouble-maker' families lived in these streets. When their neighbours moved away, no one wanted to move in. One interviewee described Leicester Avenue as a "den of iniquity", with a few families who just "let their kids get up to whatever they want". Young people from another part of the estate talked about "the Leicester Rats", alleging that none of them worked and that they were all "tramps, rubbish, smackheads", to blame for crime and drug dealing. Residents said that one family in Leyland Close had driven the others away. Five families in another street were currently considering moving because of the behaviour of one neighbouring family.

Communal space around the estate began to be perceived as unsafe, with people particularly avoiding the estate shop because of gangs of young people hanging around outside. Residents accused the council of "not vetting people", of "putting trash in" and even of advertising the homes in Durham prison. They complained that there was negligible tenancy enforcement, even when residents reported antisocial behaviour or other breaches of tenancy conditions. "I don't know why they bother having that book [tenants' handbook] because they don't enforce it" (resident).

By the time I visited the estate, some of the long-standing tenants were beginning to move away. Some of those who stayed opted to "keep themselves to themselves" or withdraw to the safe company of longer-standing friends. A sense of community was maintained, based on strong links between small groups of people, and there was an active group of older residents that was working effectively with the area coordinator, police, housing and environmental services departments to maintain estate conditions. However, they acknowledged that this was qualitatively different from the kind of community that they used to know, based on a larger number of weak links.

Knowing fewer people, they could be less confident of shared norms and standards, and less confident to challenge people who stepped out of line. In Borough View, for example, an older resident described how she had lost confidence to tackle young people who were vandalising lamp posts or urinating in the doorways of empty homes, for fear of being turned on, not just by the young people, but their families and friends of their families. In Caerphilly, a long-standing resident recalled, perhaps with some exaggeration to emphasise the contrast, a golden age of community self-policing, which had gone with the increasing transience of the area and the 'dumping' of families from outside the area.

> "We used to watch TV and say 'oh look at that, we wouldn't want to live in a place like that', and now we do. You see, we had our well-known tea-leaves, but at least we knew who they were, and we knew their modus operandi. We'd say 'oh someone's mower's gone' and you'd know who had it and you'd get it back, nothing else said about it. Now, we don't know who they are." (resident, Fairfields, Caerphilly)

Network containment and neighbourhood stigma

While intra-neighbourhood networks shrank, we found no evidence that inter-neighbourhood networks were growing. Conversations with older residents suggested that the areas had always been characterised by a certain degree of network containment. While they were certainly not islands, limited opportunity to travel and strong in-neighbourhood networks of family and kinship probably meant that in-neighbourhood ties were more common than in better-off areas, where residents enjoyed greater mobility. Large-scale local employment in factories, mines or shipyards contributed to the development of locally based networks.

Other studies in the US and in this country (Morris, 1993; Jargowsky, 1996; Wilson, 1997) have noted that dependence on local networks does not lead to a wholesale disconnection from mainstream societal values. What was remarkable was the extent to which relatively isolated communities continued to endorse mainstream norms, rather than reject them. However, network containment did impact on some elements of perception and behaviour. In our study areas, both residents and professionals commented on localised cultures built up through strong local peer groups, and on a certain degree of closure towards 'outsiders'. Communities to some extent developed an equilibrium of self-regulation which accepted "the normality of what goes on" (resident in Kirkside East), and dealt with it internally within certain limits. A police officer in Newcastle talked about "self-regulation – there are criminals who live in Sunnybank, but you won't find them committing burglaries in Sunnybank. They'd get beaten up". Provided that behaviour was within certain limits, solidarity against the authorities was accepted, with every place having what was described in East-Docks as "a culture that no one will grass anyone up".

Professionals working in the areas were struck by their apparent insularity and regarded it as a constraint on opportunities outside the area:

> "… it's a culture which is to a certain extent self-excluding. It's inward-looking. The only society they want to know about is the one in this town … people here have developed an attitude that the system is there to be beaten. Even residents who wouldn't get involved in crime know what they can buy where, and don't see anything wrong with it. The culture is completely out in the open." (youth worker, Southside, Redcar and Cleveland)

> "… people expect local jobs because all their habits and experience are local. Their social network is local. You can't leapfrog people from the Grove to the City just like that." (employment adviser, West-City, Hackney)

Such comments support the notion put forward by Putnam and others that strong in-neighbourhood networks can create 'bonding' social capital, to reinforce neighbourhood norms and provide support and solidarity, but not 'bridge' to wider opportunity networks (Putnam, 2000; Burns et al, 2001). Das et al (2003) have particularly noted that the support networks established in immigrant communities can become limiting, preventing connections to other beneficial networks. However, other responses suggest that the limited networks and social isolation of these disadvantaged neighbourhoods were the creation of stigma at least as much as of local culture.

As low-income areas, all of the neighbourhoods traditionally had relatively low status in the towns and cities around them. Social divisions had widened as neighbourhood fortunes had diverged during the 1980s and 1990s, and the increasing concentration of society's most disadvantaged and vulnerable people within the neighbourhoods had deepened their reputations as 'rough' or 'undesirable' areas.

In common with other studies, we found that residents were usually acutely aware of the reputations of their areas. On the one hand, they were anxious to play them down, emphasising the universality of problems and finding things to praise about the places they lived (Dean and Hastings, 2000; Burningham and Thrush, 2001). On the other hand, they described at length their personal experience of neighbourhood stigma. Postcode discrimination was widely reported. Residents revealed that they were unable to get credit to buy household goods or purchase items from catalogues. Some younger people thought that they would be discriminated against in the job market, and there was some evidence that this was a justified concern. In Bridgefields (Blackburn), an employers' forum had set up links with the estate partly because employers said that they were reluctant to take on any local people, because of the area's reputation. In Broadways (Birmingham) the neighbourhood forum had made dummy job applications to a range of large employers, and found less success with applications carrying the neighbourhood address rather than one from a more affluent area. Neighbourhood stigma was certainly felt, even when not directly experienced, and contributed to lack of confidence and to isolation from opportunities and networks outside the area:

> "My daughter goes to school in [another part of the city] and some of her friends aren't allowed to come and visit her, because of where we live in Middle Row." (resident, Middle Row, Birmingham)

> "I was looking for a job for six or seven months when I left school but people turned their nose up when they found out I was from Southside. People look at you funny when you say where you live." (young resident, Southside, Redcar and Cleveland)

In this sense, area contributed to social exclusion, as well as collecting the socially excluded. Over time, services had become depleted and ineffective. Public space had become contested and disordered and, while community did not disappear, community networks became too small to exert a strong enough counter-pressure against the decline in neighbourhood conditions, and too contained to bridge effectively to opportunity networks outside. Neighbourhoods that were already at a disadvantage took on characteristics that reinforced their exclusion rather than remedying it.

Summary

- 'Community' had not disappeared in the neighbourhoods in our study. There was evidence of what Putnam (2000) has referred to as 'bonding social capital'. Residents observed and valued a range of informal supportive relationships, from caring for a neighbour to trading in cheap goods in the illegal economy.
- All the neighbourhoods also had formal community organisations, running activities, managing the housing stock through tenant management organisations, or providing services funded by regeneration programmes.
- Community was sustained by family, kinship and faith networks, and because poverty limited people's travel outside their neighbourhoods and made them more dependent on each other because they lacked the means to buy goods and services in the private market.
- However, community was also made up of myriad social networks and meant different things to different people. Its existence did not guarantee cohesion, integration or social support. Networks based on long-standing residence or on community facilities, or on faith, were exclusive and isolating to some residents just as they were inclusive to others.

- There was evidence that social networks in some areas were under pressure, becoming smaller and turning in on themselves as a reaction to the disordered behaviour of a small number of problematic households, who tended to be blamed for neighbourhood decline. Defensiveness caused social networks to shrink and to be less effective in maintaining social norms and standards.
- Meanwhile, the extent of overlap with networks outside the neighbourhood was limited by poverty, local employment or worklessness, and by the traditional strength of local social networks. Social divisions had widened since the 1970s as neighbourhood polarisation had increased. Residents were inhibited, practically and psychologically, by the stigma attached to their addresses. While community existed, it did not help people to bridge to opportunities beyond their own areas.

Note

[1] Similar findings have emerged from other studies, both quantitative and qualitative (Geis and Ross, 1998; Pitts, 2000).

SIX

Attempts at regeneration

Histories of regeneration

As I demonstrated in the Introduction to this book, the need to do something about the problems of the poorest neighbourhoods was recognised by central government as early as the 1960s, and a series of 'regeneration' policies followed for the next three decades. By the late 1980s, numerous programmes were running simultaneously: major initiatives like City Challenge as well as smaller programmes of special grant aid. In all, there were no fewer than 15 urban policy funding programmes[1] in the decade from 1981, with City Challenge and the SRB following on in the 1990s (Robson et al, 1994).

Inevitably, these programmes were directed to most of the local authorities in our study. All of the English authorities except one (Thanet) received the Urban Programme. Five were affected by Urban Development Corporations (UDCs) and three by Inner City Task Forces. Six had City Challenge (Table 6.1). All of the English authorities had funding from SRB.

However, each of these authorities had more than one deprived area. Funds were not necessarily directed to the areas in our study. Among the more recent programmes, nine of the areas had benefited in some way from SRB, although sometimes only as part of much bigger schemes. Only one (Riverlands in Nottingham) had City Challenge, and only one of the UDCs (Sheffield) was directed at an industrial area close to the study area itself. It was impossible to establish the localised distribution of Urban Programme funding and Estate Action – some of the programmes having been implemented as long ago as the early 1980s.

There was no doubt that the programmes that had been completed had left lasting benefits. City Challenge, in Nottingham, was the most recently completed, investing about £7.5 million of government funds per year in the Riverlands area between 1991 and 1996. The programme had enabled the creation of new business parks close to the city centre, generating employment and also a rental income to support the ongoing regeneration of the area through a local Renewal Trust. Other investments made by City Challenge were also very much in evidence – housing and lighting improvements and traffic calming schemes. The programme mainly had a physical focus, although it did fund some welfare projects, such as training, childcare, and improvements to community facilities.

Other programmes had also left tangible physical improvements. The Estate Action programme on the Saints' Walk estate in Knowsley, which finished in

Table 6.1: Major regeneration programmes: local authority coverage

Area	Urban Programme	Urban Development Corporation	Inner City Task Force	City Challenge	Single Regeneration Budget
Hackney	✔		✔	✔	✔
Newham	✔			✔	✔
Knowsley	✔				✔
Nottingham	✔		✔	✔	✔
Newcastle	✔	✔		✔	✔
Sheffield	✔	✔			✔
Blackburn	✔			✔	✔
Birmingham	✔	✔	✔	✔	✔
Caerphilly					
Redcar and Cleveland	✔	✔			✔
Leeds	✔	✔			✔
Thanet					✔
Total	10	5	3	6	11

Source: Interviews and documentary evidence in the 12 study areas

1997, had revamped its appearance, with new brick walls and front gates, in-curtilage parking and attractive communal gardens in the centre of some of the closes. The attractive environment of the estate had boosted its popularity. Elsewhere, there had been improvements to the community infrastructure. The youth club in East-Docks (Newham) and a well-regarded women's centre in Borough View (Redcar and Cleveland) had both originally been established with help from the Urban Programme. Borough View's Urban Programme also paid for housing improvements, landscaping of an area near the shops, and a local advice office. In Nottingham, the Urban Programme funded a community worker, whose key remit was to establish a community resource. His work with a local group enabled them to secure City Challenge funding to build a new community centre in the heart of the area.

These investments were valuable and usually appreciated by residents. They brought opportunities that could not have been afforded within mainstream local authority budgets. Nevertheless, none of the programmes could have been said to have transformed the fortunes of the areas. People spoke of their contribution in terms of improvements they had funded rather than 'regeneration' or transformation.

SRB and problems with regeneration policy

By 1999, the only current major programme in England was the SRB[2]. Nine of the 12 areas had regeneration funding from this source. In four, the scale of the activity was relatively small, part of thematic programmes covering much larger areas. Kirkside East, for example, was one of several areas in Leeds to get funding for extra policing, a youth programme for young people at risk of offending, adult education and a sustained reading intervention programme in local schools. The Valley in Sheffield was the subject of a five-year SRB programme to build community capacity – supporting community organisations and attempting to reach excluded groups through initiatives such as community literacy campaigns, a family learning programme and a community health initiative. In High Moor, Blackburn, SRB funding paid for a training and employment facility in Bridgefields, an employers' forum, education/industry links and the community coordinator post. Beachville in Thanet had a small SRB programme covering the development of community facilities, childcare and education and training support in Sandyton. In these areas, in a sense, SRB was not a comprehensive regeneration programme as such but just another source of funds.

In the other five areas, however, SRB was funding comprehensive area-based programmes designed to turn around the fortunes of the areas. These involved government investment of £20 to £30 million over a seven-year period (all smaller programmes than City Challenge), plus matched funding from local government, the voluntary sector and business. The programmes varied in scale from £32 million to £106 million over seven years and the amount of matched funding also varied considerably. They covered populations of 7,000 to 46,000, giving a per capita spend of between £1,800 and £6,500. In each case, spending was controlled by a management board and managed by a dedicated team. All the programmes involved some improvements to the housing stock, investment in the economic infrastructure, improved community facilities, as well as 'people-based' schemes such as training programmes, crime reduction and youth work. Table 6.2 outlines the programmes. Most of them were in their fourth year when we looked at them in 1999.

Interviews with regeneration workers and other professionals and residents revealed many examples of valuable work being done, but also highlighted three problems. One was the difficulty of implementing programmes in a genuinely inclusive way, to overcome the barrier of mistrust between residents and professionals. The second was that the SRB approach of time-limited, area-based funding impeded a more strategic approach to area regeneration, and the third was that it was clear that regeneration focused at the neighbourhood level could only have a limited effect unless the wider forces of decline were tackled as well. Area regeneration could not, in isolation, transform areas. We looked at each of these issues in turn.

SRB: inclusion through regeneration

National evaluation of SRB has demonstrated a number of problems with its implementation: difficulties spending the money and keeping projects on track; problems coordinating SRB funds and other money levered in from other sources; the proliferation of monitoring requirements generated by its output-focused nature; and difficulties engaging the voluntary and community sectors as equal

Table 6.2: Comprehensive area-based SRB programmes

Area	Population of programme area (000s)	Total size of programme (£m)	Single Regeneration Budget (£m)	Per capita spend (£000)	Main elements
East-Docks (Newham)	15	98.5	21.5	6.5	• Redevelopment of industrial estates. Attract new employers. Business support • Training/employer links • Housing renewal
Overtown (Knowsley)	29	106	26	3.6	• Industrial estate improvements • Training schemes, community education facilities • Environmental improvements • Funding for community groups and schemes • Community health workers • Limited housing improvements
Shipview (Newcastle)	35	65	25	1.8	• Redevelopment of main shopping street • Training schemes, community education facilities and Workfinder • Funding for community groups and schemes (eg family support worker) • Housing estate improvements • Improved pool, library, play centre
Middle Row (Birmingham)	46	138	23	3	• Community-based training and employment initiatives • Business support and improved trading environment • Housing renewal scheme • Tailored initiatives for minority ethnic groups • Designing out crime • Highway/environmental improvements • Improved community facilities
Southside (Redcar and Cleveland)	7	32	18	4.6	• Training, employment advice, employer incentives • Industrial estate improvements and inward investment grants • Shopping street redevelopment • Environmental warden scheme • Demolition and estate improvements, private sector renewal • CCTV and additional policing • Community forum, improved community facilities • Detached youth work

members of the partnership (Brennan et al, 1998). From our work, the most striking implementation problem was how to ensure that regeneration was a process owned by residents, rather than one imposed on them by government and other agencies.

The residents whom we interviewed greeted SRB programmes with a mixture of enthusiasm and cynicism. While they welcomed investment in their neighbourhoods, they were not always optimistic about the outcomes. Over the years, they had seen spending programmes of various kinds come and go, while their communities continued to decline. They could all list projects that had been set up, valued locally and then dismantled when the funding ran out. Many residents were, unsurprisingly, sceptical towards new programmes run by new groups of enthusiastic professionals. In Borough View (Redcar and Cleveland), where neighbourhood conditions were deteriorating badly, some residents resented the approach of SRB workers and board members, very few of whom lived in the worst affected areas. SRB-funded projects to landscape a site where homes had recently been demolished, to design and erect elaborate railings around a former football pitch that was being redeveloped as a community facility, and to research young people's lifestyles seemed largely irrelevant to some residents living in this highly disordered neighbourhood.

> "From Hope to Reality – that's the slogan. Well they don't live in the bloody reality." (resident, Borough View, Redcar and Cleveland)

> "The problem with the SRB is that they don't live in Borough View. They drive away at night. They don't understand the conditions we're living in." (resident, Borough View, Redcar and Cleveland)

Moreover, regeneration programmes were operating in the context of widespread cynicism about the ability of public sector agencies to deliver, and about their willingness to share decision-making power. Although SRB programmes were new, their board members and staff largely came from public sector organisations (often from the local authorities) and embodied their same culture. They often found it hard to deal with residents, unsure how to value their local knowledge as against their own specialist expertise, and unwilling to engage in frank conversations for fear of being seen to make promises that could not be delivered. While residents were always represented on the SRB boards, most reported in 1999 that it had been hard work to gain the influence and the trust that they wanted.

> "... no one listens to us ... you get respect when you're a paid worker. When they realise we're truly voluntary, we're contemptible. They can say 'don't worry about them, they're not paid'." (resident activist, East-Docks, Newham)

"… it's been a difficult road for the community to take the lead in regeneration. The initial view [of the professionals] was 'ooh, the community, keep them in the cupboard'. It was token involvement. They expected us to fail. I realised early on that because we're community we have to be 200% better than anyone else because of the amount of scrutiny." (resident, representative of community organisation, Overtown, Knowsley)

"Resident forums don't feel that they have equality in the partnership. The council still has the budgetary control. If the regeneration programmes are really going to be community-led, then they must not be administered by the city. The money that comes in in the name of the community just gets sucked up by the city institutions." (resident activist, Middle Row, Birmingham)

Few programmes addressed this issue directly, but it could be done. In Overtown, the SRB partnership ran training sessions for its board members and working groups to help them to work together better. A conscious effort was made to get residents into position as chair of groups, to shift the balance of power away from organisations that were already powerful, and to engage local people as valued and equal partners.

Some of the SRB programmes were also demonstrating that they could work in ways which, in themselves, helped promote social inclusion and build local capacity, rather than simply delivering useful projects.

A first step was being locally based in the area, to demonstrate commitment and to get a first-hand understanding of the problems. In East-Docks, Newham, residents convinced the SRB board that all services funded by the programme should have a physical base in the area. A second step was to fund existing local projects or, in new projects, to employ local people, who had credibility with service users and who could help people engage with what would otherwise seem like official services. In Kirkside East, Leeds, two local women were employed as outreach workers for a young children's centre, but also distributed information and talked to people about adult education opportunities in the local area. In East-Docks, regeneration funds had helped establish a local labour hire and training project, contracting with the council to provide estate caretaking, concierge and administration staff as well as filling ad hoc vacancies for other companies. The project had its own training arm and ran courses in response to demand, including skilled trades, forklift truck operation, cleaning and security procedures, and modules such as first aid, driving, and health and safety. According to the coordinator, the main advantage of the programme was that the advisers were local people and could respond in a non-judgemental way with realistic advice. Similarly, in Birmingham, Middle Row, SRB funded an adult education programme in primary schools. Workers recruited from the local community talked to parents in the playground and at school gates about their learning needs and aspirations and encouraged them to attend courses, ranging from parenting-based topics such as 'Stay and Play' to 'A' level Urdu, provided on the school premises. Nearly 1,000 parents, mainly women, took part in 1999. One worker commented that local people were, in his view, best placed to motivate other local residents into further education:

> "It annoys me that most of the jobs created by regeneration are advertised city-wide or nationally. People say they don't want to advertise locally. It might build up expectations if people don't have the skills needed. This approach sends a message to the community that they are no good and it overlooks exactly the kind of people who are needed in these jobs." (project worker, Middle Row, Birmingham)

Including people as workers, volunteers and decision makers was invaluable in itself, not just because it helped services work better. It could offer a chance to develop individuals' skills and confidence, building the human capital that had become so depleted, and also to restore a collective belief that things could change for the better. In Overtown, Knowsley, a key principle of the regeneration programme was that local people should be helped and encouraged to help themselves and to take action themselves for the benefit of their neighbourhoods. The programme helped to build up a community-led organisation which ran SRB-funded projects and applied for its own regeneration funds. Local people who wanted to get involved were taken seriously, encouraged and given training, not just in basic skills, but in market research, 'train-the-trainer', management, and even degree courses. Their achievements inspired other people in their communities to aim high (see Box 6.1).

These local projects also highlighted a third key step in engaging local people effectively – the time and flexibility to allow services to develop in the way that suited participants, rather than offering standard packages that were too rigid for people with complex problems to negotiate. The Middle Row education project provided courses during school hours on school premises, to suit women with children. The East-Docks employment project tailored courses to meet demand. Some started with short hours in the middle of the day, then built up to full days, to cater for the fact that many long-term unemployed people simply were not used to getting up in the morning. Advisers would ring some trainees at home if they failed to turn up for courses. Similarly, in Shipview in Newcastle, training was offered by a family centre attached to a nursery school, but only on a customised basis. Through networking, an outreach worker tried to contact the most isolated parents and encourage them to come into the centre, where initial activities were simply based on building friendships and social activities. Parenting skills support was introduced gradually and adult education courses ran on-site in response to parents' requests.

Box 6.1: Building human capital: individual stories from Overtown

'**Brenda**' was 38 and had not worked since she was 15. After her fourth child went to school she wanted to do something else but thought she was too old for training and couldn't 'go back to school' after 20 years. Through being a volunteer on her estate she was persuaded to go on a community economic development course, which made her realise her skills and set her off on a range of other courses. She wrote a 'wish list' of things she wanted to achieve, all of which she had accomplished three years later. In 1999, she was working as a smoking cessation counsellor, but believed she had made a bigger contribution as a role model in her local community.

Her colleague '**Andrea**' had left school with five CSEs and remembered being branded 'educationally subnormal'! She hadn't worked for 20 years and recalls that the highlight of her day was getting the kids ready for school. Like Brenda, she got involved as an estate representative and undertook a community economic development training course, then continued her training through to the achievement of a management qualification. She chaired the community-led regeneration partnership which had grown to have a budget of over £4 million.

Box 6.2: Local, flexible and accessible: successful regeneration projects

In Riverlands, Nottingham, the community regeneration trust ran a local 'job shop'. The Employment Service provided a manager and reception and circulated the same vacancies as in its main job centres, as well as some local jobs that were uniquely advertised in the job shop. There were dedicated advisers for the black and Asian communities, and the trust also funded childcare vouchers and 'Into Work' grants – helping with equipment, driving lessons or training for people who had got a job offer. We were told that the shop was the most successful office in the city in terms of placements into work. Its manager attributed its success to its accessibility – it was local and had the 'feel' of a voluntary project, as well as advisers who understood the cultural backgrounds of black and Asian clients. Take-up of the service and the number of minority ethnic placements both improved when these workers were taken on.

In Blackburn, there had been an emphasis on community economic development. Bridgefields had one of several 'access points' in the town, based at its community and employment centre. The access point, funded by the council and SRB, provided employment advice and help with job search and CVs, as well as running courses locally, in partnership with Blackburn College. With workshops and computer facilities, courses could be run in response to local demand, and a crèche was provided. Having a local training base in the community centre was a way into training for people who lacked confidence, time or transport. The neighbourhood focus was helpful in another way. The access point manager could liaise with the local employers' forum over skill needs, and get involved with other estate-based initiatives building confidence, skills and learning, such as Parents as Educators.

> ## Box 6.3: Inclusive regeneration: key elements
>
> - Residents as equal partners in decision-making
> - Local base
> - Employing local people
> - Accessible and flexible services

Lack of a strategic approach

These examples demonstrate both the difficulty of making regeneration an inclusive process and the possibility for change, given sufficient will on the part of local authorities and other partners. They provide a ground-level view that supports the findings of a considerable body of other work on community involvement in regeneration processes (see, for example, Duffy, 1995; Taylor, 1995; Anastacio et al, 2000). However, inclusive implementation was not the only problem with SRB. In addition to problems at the implementation level, there were broader concerns about the whole approach to regeneration through area-based programmes.

Urban policy research during the 1990s consistently found that there were many pragmatic justifications for area-based programmes like SRB. Public services had to be located somewhere and targeting deprived areas was an efficient, if not a complete, way of reaching disadvantaged individuals. It produced useful activity at a local level to counter neighbourhood problems, as well as a focus for innovation, for multiagency working and for resident involvement (Brennan et al, 1998; Smith, 1999; Kleinman, 2000). However, the SRB concept of a comprehensive time-limited programme was, as a basis for regeneration policy, very limited. Its emphasis on special funding, additional projects and bidding processes seemed, for many people, to be a barrier to a strategic approach to area problems and an impediment to sustained regeneration.

The first problem was the need to bid for funds. As the problems of deprived areas became more acute and core local government services continued to be cut, local authorities bemoaned the lack of government assistance and the need to compete in bidding rounds to secure extra funds for one area at a time when problems were equally acute in others. "Bidding processes are crap", a councillor for Borough View (Redcar and Cleveland) told us. "The government should be about addressing need, not making poor areas bid against each other". In Blackburn, one of High Moor's councillors argued that top-sliced funding was "taking money from everybody and giving it to a few. It's making the poor bid against the poor. Why should Burnley lose out for the benefit of Blackburn?". There was a sense that the allocation of funds was too dependent on the time and skill devoted to bidding, rather than on the needs of the respective areas. Moreover, the programme lacked a strategic bidding framework. In order to secure funds, it was tempting to 'second guess' the government's criteria and tailor bids to these, rather than reflecting local priorities.

The need to identify small areas for regeneration funding made it difficult to take a strategic approach. Problems in the cities usually related to the entire inner city, because of deindustrialisation and depopulation, but the funding regime encouraged a fragmented approach, looking at one area at a time. In some cases, where there were many equally needy areas in a local authority, decisions about which areas to choose for funding bids were determined by political considerations, "sharing out the money", as well as indicators of need. Areas with strong community organisation and a political voice were better placed to articulate their needs for funding than those with many diverse interest groups. In Sheffield, representatives of residents and the local authority agreed that the ethnically diverse Valley area had probably lost out in regeneration funding bids to white council-owned areas, with a greater homogeneity of interests and a structure for community representation on area issues, based on tenants' associations. The Valley, by contrast, had a plethora of smaller community groups, representing religious or cultural interests. A small amount of SRB funding was eventually gained to help build community capacity. On the other hand, some resident activists in the predominantly white East-Docks area of Newham felt that their area's needs had been neglected while funding was sought for minority ethnic areas whose problems were seen as more pressing or more important politically.

Local authority structures for delivering regeneration reflected the fragmented funding regime. Small teams had been set up, sometimes within chief executive's departments, sometimes within planning or development departments, to bid for funds and to manage programmes. Some councils, like Knowsley, Birmingham and Newcastle, also employed the staff at local level who ran the SRB programmes: programme managers, monitoring and finance officers, community development staff, business advisers and similar posts. Others, like Hackney and Newham, employed specialist regeneration agencies to run the programmes. Either way, a mobile army of regeneration professionals grew up with the key skills of preparing funding bids, managing projects to timescale and budgets, and monitoring outputs.

The extent to which area regeneration was seen in a strategic sense was very mixed. Most authorities allocated some strategic responsibility to an officer or small unit, but mainly with the function of keeping an overview of funding streams and coordinating funding bids. It was unusual for regeneration to be the responsibility of a senior officer or to be integrated with other key issues: housing, education, economic development, democratic renewal, or equalities. There were exceptions. Blackburn-with-Darwen had a Regeneration Directorate. Sheffield had recently established a Regeneration and Partnership division within its chief executive's office to integrate area initiatives, external funding, community safety, equalities and community partnerships. The division reported to a Social Inclusion Board. Elsewhere, structures reflected the separation between area regeneration programmes, which were largely seen as involving bidding and programme management functions, and other corporate regeneration activities, such as anti-poverty policies and economic development. No authority had an over-arching area regeneration strategy, only plans that identified areas in need and earmarked them for future rounds of external funding. Caerphilly, with regeneration as one of the four priorities of its corporate plan, and three geographical areas identified for the development of specific local regeneration strategies led by senior officers, was a notable strategic exception, perhaps because of the lack of a major area-based funding programme similar to those in England.

Sustainability was another real problem. Local authorities welcomed regeneration funding in order to provide services that they wanted to provide anyway but could not afford from mainstream budgets. When funding programmes were complete, they often lacked the money to continue with the level of service that residents had got used to. In Borough View (Redcar and Cleveland), for example, SRB had funded a detached youth work project aiming at older teenagers and young adults. Two full-time workers met young people on the streets four evenings per week and set up social and activity groups and holiday activities. The project had a good reputation locally, but was due to close at the end of the SRB period. There were hopes that it could be extended through renewed SRB funding, because the local authority would not be able to take it over. The youth worker explained the difficulties of effecting real change in this insecure environment:

> "In practice, even in a seven-year programme, by the time it's been decided what to do and you've got up and running and recruited staff, most projects probably only have an active three-year life. It's enough to raise people's expectations, but not to achieve real change. If you're trying to change a society which is so inward looking, so ingrained, you're not going to do it in three years. You might scratch the surface and maybe help some of those who want to get out and get on, but the majority won't be affected. It's like polishing the top with no impact on the bottom. With youth work, you need to be able to work with people for 10 years, until they become parents themselves." (youth worker, Borough View, Redcar and Cleveland)

Thus while regeneration money was welcomed, it contributed to a situation of short-term rather than permanent provision and to services being driven by funding criteria, not just by users' needs. Sustained activity was possible, but it required a lot of effort to keep continuous funding, and frequent changes in provision to match the funds being offered. Voluntary organisations based permanently in the areas tended to 'bend' their activities according to what they could get regeneration funding for, changing the objectives of their youth work, for example, and adding a few new activities, in order to meet funders' objectives. One youth group in East-Docks had been going for 11 years, changing shape not just according to what the young people needed but according to the funding available – "we just do what we do until the money runs out, then we apply for something else" (youth worker). While regular reinvention was beneficial, organisations did not always feel that the interests of their clients were best served by changes driven by the imperatives of external bodies. Larger voluntary organisations even began to follow the regeneration money, setting up services in areas where they could get funding, for a period of a few years, then moving on to the next area. In East-Docks, several respondents who had lived and worked in the area for many years expressed wry amusement, mixed with resentment, about the influx, which they expected to be short lived, of new voluntary organisations and regeneration professionals: "Suddenly, voluntary organisations are all coming in to the area because they know East-Docks is the place to get the money. It's suddenly on the map", said one, while another remarked that "the government pays a lot of professionals and organisations to regenerate areas like this, but who gets the benefits? There's a lot of money to be made out of poor people".

These difficulties with the SRB approach to regeneration are summarised in Figure 6.1.

Figure 6.1: Limitations of the SRB regeneration approach

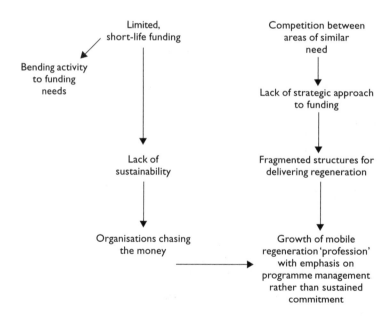

'Regeneration' and realism: the need for a broader regeneration agenda

This over-emphasis on short-life regeneration programmes was clearly problematic and limited both what the programmes could do and the extent to which funds were distributed to areas of need. But there was also another problem. It was evident that while area-based programmes were useful, they could not, even if combined with a more strategic and sustained approach, transform or 'regenerate' areas. As earlier chapters have shown, the causes of decline did not originate at neighbourhood level, but in the wider structures of the economy and society. Area-based programmes could not impact on these structures. All they could do was mitigate the effects of wider changes, or try to link areas to positive developments. Talking to SRB programme managers and board members and examining funding bids, delivery plans and progress reports, it was clear that there was a high degree of realism about the likely impact of SRB. Programmes were billed as 'regeneration' and sometimes made ambitious transformational statements about their likely impact, but in reality they had much more limited aims, determined by the wider context in which area problems were located.

Three main approaches were adopted by the SRB programmes in our study (see Figure 6.2). The first was to apply a brake to a process of decline that already had a momentum of its own and could not be stopped with the normal funding available to local authorities, police and other organisations. Halting decline was an essential prerequisite of any strategy for regeneration and in the case of Borough View in Redcar and Cleveland, it took most of the energy of the regeneration partnership. The rapid decline of the area in the early 1990s caused church and community leaders and the council to get together to discuss how the problems could be tackled, and eventually, to bid for SRB. The SRB chair described Borough View as "in a desperate state". "We needed to intervene quickly", said a local councillor, "or we would have lost it. The council just hadn't got the money, especially for the housing". Housing and community safety were the major issues in early meetings. Of £17.9 million SRB funding, £9.6 million was spent on housing, and a further £4.4 million on community, environmental and quality of life projects. Economic development and employment programmes

Figure 6.2: SRB programmes: three broad approaches

Brake	Platform	Bridge
Halt rapid decline, as precursor to renewal	Sustain areas, prevent decline and provide basis for renewal	Link areas to economic opportunity
↓	↓	↓
Housing demolitions and refurbishment Community safety	Housing improvements Community facilities Business support Training and education	Economic development Business support Employer links Training and education

accounted for just £2.7 million. Housing demolition and improvements, CCTV and extra policing managed to stabilise at least part of the area. One resident acknowledged that "Borough View wouldn't exist if we hadn't had the money". SRB did a holding job. In 1999, Borough View bid for, and gained, a further round of SRB funding to address longer-term social and economic problems: employment and training, health, educational attainment and a reduction in benefit dependency. However, even this programme was seen as only a partial contribution to solving much bigger problems.

> "The catalyst for change has been the SRB process. Had it not been for the lifeline thrown by the SRB, the decline, if that's what we're managing, would have been accelerated. It's been a bit of a stopgap. We're managing decline and it's a question of what we can do to arrest that decline. As well as resources, SRB has really contributed to improving community spirit and getting people involved. The problem is that it is insufficient. It's being asked to do things beyond its control, like poverty, lack of education. SRB can't do that." (local councillor, Borough View, Redcar and Cleveland)

The second purpose for which SRB was used was to build a platform for future recovery. When bids for programmes in Newcastle, Birmingham and Knowsley were submitted in 1994, economic revitalisation was possible, but not immediate, and social and economic problems were severe. These problems needed to be tackled to sustain the areas, stop them falling into a spiral of decline and give them a base from which to build in future. In Newcastle, the SRB funding was seen as essential to shore the area up against decline and to give it the potential for revival. The funding bid stated that investment in the area was "essential if the spiral of economic, social and environmental decline is to be halted and reversed and if the acute problems which have beset [another part of the city] are to be avoided ... our vision ... an area which can break free from the spiral of decline and take full advantage of its economic potential and ... attract private investment and stimulate enterprise". The money was used to revitalise the main shopping area, attract a supermarket and another large retail development, improve a large housing estate, and invest in community facilities: a new pool and library and community IT facilities in schools. In Birmingham, SRB was to provide a platform for sustainable economic recovery, establishing training programmes, supporting small business and improving business premises, but also providing funding for housing renewal, community safety projects, minority ethnic community needs and the improvement of the physical environment. Overtown's programme invested heavily in building human capacity, to equip people to take advantage of economic recovery and also to effect change in their local communities (Box 6.4).

Finally, SRB programmes could act as a bridge to link areas to growth and development that was already taking place or was imminent. In Newham, the

Box 6.4: Overtown: building a platform for recovery

Overtown's regeneration programme started in 1996. A total of £26 million was provided by the SRB, matched with £3.5 million from EU URBAN funds, private sector investment of £58 million and other public sector contributions amounting to £18.5 million. With extremely high local unemployment, job creation was a major issue. A total of £4 million was earmarked for improving the environment and infrastructure of the main employment centre, the Overtown industrial estate, to attract business investment, and there were plans to redevelop a former college site into a high-quality business park, diversifying employment. The programme hoped to create 2,200 new full-time equivalent jobs by 2003 and safeguard 1,600 others. By 1999, progress had been slow, with only about 40 new jobs created on the industrial estate to date and proposals for the business park still under negotiation. Labour market accounts (Table 3.4) for the period 1996-98 show that meanwhile, in Knowsley as a whole, job growth was eclipsed by an increase in net in-commuting, actually reducing the numbers of residents employed. In the short term, the SRB programme was having a negligible impact on the broader economic picture. Meanwhile, however, it was investing in enhancing skills and educational attainment, creating learning resource centres in local libraries and courses in community venues. By 1999 over 1,000 people had gained qualifications through SRB-funded courses. Social projects included a community drugs prevention initiative and a community development project involving local people in running street play activities for children. The SRB also paid for environmental improvements in the town centre and, ironically, given the surplus of social housing in the area, a small new housing development on the site of an under-used shopping parade. Funding was provided for the demolition of unpopular council flats, for energy efficiency improvements and for security improvements on certain estates.

The SRB programme manager explained that its ultimate aim was to "transform Overtown for good", but that no one thought this would happen in seven years. The success of the programme should be judged on the extent to which it produced the building blocks for future development: more facilities and infrastructure, and the capacity for the community to resolve its own problems. The programme employed a community development manager and seven development workers to promote voluntary activity, encouraging and training local people to become involved in working groups and to develop projects. Joint working groups also started to engage council departments and other organisations in a new collaboration. The SRB was a catalyst for change as well as a spending programme. "I never thought I would see organisations working together like I am today. With this, we can't fail to be successful. The money is incidental. It has helped us to get on the right track – to develop sustainable regeneration for when the money runs out" (councillor, November 1999).

purpose of the East-Docks SRB was "to revitalise East-Docks and equip its people to take advantage of new employment opportunities; transport links; the regeneration of the Thames Gateway and the Lea Valley". Although also investing in some housing and quality of life projects, this programme explicitly sought to bring new employers to the area and to work with them to set up local employment opportunities. Business advisers proactively contacted local businesses to help them to anticipate and bid successfully for contracts that would spin off from the bigger economic developments in the area. Education and training opportunities were increased with a new secondary school, an adult training centre, targeted training programmes and outreach work.

Whether SRB funds were used as a brake, a platform or a bridge depended on the relationship of each area to the market for labour and housing at the time. None of the strategies could on their own regenerate the areas, only position them better in relation to wider developments, minimising negative impacts of structural changes or maximising possible benefits. There were severe doubts at local level that a strategy for the regeneration of poor areas based entirely on competition for top-sliced funds would deliver the changes that were needed, but also a recognition that, even if SRB had been incorporated into more strategic approaches involving mainstream funding, greater sustainability and the allocation of resources according to need, its ability to transform area fortunes would have been limited. Like its predecessors, it was based too heavily on tackling the problems of the areas, rather than addressing the wider causes of the problem.

By the late 1990s it was obvious that there were implementation lessons to be learned, particularly in relation to inclusion, that there was a need for a more strategic and longer approach to area regeneration, and most importantly, that area regeneration could only work in the context of a broader set of economic, urban, regional and housing policies that would address the structural inequalities at the heart of neighbourhood decline.

Summary

- Central government funding for area regeneration has a long history in this country. All of the areas in this study had been affected by one or more area-based programmes. There was tangible evidence of improvement as a result. But the effect was ameliorative rather than transformational. Areas had been improved but not regenerated.
- Five areas had major, comprehensive, SRB programmes in 1999. Like the earlier programmes, they were delivering tangible benefits. However, it was also evident that there were problems. It was difficult for the programmes to operate in an inclusive way, and it was clear that even well-implemented programmes could only make a limited contribution to area regeneration.
- Most of the SRB programmes failed to overcome the problem that residents were effectively excluded from real power in the decisions made about their lives. Their structures and processes ensured that residents were consulted but were not necessarily influential. This was frustrating and demoralising for resident activists.

- However, some programmes worked in ways that promoted inclusion as well as delivered services. They established local bases, employed local people and were flexible in their service delivery, in order to make services accessible to people who needed them. They provided lessons for inclusive regeneration, rather than regeneration delivered from the top down.
- Even in these cases, the programmes could only make a limited contribution. SRB was an insufficient basis for regeneration. Money could not be directed to all the areas that needed it, and sustaining activity beyond the life of the programme was difficult, even though there was a need for continued investment. Competition for funds led to a funding-driven approach, concentrating on getting and spending additional funds, rather than a strategic one built around mainstream service delivery.
- However, even had these elements of regeneration policy been in place, SRB could not have 'regenerated' areas. Broader economic and social policies were needed. While billed as 'regeneration', SRB programmes had in reality adopted one of three more limited strategies, depending on the wider context for neighbourhood decline or recovery. One acted as a brake on a process of rapid decline. Three aimed to build a platform to position the area better in the event of economic revival. One, in inner London, formed a bridge to an economic revival that was already happening nearby.
- By the late 1990s, it was evident that a longer-term, more strategic approach to area regeneration was needed, within the context of broader policies to tackle the causes of area decline and polarisation.

Notes

[1] Urban Programme, City Action Teams, Section 11 Grant, Ethnic Minority Business Grant, Inner City Task Forces, English Estates, Regional Selective Assistance, Regional Development Grants, the Enterprise Initiative, Enterprise Zones, Urban Development Corporations (UDCs), Derelict Land Grant, Urban Development Grant, Safer Cities and the Garden Festival Sites.

[2] Fairfields, in Caerphilly, had a Welsh Office 'People in Communities' programme, with an SRB-style local coordinator and partnership, but very limited funding (initially just £120,000 to kick-start the initiative). Rosehill estate, in Nottingham, was beginning a programme similar in design to the SRB-funded schemes, but funded by the local authority from capital receipts to the tune of £12 million, an even more generous per capita spending programme, although the majority of the funding (£10.5 million) was earmarked for extensive housing improvements.

SEVEN

New Labour and neighbourhood renewal

Two phases of policy

The election of the New Labour government in 1997 heralded major changes in regeneration policy, most of which had hardly begun to make an impact by the time of our first visits to the areas in 1999.

The new government placed a much bigger emphasis on the problems of deprived areas than its predecessors. With its focus on social exclusion and its *Bringing Britain together* report (SEU, 1998), it raised their political profile. It also pledged to learn the lessons of the past. It would take a comprehensive and long-term approach, involving both national policies and area-based programmes, investing in both physical and social improvements, and putting communities in the driving seat, rather than imposing solutions from above.

In England, there were two distinct phases of policy development. The first, from 1997 to 2000, was, as indicated in the Introduction, in many ways a continuation and an expansion of the policies of its predecessors: a range of short-life area-based spending programmes managed by multiagency partnerships. All of these were to some extent competitive, involving a bidding process, although increasingly the government identified the areas that would receive funding subject to satisfactory spending plans. All involved similar accountability mechanisms, with local partnerships producing and monitoring delivery plans as the basis for the release of funds. Many areas benefited from several of the new programmes, representing a major injection of funds in a short time. One local councillor in The Valley described this period as like going "from rags to riches overnight".

The second phase, marked by the introduction of the National Strategy for Neighbourhood Renewal in 2001 (SEU, 2001a)[1], was a new departure, with a greater emphasis on establishing mainstream structures and funding mechanisms that would ensure a longer-term focus on the problems of poor areas, and reach a larger number of areas than area-based programmes could possibly target. Moreover, the new government also began to recast its urban, regional and housing policies in a more strategic response to the problems of the most deprived neighbourhoods.

In Wales, tackling area deprivation became a major element of the new Welsh Assembly's strategy to tackle 'social disadvantage', one of the three major themes of its strategic plan (National Assembly for Wales, 1999).

Area-based programmes

In England, area-based programmes formed the bulk of New Labour's early neighbourhood renewal programme, reflecting both the constraints on mainstream funding imposed by the government's pledge to meet the public spending targets of its Conservative predecessor, and the evidence of numerous evaluations of area programmes.

The new government's area programmes, which became commonly known as area-based initiatives (ABIs) included both comprehensive area regeneration schemes and specific programmes on health, education, employment and early years development. The government announced its intention to continue with the SRB until 2002, when the fund would be taken over by Regional Development Agencies as a part of a single regeneration 'pot', enabling integration into regional regeneration strategy. It also introduced its own successor, the New Deal for Communities (NDC). NDC originally applied to 17 'pathfinder' areas, each receiving £20 to £50 million over a 10-year period beginning in 1999/2000. It differed in several key respects from SRB, taking on board some of the lessons learned from previous regeneration attempts. The areas selected were smaller, between 1,000 and 4,000 households, and the amount of funding per area was not only larger in total but correspondingly more concentrated. The funding period was longer, 10 years, and it was an explicit aim of the programme that it should put in place the structures for sustainable regeneration after the funding period. NDC was to be seen not just as a pot of money to spend, but a chance to achieve long-term change by establishing effective multiagency partnerships with residents in the lead. NDC funds were intended to pump-prime new joint work, levering in money from other ABIs and from other mainstream funds bent towards the NDC areas.

Local partnerships would tackle five key strategic areas: worklessness and poor prospects, improving health, tackling crime, raising educational achievement, and improving housing and the physical environment. They would do so by building partnerships with other organisations, not just by spending their own funds. Areas that could not demonstrate community involvement or links to other programmes and agencies were not to be granted funding, although in practice, every area did so. NDC also had the flexibility of a 'year zero', a first year in which no money need be committed or spent, so that partnerships could take time to consult properly and identify priorities. In this way, it was hoped that more time could be spent on building the capacity of residents to participate on an equal footing with professionals, and that it would be less necessary to direct funding to those organisations already geared up to receiving and spending money, namely statutory and large voluntary organisations rather than community-run bodies.

As well as the NDC, the government also announced thematic area-based programmes. The first were the Health Action Zones (HAZs) and Education Action Zones (EAZs), launched in 1998. EAZs were designed to tackle under-achievement and low standards in deprived areas – to 'level-up' the standard of education in the most difficult areas. They initially covered 25 areas – small geographical areas similar in size to the ones we describe in this study, and usually including two or three secondary schools and their feeder primaries. Later the scheme was extended to another 48 zones. Each Zone received £750,000 per year government funding, topped up with £250,000 private sector funds, and was also granted priority access to parallel initiatives, such as out-of-school hours learning projects, specialist schools and literacy summer schools. Their work was not prescribed – a key theme was innovation – with local education authorities working in partnership with the private sector to try new ideas. HAZs covered wider areas, typically the size of a health authority. Seventy-three local authority areas (about one fifth of the total) were included in the 26 Zones, which were designed to cut inequalities and deliver measurable improvements in public health and health outcomes and the quality of treatment and care. The principle was that of a new approach to public health – linking health with regeneration, employment, education, housing and anti-poverty initiatives, not just health service provision. Given the breadth of the areas covered, the HAZ funding programme was small – just £320 million over three years.

EAZs and HAZs were followed, in the Comprehensive Spending Review of September 1998, by Sure Start, a programme designed to work with families with children under the age of four, improving the provision of family support, advice on nurturing, health services and early learning provision. About £200 million per year was made available to local programmes, each designed and delivered by a multiagency Sure Start partnership, including parents, and with a local coordinator. Sure Start would be rolled out to over 500 different neighbourhoods by 2004. In 1999, the government announced 'Excellence in Cities', a programme to raise educational standards in urban areas. Initially targeting six clusters of local education authorities, the programme would eventually be expanded to cover one third of secondary-age pupils. It introduced information technology (IT) learning centres, learning mentors, learning support units for children with behavioural problems, and better opportunities for gifted and talented children. The following year, Employment Zones (EZs) were introduced, areas of high long-term unemployment that would benefit from extra funding to get older unemployed people into work. The EZs were a pilot for the idea of the individual job account – an individual pot of money consisting of benefit payments and training grants that could be used flexibly to get a person back into work. Funds could be used for training, transport, clothing or other needs, agreed after individual guidance and counselling to identify and remove barriers to employment. EZs could be run either by public sector bodies (the Employment Service or local authorities), or by private sector organisations.

Such was the plethora of zones and programmes, summarised here in Table 7.1, that the government even sponsored research to examine how well they were being coordinated (NRU, 2002). By the time this had reported, policy had already entered a new phase.

The National Strategy for Neighbourhood Renewal

2001 marked the adoption of a new approach to the regeneration of deprived areas. Special funding programmes were given much less emphasis, mainstream programmes much more, in a systematic attempt to close the gap between poor neighbourhoods and the rest. The Action Plan for the National Strategy for Neighbourhood Renewal was entitled *A new commitment to neighbourhood renewal* and made a bold new commitment: that within 10 to 20 years no one should be seriously disadvantaged by where they live (SEU, 2001a).

The new approach had five key elements. The first, echoing the approach of the Urban Programme 30 years previously, was a principal focus on specific local authority areas: in this case the 88 most deprived according to the IMD[2].

The second was a focus on mainstream services as well as additional programmes, within a strategic and coordinated approach. The 88 authorities were required to establish Local Strategic Partnerships (LSPs), single coalitions of public, private, voluntary and community sectors, operating as equal players. In practice, many districts already had a partnership of this kind[3], but their existence was now obligatory. LSPs were seen as a key tool for strategic multiagency working across many issues, but they had a specific role in respect of neighbourhood renewal. They would be obliged to produce neighbourhood renewal strategies, by which to prioritise and implement action in the most deprived neighbourhoods in a coordinated way, linking to the existing strategies of the partner organisations. The strategies would be the basis for funding from a new Neighbourhood Renewal Fund (NRF), designed to target the improvement of mainstream public services in the poorest neighbourhoods.

The third element was the concept of minimum standards below which no neighbourhood should fall. The government described these as 'floor targets'. For example, no school should have fewer than 25% of pupils getting five higher grade GCSEs, and no district should have a burglary rate more than three times the national average. The performance of the poorest 10% of wards, monitored by a new set of neighbourhood statistics, would be the benchmark for the strategy's success. Specific strategies would be aimed at different areas. For example, the DfES was given targets to raise employment rates in the 30 local authority areas with the poorest initial labour market position, while other programmes, such as Sure Start, NDC and Excellence in Cities, would continue to be targeted at a smaller number of smaller neighbourhoods.

Fourth, there were new mechanisms by which to focus on poorer

Table 7.1: New Labour area-based programmes

Programme	Number of areas	Size of areas	Criteria	Deprivation index used or specific indicators	Other factors	Competitive bids between areas
SRB rounds 5 and 6	65 districts (18%)	Whole district (thematic programme) or smaller area within	Deprivation: districts that came in top 50 on any domain	Index of Local Deprivation 1998	20% of funding goes to other areas, particularly those identified by Rural Development Commission	Yes
NDC	39	Neighbourhoods of 1,000-4,000 households	Deprivation	Index of Local Deprivation 1998	At least one in each DETR/RDA region. Some flexibility	No
EAZs	99	Clusters of schools	Innovation, delivery potential, need	Specific indicators: free school meals, low achievement, absence		Yes
HAZs	26 in 73 districts	Health authorities	Deprivation Quality of bid (one aim is to modernise services)	ILD 1998 and specific indicators		Yes
Excellence in Cities	58	Districts and district clusters	Deprivation Low educational attainment	Specific indicators: free school meals and attainment		No
EZs	15	Districts and district clusters. Up to 48,000 people	High long-term unemployment Low employment rate	Specific indicators: unemployment rates		No
Sure Start	Over 500 by 2004	Neighbourhoods with 400-800 children aged 0-4	Child poverty	ILD 1998 and IMD 2000 boosted with specific indicators – low birth weight and teenage pregnancy	Regional spread and spread of types of areas: inner city, suburban, rural and coalfield	No

Notes: The government also made available new funding streams to which area-based organisations could apply, such as the Crime Reduction Programme. These are not included here since they do not constitute programmes as such.

Sources: Various government departments

neighbourhoods and to integrate the policies of different organisations, and different levels of government and management – central, regional, district and neighbourhood. At national level, a Neighbourhood Renewal Unit (NRU) was established in government to implement the programme and spread knowledge of 'what works', with Neighbourhood Renewal Teams in each region to oversee local renewal strategies, administer funding and join up government policy. LSPs provided a new coordinating mechanism at the local authority level. At the neighbourhood level, the government promoted the idea of neighbourhood management – putting a single neighbourhood manager (or team) in charge. Neighbourhood managers would provide a central point to focus on neighbourhood concerns – making service-level agreements with other organisations, managing devolved budgets or lobbying higher tiers of government. Central government funded a number of neighbourhood management pilot projects.

The fifth element was a new emphasis on supporting communities – the residents of disadvantaged neighbourhoods. Communities would have to be involved in LSPs, in NDC partnerships and in neighbourhood management. The government also set up a Community Empowerment Fund, to support community involvement in LSPs in the 88 NRF areas, and Community Chests, to go directly to community groups in these areas.

Building on this approach, the strategy included over 100 specific elements, some of them new, some already being done. They included business brokers, universal banking services run through the post office network, extra funding for childcare, a new urban bus challenge scheme, more funding for neighbourhood wardens, the development of neighbourhood learning centres, 'no harassment' clauses in social housing tenancies, and so on. It was a vast programme (Box 7.1).

Urban, regional and housing policy

By the time the Neighbourhood Renewal Strategy was published, it was able to incorporate most of the government's major changes in urban, regional and housing policy. The Regional Development Agencies Act of 1998 had created a stronger regional role in regeneration, with the establishment of Regional Development Agencies (RDAs) to coordinate regional economic development and regeneration and develop regional economic strategies and skills action plans. Future local regeneration plans would have to dovetail with regional strategies in order to gain funding. At the end of 2000, the Urban White Paper and the new Housing Policy Statement signalled big changes for urban areas. The Urban White Paper reflected a determination to revitalise cities and reverse the urban-to-rural population drift through private investment and the creation of attractive living and working urban environments. As well as the neighbourhood-based initiatives already described, Urban Regeneration Companies would be set up to stimulate private investment, alongside an English Cities Fund for mixed use

Box 7.1: Main elements of the Neighbourhood Renewal Strategy

Employment and economies

Making the New Deal permanent; new tax and benefit measures to make work pay; creating 32 new Action Teams for Jobs in high unemployment areas; £379 million from the National Lottery for childcare; a £96 million Phoenix Fund to support business start-ups in deprived areas; more flexibility and more funding for RDAs.

Crime

Drug treatment funding to increase by some 10% a year in real terms. Spending on police to be £1.6 billion higher by 2003-04. A new National Drug Treatment Agency; a new responsibility for Crime and Disorder Reduction Partnerships to tackle anti-social behaviour and improve reporting of racist crime, and an £18.5 million fund for Neighbourhood Warden schemes.

Education and skills

Extending Sure Start to cover a third of infants by 2004; extending the Excellence in Cities programme; a new entitlement to out-of-hours Study Support for secondary pupils; a Children's Fund to work with vulnerable five- to 13-year-olds; and creating a Connexions Service to keep 13- to 19-year-olds in learning. For adults, measures include creating 6,000 new online centres, and an Adult Basic Skills strategy aimed at helping 750,000 people improve basic skills by 2004.

Health

New incentives to recruit and retain primary care staff in deprived areas; 200 new Personal Medical Service schemes, mainly in deprived areas; a free national translation and interpretation service available in all NHS premises; new help for smokers, including goals for reducing smoking by 2010; and a National School Fruit Scheme to provide young school children with a fresh piece of fruit every school day. A target to halve the rate of teenage conceptions among those under 18 by 2010.

Poor housing and physical environment

An extra £1.6 billion investment in housing; expanding the transfer of local authority homes to housing associations; and an extra £80 million for housing management by 2003-04. A clearer role for local authorities in preventing and tackling abandonment; Housing Corporation pilot on funding demolition to ensure supply does not exceed demand.

developments in areas on the fringes of towns and city centres that would not normally attract private investment. Years of under-investment in the public housing stock would be reversed through a new Private Finance Initiative, the transfer of council housing to registered social landlords and the establishment of arm's-length management companies with more scope to borrow than local authorities. Finally, the needs basis for social housing lettings, which had created concentrations of the most vulnerable, would be phased out through the piloting of choice-based lettings. Changes at the neighbourhood level were thus underpinned by moves towards more strategic and coordinated regeneration, a revitalisation agenda for cities as a whole, and an attempt to reduce poverty concentrations and diversify tenure.

Tackling area deprivation in Wales

In Wales, the policies of the new Assembly reflected similar policy objectives, emphasising participation and partnership, integrated and long-term approaches. Area-based policies in Wales had to respond to the country's particular socioeconomic geography, with many of the most deprived areas being small, isolated communities rather than large clusters of poverty located in major cities. Funding was widespread and targeted on small communities, with a strong focus on locally developed solutions. The first programme, People in Communities, launched in 1998, was limited, targeting just eight areas and offering a small amount of government funding principally for the appointment of local coordinators tasked with forming local partnerships and developing multiagency approaches to community problems. The programme embodied the ideas of local partnership groups and neighbourhood-level coordination that later emerged in England in the Neighbourhood Renewal Strategy, as well as the idea that neighbourhood problems needed to be tackled mainly by mainstream funding rather than by short-life regeneration funds.

In 2000[4], the principles of People in Communities were extended into a larger programme, Communities First. Communities First funding was available for the most deprived 100 electoral divisions according to the Welsh IMD 2000. It was to be a 10-year programme at least, designed to develop integrated approaches to the problems of disadvantaged communities, mainly funded through mainstream funds, and based on community participation and local partnership. To be eligible for funding, each area had to set up a partnership and appoint a coordinator, and develop 3-, 5-, and 10-year community action plans, and plans for community capacity building. They could then apply for a share of Communities First funding, initially £80 million over the first three years, provided that they could demonstrate that their plans were predominantly to be funded from other sources. This was a flexible programme, with funding available for any capital or revenue purpose, but depended on the ability of local partnerships to gain committed funding from other government departments, European Funds or mainstream agencies.

In 2001, Wales' first national housing strategy, *Better homes for people in Wales* (National Assembly for Wales, 2001), set out policies to improve quality and choice in housing. These reflected many of the same policy objectives as in England, but with differences: more emphasis on protecting the economic interests of tenants in stock transfer and the development of the community mutual model; the development of a national lettings framework rather than the promotion of choice-based lettings (although some choice-based schemes were to be piloted); and a strong emphasis on renewing private sector stock. 'Tenure neutral' housing was to be facilitated by flexible use of the Homebuy scheme to enable residents to move between renting and owning, and to enable social landlords to buy back homes bought by tenants. As in England, area-based policies for area regeneration were underpinned by broader moves to improve living conditions and build mixed and sustainable communities.

Broader social exclusion policies

These were policies with a spatial element. At the same time, the government was also implementing a range of broader policies to reduce poverty and social exclusion overall. From the start, it gave a high priority to this area of work, establishing its Social Exclusion Unit (SEU) at the heart of government in the Cabinet Office. The SEU was tasked with targeting specific at-risk groups, such as school non-attenders and rough sleepers, many of whom, of course, are clustered in higher proportions within the poorest neighbourhoods. However, there were also more generic policy interventions, implemented by specific departments. Three distinct approaches could be identified. The first was *protection* against social exclusion through the provision of better standards of public services across the board. The introduction of floor targets as part of the National Strategy for Neighbourhood Renewal was an example of such an approach. So too was the new requirement on local authorities to provide full-time education for young people excluded from school. The second approach was *prevention* of poverty and social exclusion by intervening with groups who were vulnerable. As well as targeted initiatives like Sure Start and the New Deals for the Unemployed, New Labour also introduced a minimum wage, a tax credit for working families and a new children's tax credit, increases in Child Benefit and Income Support for children, and a pensioners' Minimum Income Guarantee. Finally, there were policies of *re-integration*, such as the expansion of drug treatment services, and provision for rough sleepers. All of these policies could be expected to impact on individuals in the poorest neighbourhoods, closing the gap between them and others by intervening at an individual and not a neighbourhood level.

Policy limitations

The new government's policy agenda for neighbourhood renewal was certainly broader than that of any of its predecessors, and seemed to have learned some of the lessons of the past. Renewal was to be long term, led by mainstream services, and inclusive. Area-based programmes were to be integrated with city and regional strategies, with funds directed to areas of need rather than on the basis of competitive bids. Broader strategies for revitalising cities, reversing population losses and breaking up concentrations of low-income housing would address some of the underlying causes of spatial polarisation, while the social exclusion of individuals would be tackled by investment in education, welfare-to-work programmes, tax and benefit policies, and multifaceted interventions to tackle the complex problems of high-risk individuals and groups.

Critics of the government's approach have focused less on the substance of the National Strategy for Neighbourhood Renewal than on the overall package. There are three main criticisms. One is concerned with the implementation of the strategy, and in particular with the extent to which communities can really take the lead in regeneration, when government and local mainstream agencies still hold the purse strings. As the NDC was launched, critics were already asking whether it was more idealistic than practical. Could residents of low-income areas, so long disempowered, really be expected to design and manage multimillion pound programmes within a year? What would happen when residents of the NDC areas, in a majority on their boards, wanted to pursue strategies that were contrary to the government's broader objectives? Could their local strategies be carried through when major elements, such as housing and education plans, depended on decisions and funding streams outside their control? Some aspects of the Neighbourhood Renewal Strategy, like neighbourhood warden schemes, seemed straightforward to deliver, but how would their funding be sustained in the long term? And could the strategy as a whole, covering so many different elements, be successfully implemented? Would LSPs, operating at a local authority level, be an effective mechanism for coordinating services at the level of neighbourhood, and how would neighbourhood management posts be funded on a wide scale? Could local authorities and other agencies really bend their spending towards deprived areas on a long-term basis without depleting services in areas with more political influence?

These are questions about whether the government's agenda is doable. Other criticisms centre on the belief that it is ill-conceived, focusing too much on dealing with the problems of poor neighbourhoods, and too little on the extent of residential segregation. One argues that area-based policies, which often involve the building of new social housing and the development of community, actually contribute to reinforcing segregation. More effort needs to be given to enabling people on low incomes to access housing in higher-value neighbourhoods, developing transport and concessionary access to services so that they can be included in out-of-neighbourhood jobs and leisure activities, and increasing the permeability of low-income residential neighbourhoods to other people by design and by the situation of shops, leisure and visitor attractions (Kintrea and Atkinson, 2001).

Another line of criticism argues that it is a mistake to focus on spatial concentration of poverty, since this is only a symptom of more fundamental inequalities. Oatley (2000), for example, has suggested that the root causes of the problems of deprived neighbourhoods are structural: "related to inequality, the distribution of wealth and power" (p 93). The structure of work means that large numbers of people are only required in the labour market in a marginal and insecure capacity, and cannot achieve from it the rewards that are necessary to secure a relatively good standard of living. Thus Byrne (1999) has argued that social exclusion is "a necessary and inherent characteristic of an unequal post-industrial capitalism founded around a flexible labour market and with a systematic constraining of the organisational powers of workers as collective actors" (p 128). Drawing on Giddens' concept of 'risk-producing' modern societies, Young (1999), similarly, argued that social exclusion is a 'manufactured risk', the direct outcome of modernising trends, notably global competition between international companies:

> ... businesses (and in some cases whole sectors of national economies) are being forced to improve the quality of their products and in some cases reduce their prices if they want to survive. To achieve these goals more dedicated, more skilled, and more knowledgeable workers are needed. This means that there are fewer and fewer jobs for those lacking such skills and knowledge and the economic basis is laid for the social exclusion from work of those without qualifications. (Young, 1999, p 218)

For these critics, it follows that social exclusion, and spatial concentrations of social exclusion, cannot be tackled within an overall policy framework that accepts the logic of globalisation and the free market economy. Rather, they have argued for two sets of broader policies. The first would attempt to transform the global economic system in order to make it more sustainable and more equitable: policies such as greater global governance, regulatory reform, debt cancellation and controlled technological development that weighs social, not to mention environmental costs, against business benefits (Douthwaite, 1992; Gray, 1998; Oatley, 2000; Hutton, 2002b).

The second would attempt to protect against the inequitable effects of the current economic system by more redistributive policies at home. Although Powell (2002) argued that New Labour has not altogether abandoned redistribution, he also noted marked differences from Old Labour manifestos. Levitas (1998) suggested that New Labour has rejected redistribution in favour of a *social integrationist discourse* which effectively concentrates on attempting to link everyone into society, delivering equality of opportunity, rather than altering the structure of advantages and rewards. Giddens (1998), Barry (2002) and others have all suggested that social exclusion has to be seen as a dual process, in which the voluntary exclusion of the rich contributes to the involuntary exclusion of the poor. Most of New Labour's policies have aimed to bridge the opportunity gap by interventions in the lives of the poor (such as good pre-school provision, education and training, and tax credits), rather than in the lives of the rich. Increasing higher-rate income tax or inheritance tax, valuing non-paid work through state benefits, boosting the salaries and status of public and voluntary sector workers, and dismantling markets for health and education, are all proposed alternatives.

These policies are not central to New Labour's social exclusion or neighbourhood renewal agenda, in which the promotion of greater inclusion and social cohesion "does not imply a repudiation of neo-liberal principles of privatisation nor a move away from greater reliance on individual responsibility in place of governmentally provided social welfare benefits" (Fainstein, 2001, p 1). Without changes like these, New Labour's critics have argued, pragmatic strategies like the National Strategy for Neighbourhood Renewal could only be expected to have a limited impact.

In this policy context, and in the light of these criticisms, we returned to the 12 areas in 2001. We wanted to see how New Labour's policy changes were impacting on the ground, what difference they were making and whether they could indeed change the trajectories of the areas in the face of broader social and economic changes.

Summary

- The New Labour government elected in 1997 introduced major changes to area regeneration policy, with a much bigger investment in this area of work than any of its predecessors. The problems of the poorest neighbourhoods were raised high up the political agenda.
- There have been two main phases of policy. The first, from 1997 to 2000, was concerned with the introduction of a new range of area-based policies, including a new comprehensive area regeneration programme (NDC) and specific initiatives such as EAZs, HAZs and Sure Start.
- The second phase of policy was launched with the introduction of the National Strategy for Neighbourhood Renewal. The strategy marks a change of emphasis from additional initiatives to mainstream services, and to strategic, long-term interventions rather than isolated, short-term initiatives for selected areas.
- Area regeneration policies are nested within broader policies to tackle revitalised cities and to break down concentrations of social housing, as well as within broader policies to tackle social exclusion through welfare-to-work programmes, tax and benefit policies and intensive investment in services for at-risk groups.
- The new policies reflect many of the lessons of previous regeneration policy. Their focus is longer term, on mainstream services that are more strategic and more inclusive. However, the wider policy context is one in which the economic implications of global free market capitalism have not been challenged, and one in which market values are accepted as the basis for the organisation of economic and social institutions and the provision of social welfare. Critics on the left have argued that, provided they operate within these parameters, policies to tackle the spatial concentration of social exclusion and narrow the gap between poor neighbourhoods and the rest can only have a limited effect.

Notes

[1] The National Strategy was finally launched as an Action Plan in 2001 but had been in development since September 1998, when the Social Exclusion Unit's report *Bringing Britain together* documented conditions in the poorest neighbourhoods and established 18 Policy Action Teams (PATs) to develop strategic responses. The PATs reported during 1998/99 and the strategy was produced as a consultation document in 2000, prior to its final launch the following year.

[2] These included 81 authorities that ranked in the top 50 on any of the domains of the IMD, as well as seven other authorities which had ranked very highly on previous indices.

[3] Partnerships had developed for different reasons: public–private partnerships for economic development, City Pride partnerships, and bodies constituted to coordinate bids for regeneration funding. The LSPs had also been foreshadowed by the New Commitment for Regeneration (NCR), a pilot programme initiated in 1997 to achieve a more strategic approach to regeneration. NCR established strategic partnerships with a leading role for the local authority.

[4] Communities First was launched with a consultation paper in 2000, but final plans and guidelines were not finalised until September 2001.

EIGHT

Making a difference?

Back to Bridgefields

Our investigation in 2001 began, as it had in 1999, in Bridgefields, Blackburn. At first glance, the estate seemed much as it had been two years previously. Rows of shuttered houses with their roofs missing, fences vandalised and piles of rubbish in their gardens made a dismal impression. After protracted negotiations, the proposed redevelopment had fallen through. A new set of plans was unfolding. Local authority tenants in Blackburn-with-Darwen had recently decided to vote for the transfer of the entire housing stock to a registered social landlord, which had pledged to carry out demolition of 1,100 surplus council homes in the borough, to attempt to bring supply in line with demand, and to begin a programme of improvements to the remaining homes. Of the homes earmarked for demolition, 149 were in Bridgefields, and it was hoped that their removal would bring the number of empty homes on the estate to less than 40.

Meanwhile, several of the worst streets, full of long-term empty homes, had already been demolished, shrinking the estate and making room for a children's playground in the middle. Other youth facilities had improved, with the voluntary youth project expanding into a larger and more visible venue, and more outreach work being provided. The local school had received funding for learning mentors and out-of-hours study support from the EAZ. However, the housing office had closed, because the number of properties no longer justified its presence, and so too had the general store, leaving the estate without a shop for the first time in over 15 years. Some respondents put the closure of the shop down to intimidation and thefts. "They even had to keep the coffee behind the counter", one said, while others argued that it had just become uneconomic, partly because of the dwindling numbers of residents and partly due to the high level of black market sales of tobacco and alcohol, which otherwise would have generated some profit. Attempts had been made to attract other retail chains to run the store, offering subsidised business rates, but no one was interested. The resident-run food co-op had also folded.

Listening to people associated with Bridgefields, a sense emerged that the estate had 'quietened down'. There were fewer people, less transience, and fewer incidents of severe antisocial behaviour. It had an air of sadness about it. It was "quiet, in terms of people. No, I think I mean derelict. Derelict, the whole area is depressing" (resident). Several respondents felt that the estate had lost some of its stigma and was getting less attention in the local press. One local worker attributed this to positive management and beneficial changes:

> "It's still got a stigma, but it's probably viewed in a brighter light than it was – that's partly the physical changes, the demolitions and the play area. Also we've done up the main roads so it looks better when you come in. We did the houses up and had the shutters taken off and put alarm systems and curtains in instead ... we've also promoted the estate positively through the housing association and the press. People see this as an area where things are changing and where things get done."

Others saw it as a sign of the decline of the estate almost to an insignificant size:

> "It used to be infamous but now it's lost its teeth. It's just seen as a sad place. It's still got a name, but mainly by historical association ... more boarding up, more vandalism, run down, the shop's closed. It doesn't feel like a place of resurgence. You only see bulldozers. And the playground, everyone's saying how wonderful it hasn't been vandalised. If that's the level of expectation it shows we're at our very lowest ... they're talking about what's going to happen to the estate and people are just thinking 'here we go again'. They're either staying on for a payout or seriously thinking of moving on." (vicar)

> "It's not in the press so much. It's more of a nuisance now, not the threat it used to be, because it's smaller. People just think it's a sad place, not a threatening one." (resident)

Attempts to manage conditions on the estate had certainly improved. The anger and demoralisation that resident activists had felt towards the council in 1999 had diminished. Lettings had been resumed on the estate, and the council had listened to tenants' concerns that problem families would be 'dumped' there. A local lettings policy had been introduced, with tenants involved in the interviews of prospective new residents. Forty homes had been re-let, with only one antisocial household among them.

With the help of the community coordinator, an estate agreement had been established, with all agencies agreeing to a certain level of service against which they could be held accountable by tenants. A local crime and disorder panel had been set up, working proactively to tackle problems quickly, and the police had also adopted a problem-solving approach. The panel was investigating a joined-up solution to crime problems in the alleyway at the back of the shops. Senior managers from the housing association had begun to undertake a monthly walkabout with residents to identify areas for improvement. Most respondents agreed that not only had residents got more opportunity to influence estate

"... derelict" and "... depressing".
Empty houses, rubbish and fire-setting

The bright new play area

management, organisations were working together better too. There was a sense, however, of managing decline, handling the transition to an estate that was going to be smaller, and possibly not even exist at all in the future. The lack of housing demand in Blackburn generally made it unlikely that Bridgefields would ever be 'regenerated' in the sense of restoration to its former state.

In High Moor as a whole, demand for social housing was just ticking over and the number of vacant properties appeared to have stabilised. Demand and prices in the private sector terraced housing in the inner part of the area remained very low. New private housebuilding on the edge of the town continued, albeit at a slightly slower rate than in the late 1990s, offering attractive options for people living in the older terraced stock to trade up, and depressed prices in those areas. In 2001, the average house price in High Moor was just £35,000, compared with £49,000 for the district as a whole and £120,000 nationally. Prices had risen since 1999, but much more slowly than nationally. People leaving the older stock often could not sell, fuelling an increase both in private renting and empty properties. Lower-income residents in these areas were trapped, without the resources to move somewhere more expensive, or to invest in improving property that had, in any case, a low market value.

Economic prospects for High Moor residents had, in theory, improved since 1999, with the completion of the three business parks, all of them in close proximity. By July 1999, only one unit remained unoccupied. However, growth on these sites, mainly in distribution, call centres and ICT, were offset to some extent by continuing losses in textiles, engineering and other manufacturing. Nevertheless, unemployment in the borough continued to fall, although slightly less quickly than the national average, and unemployment in High Moor fell in line with the national average. Our respondents noted that job growth combined with advice, training and better transport had helped people into work, but that the continuing sectoral changes in the economy made many of the new jobs unattractive, unrewarding and unreliable. Anecdotally, it was suggested that economic inactivity continued to rise, leaving a group of people, mainly men, who were not actively seeking work, and a larger proportion of the unemployed churning in and out of unemployment as they failed to find secure work.

"What we find from our survey is that there's a group of people who are just being recycled. They've been unemployed four or five times in two years. They'll get a job, then lose it, do some training, get a short-term contract and so on. It's just the same people. They're not unemployed, but they're not in continuous employment either … for some people New Deal's been an excellent route to work but for some people it hasn't helped. They sign up, do some training, drop out, go off the register for a while and then reappear a bit later. I'm not sure unemployment will get much lower." (economic analyst)

"Don't get me wrong, we are getting people into work, and I think there are more jobs out there, but a lot of it is the lower-skilled jobs and a lot of it is temporary. New Deal? It's been very successful with the ones who have a work ethic, mainly the younger ones. But the over 25s, we really struggle with them. The personal adviser role does give us a chance to talk to people and find out why they're not working. I mean, we'll say to them, 'You've not worked for a very long time, there must be a reason. Do you actually want to work?'. And sometimes there is a reason why they don't want to work, like that they're caring for an elderly relative, but not getting any benefits for that and not wanting to say in the job centre that they don't want to work. So in those cases, we can help sort out their benefits. So some of them we can help, but with some they just don't want to work and until they wake up to reality, there's nothing you can do." (employment adviser)

Whether, on aggregate, the economic fortunes of Bridgefields' residents had improved since 1999 was unclear. While one respondent noticed "more cars" on the estate, perhaps a sign of more people in work, another said that "people are getting poorer, struggling more on benefits than they used to. There's a widening gap between the cost of living and benefits, and it's getting more obvious because of the substantially priced properties all around" (resident).

So Bridgefields in 2001 was fairly similar as a living environment to 1999, with evidence of better management, and with the prospect that its transition to a smaller size could at last be made, through the injection of funds enabled by Blackburn's housing stock transfer. For some, economic upturn and labour market initiatives had helped, but poverty among the non-working poor remained, as did labour market alienation, promoted rather than alleviated by structural economic changes. Would we find the same picture elsewhere?

Summary

- As a living environment, Bridgefields in 2001 had changed little since our first visit in 1999. Improvements in one area were countered by decline in others.
- The estate still had large numbers of empty and vandalised properties. The original redevelopment plans had fallen through and new plans for demolition and improvements were being discussed with the new social landlord to whom the council had transferred its entire housing stock.
- Residents were more involved in estate management, and interagency working had improved.
- There had been further job growth on the industrial estates close to Bridgefields and unemployment continued to fall.
- However, the demand for housing in the town as a whole was still much lower than the supply, and the decline of manufacturing industry was continuing. Low-paid and insecure work was continuing to trap people on low incomes and to push people into economic activity. Thus, while the estate was being better managed and its longer-term future decided, there had been little change in the wider economic and housing market trends that were driving its decline.

NINE

Getting it together: new money and better partnerships

Signs of progress

Without a doubt, levels of expenditure and activity had increased since 1999, as the government's new initiatives began to hit the ground. EAZs and HAZs had already been initiated when we first visited, affecting 10 of the areas (with nine HAZs and three EAZs). By 2001, most areas had Sure Start and Excellence in Cities. Three were in NDC and five in EZs. All except one of the English authorities was beginning to receive money from the Neighbourhood Renewal Fund. Six areas had new SRB programmes. One of these was area based, another round of funding for the regeneration work in Southside, Redcar and Cleveland. The rest were thematic programmes funded under SRB Round 6, which planned to develop strategic employment sites and to link local people to them through training, employer links and local learning plans. Overall, some areas had as many as seven or eight ABIs or funding streams (Table 9.1).

All of this activity had led to an increase in the services and facilities available, but not by very much, because all of the programmes were still very new and had had little time to move beyond the planning stages. There was still some evidence that core services were being cut while new funding streams were creating new short-term activity. It was clear that implementation, even of short-life programmes, could be a lengthy business, and it was still far too early to tell whether the programmes would achieve their intended outcomes. However, it was obvious that they were part of a broader approach to neighbourhood renewal that was starting to deliver better joined-up working and greater resident involvement. The signs of progress were there even though it was taking a long time to see real change at ground level.

Services and facilities

As in 1999, we examined services and facilities at neighbourhood, rather than area-level. We used service plans and annual reports, and our own observations, to assess change, and also asked respondents to comment, overall, on what had happened.

There was no neighbourhood where the majority of people we spoke to considered that services and facilities had got worse in the two-year period. In

Table 9.1: Regeneration programmes in the study areas (2001)

Area	SRB – area-based	Other SRB Budget	NDCs	HAZs	EAZs	Sure Start	Excellence in Cities	EZ	NRF	Neighbourhood Management pilot	Total
West-City (Hackney)			✓	✓			✓		✓		4
East-Docks (Newham)	✓	✓		✓	✓	✓	✓	✓	✓		8
Overtown (Knowsley)	✓		✓	✓		✓	✓		✓		6
Riverlands (Nottingham)		✓		✓		✓	✓	✓	✓		6
Shipview (Newcastle)	✓			✓		✓	✓		✓		5
The Valley (Sheffield)		✓	✓	✓	✓	✓	✓		✓		7
High Moor (Blackburn)		✓			✓		✓		✓		4
Middle Row (Birmingham)	✓			✓		✓	✓	✓	✓		6
Fairfields (Caerphilly)						✓		✓			2
Southside (Redcar and Cleveland)	✓			✓		✓	✓	✓	✓		6
Kirkside East (Leeds)		✓		✓		✓	✓		✓		5
Beachville (Thanet)		✓				✓					2
Total	5	6	3	9	3	10	10	5	10	0	

Note: Fairfields had a Welsh National Assembly regeneration programme, People in Communities. Riverlands also had a Community Renewal Trust, set up to continue regeneration after City Challenge. Several areas had funding from European funds.

eight cases, respondents reported a definite improvement. In particular there was more childcare and early years provision and more opportunities for adult education and computing in community settings (Table 9.2).

Most of the new activity was funded through special funding programmes, the 'funny money' as it was often referred to. This was important to note, for two reasons. The first was that it meant that what we were observing was only the start of a much bigger programme of investment in new services and facilities. The majority of programmes were still very new. It was taking time to consult locally, to develop delivery plans and to recruit staff.

In particular, the major area-based programme, the NDC, had as yet delivered very little. Both the Sheffield and Knowsley programmes had taken longer in the planning and approval stages than expected and had only received final approval in the summer of 2001. The Hackney programme had been in place a year longer. Consultation and planning had inevitably taken time, and the programme had also been held back by disagreements with the government over its housing plans. The residents we spoke to were disappointed with the slow progress that was made, and professionals were concerned about how to retain interest and voluntary commitment. In all three areas, active residents who had taken the opportunity to become involved with the programmes had found the level of commitment exhausting and some reported being close to 'burn-out'. They found themselves in an invidious position as partnership members; involved in the lengthy decision-making processes but also accountable to other residents who demanded quicker action and had less understanding of the processes involved.

> "… people are dischuffed with New Deal because they've worked really hard and there's no money to do anything. Managing people's expectations is going to be really difficult, keeping them on board so that they do have the energy when the money does come through." (NDC worker and resident, The Valley, Sheffield)

> "You asked what would have happened in this area without New Deal? You've got to say what's happened with New Deal? Nothing's happened yet. Most ordinary people [who aren't involved] would say 'sweet FA'. I knew it was going to be a long hard struggle but no way has it reached my expectations. It's because we haven't gone along with conventional regeneration, letting the professionals do it, so it's taken a lot longer." (tenant activist involved in NDC, West-City, Hackney)

> "Nothing much has happened. If you'd knock on someone's door and ask them what had changed, they'd say 'bugger all', but behind that the infrastructure is changing, to deal with health and so on. It's

Table 9.2: Changes in public services and facilities (1999-2001)

	New services and facilities	Old services now no longer there	Overall impressions of change in services and facilities
West-City (Hackney)	Detached youth work		Little change
East-Docks (Newham)	Secondary school New building for primary school Childcare centre Community rooms One-Stop Shop	Housing office (replaced by One-Stop Shop slightly further away)	Improvement
Overtown (Knowsley)	Childcare and under-5s provision Voluntary youth clubs Resource centre Local learning and community resource centres	Council youth club	Improvement
Riverlands (Nottingham)	Community ICT suites and courses Targeted health services Community and children's activities	Community work provision cut	Improvement
Shipview (Newcastle)	Under-5s provision New pool and library IT learning facilities		Improvement
The Valley (Sheffield)	Post-16 education provision Children's activities Community Trust offices – training and advice Improved football pitch	One primary school due to close Community work cut	Slight improvement
High Moor (Blackburn)	New play area Detached youth work CCTV for some areas	Housing office	Little change
Middle Row (Birmingham)	Community Forum office Improvements to park		Little change
Fairfields (Caerphilly)	Community centre with GP and other itinerant services Youth worker for under-12s Furniture recycling centre Expansion of adult education		Improvement
Southside (Redcar and Cleveland)	Two local cleansing workers New play areas and green Sports and community facility Community safety wardens	Church	Improvement
Kirkside East (Leeds)		Under-13s youth provision reduced	Little change
Beachville (Thanet)	Improved asylum seeker services Community learning centre Expansion of community centre work One-Stop resource centre		Improvement

Source: Interviews with service managers and frontline staff and fieldwork observations (2001). It is impossible to claim that this is an exhaustive list. It reflects the main developments mentioned by most respondents

happening but you can't see it yet. There's optimism and there's frustration." (community worker, West-City, Hackney)

NDC was particularly slow to get going because of its ambitious scope and aims. Other programmes had a smaller lead-in time. Table 9.3, which catalogues the main area-based programmes in The Valley, Sheffield, demonstrates that programmes that were tightly focused and largely the responsibility of one agency (such as Excellence in Cities) achieved local outputs relatively quickly. Those

Table 9.3: Progress of area-based programmes in The Valley, Sheffield

Programme	Funding announced nationally	Funding announced locally	Progress by 2001
HAZ	1998	1998	Started April 1999. Projects 'rolled out' across various areas of city. Projects developed in The Valley from 2001. Limited funding in 2001/02, for small projects including: health promotion events, tenancy support team, community development and health courses. More funding forthcoming in following year
EAZ	1998	1998	Started January 1999. Significant work on school improvement by 2001. Examples include: school consultant in every school to help school improvement; training for teachers, especially on literacy and numeracy, and for support staff; help to schools with recruitment; rewards for pupil motivation and behaviour
Sure Start	1998	1999	Delivery plan approved 2000. Outreach team in post about three months. Beginning to make contact with families
NDC	1998	1999	Delivery plan approved summer 2001. Only small 'quick win' projects implemented before this, for example, summer holiday activities. Senior staff still to be recruited
Excellence in Cities	1999	1999	Started 1999. Learning mentors in local schools. Learning Support Centres based at local secondary and one primary school. Gifted and talented coordinators in each school
NRF	2000	2000	First funding (£4.8 million city wide) allocated for year 2001/02, therefore no noticeable impact by summer 2001. Funding locally to pay for support worker for Area Panel and community capacity building in one neighbourhood in The Valley

Note: The Valley also had a small SRB programme working on community capacity building.

Source: Interviews in The Valley (1999 and 2001)

that required partnership formation and extensive public consultation, like Sure Start, took longer to initiate action. Sure Start, which had been announced nationally in 1998, was still only in its early stages in The Valley by the autumn of 2001. It was evident that several more years would be needed before we could evaluate the level of activity generated by the government's investment in poor neighbourhoods, never mind their impact[1].

The second reason that the 'funny money' observation is important is that it draws attention to what was *not* happening, which was an increase in core local authority, police or health services. As Table 9.2 shows, some areas continued to suffer cuts in core local services. In some cases, the reason was funding. In Knowsley, for example, a council-run youth club had been closed. In others, changes reflected altered priorities, as councils looked to provide more accessible and more streamlined services. In Nottingham, we were told that the size of community work teams had been cut but the local authority had created additional posts in its area coordination teams: officers who worked with local area committees to address local priorities and to coordinate the input of the different council departments and other agencies. In East-Docks, the functions of the local housing office had been taken on by a One-Stop Shop, a little further away, where residents could access several council services, and by a telephone service for repairs. Sometimes, population losses were the main driver, as in Blackburn, where the council had decided that the size of the Bridgefields estate no longer justified a dedicated housing office.

There had been no significant change in the area of frontline supervision and enforcement, which we had looked closely at in 1999 because of its importance for social order and community confidence. Community policing resources, in general, had not increased. We recorded only minor differences, as local commanders increased or reduced the size of their teams to respond to changes in crime trends or to introduce new forms of organisation. In Newham, close working with the local authority had resulted in community teams being re-formed to match Community Forum areas, leading to a slight increase in staffing for East-Docks (Table 9.4).

Table 9.4: Changes in community policing resources (1999-2001)

Change	Number of areas	Notes
Increase in resources	2	Newham: increase in size of East-Docks Community Team
		Nottingham: intending to move to 24-hour cover for community beats but facing recruitment difficulties
No change	7	
Decrease in resources	3	Thanet: team reduced and deployed to larger area.
		Caerphilly and Leeds: slight reduction due to overall reduction in staff

Although neighbourhood warden schemes were widely spoken about, only two areas, Middle Row in Birmingham and Southside in Redcar and Cleveland, had yet been able to implement such a scheme. Both were funded in part by the NRF and had an initial three-year life. Another was operating just outside our study area in Overtown, Knowsley, funded by the Home Office as part of its pilot scheme.

It appeared, therefore, that the focus on mainstream services that had emerged as one of the key planks of New Labour's strategy was not yet having an impact in 2001. Most of the activity was still project-based. In a sense, this was not surprising, since the strategy had only been announced in January 2001, and the new funding stream to enable bending of mainstream services, the NRF, was only in its first year when we visited. However, beyond the NRF, there had been no changes to local authority funding or to the prevailing contract model of public service delivery that might enable the changes that were needed.

Other elements of the strategy were, however, having a more immediate effect. Both resident involvement and joined-up government were very much more in evidence than they had been when we visited in 1999.

Resident involvement and resident frustration

In Bridgefields we had observed, over a two-year period, the development of more collaborative relationships between residents and professionals. Over time, people from the estate had begun to feel that they had opportunities to influence decisions about their future, and that their opinions were being listened to and valued. From a position of disempowerment and conflict over the original housing plans, trust had been developed partly through the creation of structures for resident representation, such as the crime and disorder panel, and partly through growing willingness on the part of politicians and professionals to take residents seriously.

Similar developments were taking place elsewhere. The proliferation of partnerships to deliver programmes like Sure Start and NDC also led to a proliferation of opportunities for residents to be represented. All of the programmes had management boards on which community representation was a requirement, and most conducted extensive consultation exercises.

These developments had come about for two reasons. They certainly reflected resurgent concerns, at the end of the 1990s, for democratic renewal and public accountability, but this came on top of a decade in which there was increasing focus on customer orientation, originating in the Conservative rights-based model of public service provision (Docherty et al, 2001). Over time, public sector workers had, by and large, come to accept community consultation as part of the planning process involved in new services and, to a lesser extent, as part of the ongoing process of service delivery. Even outside the board structures, there was an increasing number of user groups, resident panels, public meetings, and other ways of opening up communication. For example, the housing service in West-

City had estate committees for each estate and had extended its opening hours to suit residents. In Sheffield, the housing department had conducted a 'maintenance planning event' whereby residents joined officers on a tour of the area and a debate over maintenance priorities. A panel was being set up to monitor the maintenance programme on an ongoing basis. In Knowsley, designated police community beat officers were being given mobile phones and e-mail addresses which would be given out in the community. In every single area, both residents and professionals acknowledged the reality of increased opportunities for consultation.

They also recognised that formal structures did not necessarily widen participation, because only a limited number of people were interested in giving up their time, or had the confidence to take part. Representation was a first step, but it did not in itself expand participation in democracy nor develop community capacity as a whole.

> "There are certainly more opportunities. All the initiatives have boards with local people on them. But it's the old problem of whether you can involve people on an ongoing basis and whether you ever involve anyone apart from the usual activists." (regeneration professional, Riverlands, Nottingham)

Nor did it necessarily transfer power from professionals to residents. Changing a long-standing culture would take time. Some respondents still felt that consultation was a token exercise and that, when the important decisions came to be made, residents' opinions would still be ignored. Others felt that the requirement to consult meaningfully sat uneasily with the deadlines imposed by bidding processes.

> "It [the partnership board] is a good initiative but I feel excluded. I mean, I've done a degree, so I'm not what you'd call dull, but sometimes I can't even get all the language they use. And they seem to favour what the business people say. It's like you're there to keep the numbers up and so we can say we've got tenants on the board. The balance is wrong. I don't know whether it's because they think people like me aren't up to it or can't be trusted to make the right decision. And they don't seem to see that, although I talk in the singular, I'm saying the things that other people are saying to me – maybe it sounds like it's just me." (resident representative, Fairfields, Caerphilly)

> "… in theory, yes [residents do have more influence] … but what everyone would shout back is just look at the way the council has handled the housing issue. If they were really serious about consultation they wouldn't have done that." (vicar, East-Docks, Newham)

"No, there's a lot more talk about customer charters and one-stop shops etc but there's no real difference. One of the reasons people like the SRB is because other organisations don't respond and here they know we will. The mechanisms [for involving people in bigger decisions] are there but the council still has all the power. The council has no idea of either the risk or the work involved in really involving people." (regeneration professional, East-Docks, Newham)

"Now, we've got a change of culture. We've talked long enough and hard enough that they will now say 'oh let's ask the community', but that can still be undercut by the fact that you've got to get your bid in by this or that date. To talk to the community in any meaningful way takes time and though you've got ears now, you haven't got time within the funding regimes that they're responding to." (community worker, Beachville, Thanet)

Resident involvement was increasing, but there was still a long way to go.

Better joined-up working

In common with resident involvement, recognition of the need to coordinate the work of departments and agencies was a theme of the 1990s, not just of the New Labour government. But 'joined-up' government took on a new prominence under New Labour and was a major theme in the National Neighbourhood Renewal Strategy. Developments in the study areas suggested that the new emphasis made a difference. Partnership working was evident in 1999 but much more embedded in 2001.

The increase in joint working was happening at strategic level (principally through the establishment of the LSPs), at middle management level, through the boards of the various initiatives and partnerships, and at frontline level. In every area, the professionals we interviewed commented on better interagency working. The rhetoric of partnership, the establishment of partnership groups, and the need to bid jointly for funding meant that collaborative working was becoming the ingrained culture.

"Certainly people know a lot more that they should work together and there's an awareness that you can get small projects off the ground if you do. I suppose it starts because you can't get any money unless you get people to sign up, which is a bit frustrating, but then it becomes a habit, possibly." (local authority officer, Nottingham)

"It's definitely changed. The right noises are coming from senior managers but we're also getting effective troubleshooting between staff working on the ground – health visitors and social workers talking to each other. Sure Start helped with that." (health worker, Sheffield)

"There has been a gradual change in the way people are working. It's more natural to contact people in other agencies at the planning stages, and I think the partnerships are probably stronger than they were. Really it's born out of necessity – partly the government's insistence that this is how it should be and partly Best Value which has made organisations look critically at service delivery." (regeneration professional, Redcar and Cleveland)

"… oh yes, a huge difference. It used to be at ground level but the difference is now that you're seeing jointly commissioned and planned services. You're really seeing joint working at middle management level. I think I see more of my colleagues from other agencies now than I do my own staff. Why? It's two things – a combination of an acknowledgment from central government that this is the driver for change and actually, individuals who want to make it work. But there are lessons to be learned from all of this. There are so many different initiatives, all with different funding and different partnerships. I honestly struggle to keep it in my head who's doing what and which funding pays for what, and then it's the same people involved in all the different partnership meetings." (social services manager, Thanet)

At the most local level, this was having its effect in joint approaches to neighbourhood problems. Police in Newcastle had changed their beats to match housing areas and had introduced a multiagency problem-solving group of police, housing and community representatives. Kirkside East in Leeds had a Combined Response Team of police and housing officers. In West-City, the council and the housing management company had carried out a joint tenancy audit to check who was living in their properties. While the residents we interviewed had rarely noticed any improvement in joined-up working as an abstract concept, they were aware of these practical outcomes.

The ultimate expression of joint working, neighbourhood management, was also beginning to emerge. In 1999, none of the neighbourhoods had anyone in position as a neighbourhood manager, although plans were in place for such a post on the Rosehill estate in Nottingham, as part of a council-funded estate regeneration scheme. This had been established by 2001, and in Birmingham, a manager had been appointed for part of Middle Row as one of the government's neighbourhood management pilots. The community coordinator in Bridgefields effectively worked as a neighbourhood manager in many ways.

Neighbourhood management was also being considered in a number of other areas, but not necessarily as an addition to existing structures. It was not evident that funding for such a model could be sustained, nor how neighbourhood managers would operate in relation to service managers who often operated on different boundaries. For some authorities, neighbourhood management was to be considered as part of a bigger restructuring of services, or of democratic structures, or both. Some had already made moves towards devolved political structures, with area coordinators rather than managers. Nottingham, Newcastle, Sheffield and Leeds all had local area or ward committees which aimed to identify local issues and bring together service providers to tackle them. Three had small budgets to spend on environmental work, facilities and community activity. Area coordinators would follow up issues raised at area committees and engage other organisations in problem solving (Table 9.5). In Caerphilly, a community regeneration officer played a similar role, supporting Valley Top's Partnership Board (a group of residents, business representatives, councillors and other organisations) to develop regeneration projects but also working with smaller groups to help them to secure funding or to make sure that day-to-day problems were brought to the attention of the right organisations and followed up. Caerphilly, along with Sheffield and Hackney, had also allocated area responsibilities to senior council officers who acted as area champions.

Such arrangements represented a structure into which both neighbourhood management and neighbourhood regeneration could be integrated. In The Valley

Table 9.5: Area committees with support from coordinators

	Area covered by committee	Composition and role of committee	Coordinator job title
Riverlands (Nottingham)	Area (three wards)	'Area committee' of councillors, tenants groups and other organisations. Aim to consult people about services, develop projects (small budget), encourage service providers to work together and lever in resources	Area coordinator
Shipview (Newcastle)	Ward	'Ward committee' of ward councillors to communicate council decision to residents, identify local needs and priorities and allocate small budget for minor community schemes	Community coordinator
The Valley (Sheffield)	Area (slightly bigger than ward)	'Area panel' of ward councillors but open to public. Aims to improve and coordinate local services and provide a framework for regeneration and additional funding. No budget	Area coordinator
Kirkside East (Leeds)	Locality (three wards)	'Community involvement team' of ward councillors. elop and implement local community plan, through local partnerships. Small grant fund for community groups	Locality coordinator

in Sheffield, where some of the area was covered by the NDC, the area coordinator had helped develop a multiagency regeneration board for a neighbourhood outside the NDC area, which was developing its own regeneration strategy and attempting to bring in funding. In the city as a whole, NRF money was being used to strengthen Area Action teams, as a means of coordinating local mainstream services with a neighbourhood focus.

Developments such as these were indicative of a new strategic approach to neighbourhood renewal. When we visited in 1999, no local authority had had a neighbourhood regeneration strategy. The requirement upon LSPs to develop such a strategy meant that by 2001, 10 of the areas, all of those included in NRF funding, had them in place, or were developing them. In more than half, neighbourhood renewal was being seen not just as an exercise in coordinating spending programmes but as integral to revitalising local democracy. Neighbourhoods would be regenerated not by being given money, but by being given the power to influence decisions about their future and to shape mainstream services to their local needs.

Some authorities were developing plans for local or neighbourhood partnerships. Councillors in Birmingham were considering proposals to set up 11 constituency partnerships with devolved responsibilities and budgets to deliver local services, and taking the lead on neighbourhood renewal, funding and developing strategies for smaller neighbourhoods or wards. The majority of the NRF would be determined locally, with organisations bidding to ward or constituency panels. Newham Council had already established local community forums when we first visited. In 2001, facilitators were being appointed to support each of the forums to develop and implement local plans, working to a Neighbourhood Renewal Coordinator. Blackburn-with-Darwen was implementing Community Regeneration Zones (CRZs), covering 10 deprived areas in the borough, and each consisting of a board of councillors, residents and business and voluntary representatives. Each CRZ would develop its community strategy and, initially, have a small amount of funding for community and environmental projects.

Like many of the area-based programmes, these strategies were, in 2001, only at the early stages. Real changes had not yet impacted at ground level. But, like the programmes, they represented signs of progress, of new activity and new directions, seemingly informed by the lessons of the past. Meanwhile, however, the fortunes of the areas and their residents were also being affected by wider developments in population make-up, housing markets and the economy.

Summary

- New Labour's new focus on area regeneration was bringing new investment to all the areas by 2001. Some were benefiting from as many as seven or eight new initiatives or funding streams.

- Most of the programmes were very new and had not been fully implemented. We were able to look more at process than impact.
- In a majority of areas, the new funding streams had resulted in additional services and facilities, particularly for childcare and early years education and for adult education. However, the emphasis on mainstream services that had been a feature of the National Strategy for Neighbourhood Renewal had not yet had any impact on frontline services such as policing, estate management or youth work. It was not clear that they necessarily would do, given that the same funding regime and the same contract culture were still in place.
- The new programmes all had an emphasis on community involvement and provided new opportunities and better structures for local people to influence decisions. However, there was still a long way to go. Culture change was still needed within public agencies to enable genuine public participation and influence.
- In every area, partnership working between agencies had improved. This was making a difference at management level, with joint planning and commissioning of services, but also at ground level. Joint initiatives between police, housing and the community were the most common examples.
- Neighbourhood management was beginning to emerge. Two areas had neighbourhood managers for specific patches, while some local authorities were considering how neighbourhood management could be introduced more broadly as part of a restructuring of services, or democratic structures, or both. Area committees in the larger authorities provided a possible structure for the integration of a neighbourhood management approach.
- Thus, in the way that regeneration was being tackled, it appeared that some of the lessons of the past had been learned. There were positive signs of change.

Note

[1] CASE's research in these areas has been funded by the ESRC until 2006, allowing time to evaluate impact as well as implementation.

TEN

Drivers of change: population, housing and the economy

Two faces of population change: Middle Row and Overtown

In 1999, we saw how the context for neighbourhood regeneration in different areas was diverging. Many northern areas and former industrial areas were seeing falling population and housing demand, while London and some other inner-city areas were under housing pressure, mainly from growing minority ethnic communities and from the homeless and recent immigrants, but also, in London, from higher-income professionals. These differences, and their consequences for neighbourhood renewal, were even starker in 2001. The stories of Overtown in Knowsley and Middle Row in Birmingham illustrate the contrast.

Overtown was a white working-class area in Merseyside, dominated by estates of council housing built in the 1930s and 1940s to accommodate overspill and slum clearance from Liverpool. The decline of its manufacturing industries had led to some of the highest unemployment and deprivation levels in the country. Wards in Overtown ranked in the top 20 out of over 8,000 wards on the IMD 2000. Lack of work also precipitated population decline throughout the 1970s, 1980s and 1990s, and lack of demand for council housing was exacerbated by the council's policy of releasing land for new housebuilding, in an attempt to meet people's housing aspirations and diversify housing choice and population.

Against this backdrop, less popular estates were vulnerable to rapid decline. When we first visited Overtown in 1999, the Saints' Walk estate was slightly more popular than other estates in the area, although it still had no waiting list. It had been refurbished through Estate Action funding, and offered a relatively attractive environment. A residents' association was beginning to organise community events and build community spirit. However, this estate had experienced a calamitous decline in the early 1990s, when nuisance and intimidation by drug dealers drove other residents away and made the estate a no-go area for police and for the housing refurbishment contractors. A quarter of the homes in one crescent quickly became vacant and some were seriously vandalised. The estate's bad reputation deterred would-be residents, and it was only a combination of saturation policing, estate redesign, environmental improvements and community development activity that turned the situation around.

By 2001, Saints' Walk was still stable, although residents that we spoke to reported that the estate was "worse, definitely" with the re-emergence of the drug problem and problems with youth disorder. However, the underlying demand for most of the estates in the area was still negligible. In the borough as a whole, the percentage of empty properties available for letting nearly doubled from 1.7% to 3.1% between 1999 and 2001. Low demand overall made all the less popular estates vulnerable to the decline that had afflicted Saints' Walk, and by 2001, another estate, known as Crescent Road, had declined rapidly. Crescent Road had also had Estate Action improvements in the early 1990s and had 'held its own' for several years, before serious antisocial behaviour problems emerged in about 1998. Large gangs of youths were reported to be dominating the estate and "tearing up its physical and social fabric" (housing manager). In 1999 demand was low, pockets of empty properties were appearing, becoming targets for vandalism, and the estate was beginning to cause serious concern. Residents blamed the decline of the estate since then on "bad housing management – simple as that". Under pressure to fill voids, they say, the housing manager "dumped" a number of problem families "that other areas wouldn't have". "She [housing manager] couldn't see that filling one void created five others", alleged residents, as people were driven out by the behaviour of these families.

A senior housing manager explained how it was impossible to keep difficult families off the estate, because there was no demand from any other source. Numerous attempts had been made to try to stimulate demand by advertising council homes in the local press and other marketing activities, but to no avail. "We've tried all sorts of initiatives", he said, "but when we're faced with a slippery demand base, it's really hard. I defy anyone to do anything about it". As Crescent Road declined, the council faced a difficult choice and the manager admitted that it sometimes seemed better to allocate potentially difficult households to that estate rather than to other more stable estates where similar problems might develop. At the same time, the loss of rental incomes across the borough necessitated cuts in the housing maintenance service, meaning that only emergency repairs could be carried out. On Crescent Road estate, damage escalated. By 2001, rows of homes were almost completely empty at the heart of the estate, some of them seriously vandalised. Rubbish, some of it fly-tipped, lay uncleared for months. Young people still congregated in large numbers and tore up and down the estate on motorbikes. While long-term plans for the transfer of the council housing stock were being laid, the familiar cycle of decline underpinned by low housing demand continued to play itself out.

Middle Row, in Birmingham, was quite different. This was also an area traditionally dependent on manufacturing industry and had also suffered major economic decline and out-migration. However, it was an inner-city area, with much of its pre-1919 private sector terraced stock still in place, alongside larger homes that were subdivided for letting when the middle classes moved out in large numbers to the suburbs. The housing stock meant that it was repopulated by immigrant families who could originally not get access to council housing. Its population actually grew between 1971 and 1991 when the city's population

*Arson and rubbish dumping beset empty
properties on the Crescent Road estate,
Overtown, (Knowsley) (2001)*

was declining, and continued to grow
during the 1990s. By the late 1990s, the
area had become predominantly
Pakistani, although there was a significant
Bangladeshi community and many other
smaller minority ethnic groups. As I
showed in Chapter Three, many
members of these minority ethnic
communities were at a severe disadvantage in the labour market and on very low
incomes. Claimant unemployment in 1998, at 24%, was nearly three times the
national average and the ward ranked within the top 40 on the IMD.

When we visited in 2001, there had been little change in this overall situation, but
there had been two new developments. On the one hand, there had been a large
growth in the number of asylum seekers and refugees, because of the government's
policy to disperse asylum seekers away from ports of entry. Somalis and Afghans
were among the largest groups, but the Employment Service manager reported that
29 different languages now had to be spoken by staff and interpreters. One third of
new Jobseeker's Allowance claims (about 200 per month) were from asylum seekers
or people with refugee status. This was putting new pressure on a housing stock that
was already in demand and overcrowded. As one resident reported:

> "The biggest change since you were here before is the asylum seekers.
> No one knows how many but I'm saying 3,000[1]. You see if you try
> to put asylum seekers in middle-class areas you get a protest, so we
> get them in places like Middle Row. There's been a major impact.
> We've already got a housing problem here and the council and the
> RSLs are saying there's no houses but all of a sudden there seem to be
> houses for all these asylum seekers." (resident activist, Middle Row,
> Birmingham)

On the other hand, there was some anecdotal evidence of a limited number of
moves into one part of the area by middle-income professionals, attracted by the

older housing stock and proximity to the city centre. Thus demand was increasing not just from low-income homeowners in the Asian community but from more affluent purchasers. House prices had risen by 38% in the period, more than the national average. The same respondent suggested that even the growth in the asylum-seeker population had had an inflationary effect on house prices:

> "It's made the house prices go up. Two years ago you could get a two-bedroomed house here for £36,000. Now it's £70,000, because people are buying them to let them to asylum seekers. There's a big subsidy on asylum seekers. Some landlords have even got rid of their existing tenants to get asylum seekers." (resident activist, Middle Row, Birmingham)

The growing population meant that Middle Row came under none of the pressures that were evident in Overtown. There were no empty houses to become the target for vandalism, arson or rubbish dumping, and there were more people around to provide informal supervision and surveillance. But the concentration of poverty did not appear to be decreasing. Despite job growth, and the most successful New Deal employment team in the city, there had been no significant change in the number of unemployed people, because of the continued influx of people with labour market disadvantages. Household overcrowding was severe. Population growth was insulating Middle Row from a spiral of decline but doing nothing to diminish its highly concentrated poverty.

Rising house prices and inner-city polarisation

Middle Row was not the only inner-city area where the polarising trends of gentrification and high poverty immigration were beginning to play themselves out. There was some evidence of similar trends in The Valley in Sheffield, where house prices rose in excess of the national average between 1999 and 2001 while the number of asylum seekers considerably increased. However, the most dramatic changes were in inner London, where economic growth was the driver of burgeoning house prices and a continuation of the gentrification that had begun to be evident in 1999. House prices in West-City in Hackney rose by 35% between 1999 and 2001, and by 47% in Newham's East-Docks, compared with a national average of 22%.

The rapid rise in the areas' popularity among middle- and higher-income groups had several impacts. First, it resulted in a lot of new building, with private developers looking to convert derelict pubs and warehouses, or to put up modern flats on vacant sites. In Hackney, the cash-strapped local authority responded to this demand by selling plots of vacant land. Local workers told us that a planned youth project for The Grove estate was likely to be shelved because the council had decided to sell the land for housing.

Second, it led to increasing income polarisation. Not all the developments were private. Housing associations were also building, and some of the larger new developments offered a mixture of flats for private ownership, shared ownership or housing association rents. Nevertheless, there was a powerful sense of the area being physically transformed by the investment of private capital, while social housing improvements were stalled. Particularly in West-City, which had a stock of warehouses ripe for conversion, the polarisation of incomes within the area was stark.

> "It's a gold rush – it's like the Klondike – everyone rushing to buy up the prime land!.... How's the area viewed by people who don't live here? Depends what papers they read. If they read the arty farty magazines, it'll be loft living. There are two completely different worlds here." (tenant activist, West-City, Hackney)

Polarisation was not just being caused by high-income newcomers, but by sustained, and in West-City's case, increasing demand for housing from people in very low-income groups, homeless families and asylum seekers. In East-Docks, we were told that 70% of social housing lettings went to homeless people. The housing manager in The Grove reported that demand was "increasing rapidly. The extra demand is coming from homeless families – either immediately homeless or in temporary accommodation, and asylum seekers. About 90% of all our lettings are from the homeless list, hardly any transfers. This does have implications because if you're getting all homeless people you are getting people who have other needs apart from housing". It also fuelled resentment among long-established families in the area, who could not transfer to better or more suitable accommodation, and whose children had little prospect of being able to stay locally.

The third effect was to alter tenure patterns, officially and unofficially. The Grove's housing manager reported an increase in Right to Buy sales, by which council tenants could make enormous profits. In Hackney as a whole, the number of Right to Buy sales in a year doubled between 1999 and 2001. Right to Buy values were in the region of £25,000 to £30,000 while the market value of flats could be in excess of £200,000. Rental values were also high, leading to unofficial private renting by council tenants who had moved to other addresses. In effect the council stock was being further squeezed while demand rose.

Thus inner-city areas, on the whole, were beginning to see some increase in private sector housing values and demand. Away from the inner cities with their intrinsically attractive Edwardian and Victorian housing stock, private sector sales were not picking up, except in Thanet, where the private market experienced a knock-on effect from the rapid growth in housing prices generally in the South East (Figure 10.1). Here, demand from asylum seekers had diminished considerably, because of the government's policy of dispersal away from ports of entry.

Figure 10.1: House price rises (1999-2001)

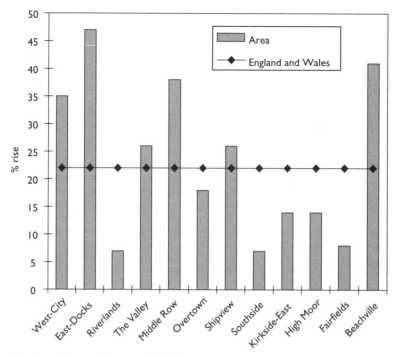

Note: Inner-city areas shown to left of figure.

Source: HM Land Registry

In East-Docks (Newham) a derelict pub in
1999 is converted into flats by 2001

In West-City (Hackney) a site earmarked for a youth project in 1999 is up for sale in 2001 as prime housing land

Low demand and neighbourhood decline

Outside London, levels of social housing demand were still low, with the demand from asylum seekers causing a small increase but not changing the overall picture. Table 10.1 shows levels of social housing demand in our smaller study neighbourhoods in 2001.

Apart from inner London, no neighbourhood was in a situation better than 'just about ticking over' in which it was possible to let homes from a small waiting list. In these situations, the number of empty properties would remain stable. In Borough View (Redcar and Cleveland), Sunnybank (Newcastle), just as in Saints' Walk in Knowsley, the situation was even worse, with no waiting list and difficulty filling any property that came up for letting. In these situations, the potential for the number of empty properties to increase was very high.

Local authorities and housing associations had responded in three ways to problems of low demand. The first was to work hard to increase the attractiveness of properties and to market them to a wider audience. In four of the low demand areas, Sheffield, Newcastle, Leeds and Knowsley, significant effort was being made in this direction. Properties were being advertised in the press. In Leeds, the City Council had set up a 'property shop' in its housing advice centre, and was advertising council housing on buses, on bookmarks in libraries and on the Internet. The local housing office in Kirkside East had a full-time rehousing officer who would proactively contact those claiming private sector Housing Benefit and who would act in an estate agent role, accompanying viewings and trying to match properties to clients' wishes. Several authorities were furnishing flats or decorating them to make them more attractive and reduce the initial investment for prospective tenants. In Sheffield, this scheme had worked successfully with 150 flats in The Valley and has been extended to cover 275 properties. Carpets were provided in some cases, with the housing department moving towards the practice of tailoring lettings, providing whatever was needed to secure a letting. In Blackburn, the local lettings policy in Bridgefields was also helping to stimulate demand and to increase the sustainability of lettings.

Housing managers involved in these schemes were positive about their effect on demand for specific blocks or property types, but saw them at best as

Table 10.1: Indicators of social housing demand (2001)

	Level of empty properties in neighbourhood (2001)	Description of level of demand by local housing manager
The Grove (West-City, Hackney)	<1% (none long term)[a]	"Massive."
Phoenix Rise (East-Docks, Newham)	No accurate figures – distorted by redevelopment sites	"Unpopular. Lower demand than the rest of the borough but always possible to let."
Rosehill (Riverlands, Nottingham)	No accurate figures – distorted by development	"The beginnings of a waiting list."
Saints' Walk (Overtown, Knowsley)	8%[a] (worse in pockets)	"... low – there's no waiting list."
Sunnybank (Shipview, Newcastle)	9%[a] (mostly in clearance area)	"No demand, not as such."
East Rise (The Valley, Sheffield)	Houses 2% Flats 29% (of which more than half in clearance area)	"... low. No more than six months' waiting time for most properties, but it's ticking over."
Bridgefields (High Moor, Blackburn)	37%	"A small local demand from within the estate."
Borough View (Southside, Redcar and Cleveland)	Council estate 4% Street properties 21%	Council estate: "We can't kid ourselves that there's people queuing up but generally we can let." RSL street properties: "... poor. The only people we can get are emerging families."
Southmead (Kirkside East, Leeds)	Not known	"... at best it's steady. I wouldn't say it's a rush but we're keeping up with terminations."

Notes:

[a] Indicates that figures are for a larger housing area and cannot be broken down further.
Did not interview housing managers for Broadways (Middle Row, Birmingham) or Sandyton (Beachville, Thanet), where the neighbourhoods are primarily privately owned, or Valley Top (Caerphilly) where the housing manager was unavailable for interview.

Source: Interviews with housing managers (2001)

contributing to stabilising particular areas that might otherwise have emptied quickly because of underlying low demand. Several managers referred to the fact that teams in different areas of the city and different social landlords were all competing for a diminishing pool of tenants. Thus the effect of local initiatives on the overall situation was marginal.

The second response was to try to limit the extent of movement between landlords that low demand enabled. The most developed scheme was in the multi-landlord area of Borough View (Redcar and Cleveland). Social landlords had entered into a housing partnership, adopting a common housing register and a single application form. Each partner could have access to pre-tenancy checks, and information about evictions and rent arrears. The message to tenants was that if one tenancy was unsuitable, they should contact the partnership to arrange something else, rather than leaving with no notice. Support was offered to sustain tenancies, by restructuring debt and giving advice with budgeting and benefits. The difficulty was in involving landlords from the large and fragmented private sector. As part of the regeneration of the area, the housing renewal team was attempting to establish a private landlords' forum and offer an estate agent service of advertising, viewings and pre-tenancy checks, but there was little incentive for landlords to become involved. In The Valley, Sheffield, a tenancy support scheme had been introduced, funded by the HAZ. It was working well, although only with a small number of people (about 20). Key workers supported council tenants who were finding it difficult to cope in their accommodation, helping them with making benefit claims, obtaining furniture and household equipment, gaining practical skills such as cooking and budgeting, contacting other agencies, and understanding their tenancy agreement.

The third response was to undertake demolitions in order to bring supply in line with demand. In all of the low demand areas, some of the housing stock had been demolished between our initial visit in 1999 and our return in 2001. Unpopular blocks of flats and long-term vacant houses had been 'taken out' because, in the long term, there was not the demand to sustain them. In every case, these could be described as 'tactical' demolitions, designed to manage local problems, while longer-term strategic decisions about the future of the housing stock were considered.

In 1999, tactical demolitions were all that was evident. They were slow to implement. In most cases, some properties in a largely empty block were occupied and arrangements had to be made to rehouse the occupants elsewhere. In private sector areas, compulsory purchase orders had to be obtained and sale values negotiated. A year or 18 months could easily elapse between the decision to demolish and the work taking place. In the meantime, 'clearance areas' of empty properties were an eyesore, a target for vandalism and a symbol of decline. After demolition, sites were not always put to another use quickly, partly because of the length of time taken in consultation and partly because of lack of funding or lack of project coordination. They remained unsafe and uncared-for building sites, littered with rubbish and rubble, contributing to neighbourhood decline as well as, in one sense, putting a brake on it.

Despite implementation problems and the sense of the overall futility of localised tactical initiatives, the combination of demolitions and lettings initiatives meant that none of the 12 neighbourhoods we looked at had more empty property or lower demand than in 1999 (Table 10.2). In some cases, of course, the demand in 1999 had been zero and could not fall any further.

Table 10.2: Levels of empty property in low-demand neighbourhoods (1999 and 2001)

	% of properties empty in neighbourhood (1999)	% of properties empty in neighbourhood (2001)
Saints' Walk (Overtown, Knowsley)	7	8
Sunnybank (Shipview, Newcastle)	10	9
East Rise (The Valley, Sheffield)	Houses – few Flats 25	Houses 2 Flats 29
Bridgefields (High Moor, Blackburn)	38	37
Borough View (Southside, Redcar and Cleveland	Council estate 3 Street properties 31	Council estate 4 Street properties 21
Southmead (Kirkside East, Leeds)	7	Not known

Note: No accurate data for Valley Top (Fairfields, Caerphilly).

Source: Interviews with housing managers (2001)

In Newcastle, properties in Sunnybank's clearance area suffer from vandalism, graffiti and discarded rubbish (2001)

In Borough View (Redcar and Cleveland), SRB funding ensures that demolition sites are immediately landscaped or put to other use

In Kirkside East (Leeds) a demolition site is left empty. There were ideas for a park but no funding (2001)

Improvements in joint working had also helped, having a stabilising effect on neighbourhood conditions, so that none of our original study neighbourhoods, according to a consensus of our respondents, had worse living conditions in 2001 than in 1999, although for some, like Bridgefields, the status quo represented a very poor living environment. In some cases, residents could point to direct interventions that had slowed the pace of decline. In Sunnybank, for example, residents had regular meetings with the environmental services department, conducted walkabouts with councillors and senior managers, and had established a direct route for reporting environmental problems to a senior manager who had taken dedicated responsibility for the estate. Despite continuing problems with drug dealing and antisocial behaviour, the appearance of most of the estate had been maintained, which helped stabilise the lettings situation. In most of the neighbourhoods, therefore, it was possible to say that a low demand situation was being effectively managed even though the underlying problem remained.

By 2001, strategic stock reduction plans were emerging (Table 10.3). The extent of the demand problem was all too evident, and the transfer of council

Table 10.3: Tactical and strategic demolitions in low housing demand areas

	Tactical demolitions in neighbourhood (1999-2001)	Longer-term plans (2001)
Saints' Walk (Overtown, Knowsley)	None, but 64 flats demolished in wider area and two further blocks earmarked	Transfer to housing trust. Demolish 4-500 across borough within five years
Sunnybank (Shipview, Newcastle)	16 houses	90 more houses in Sunnybank. Consulting on plans for demolition of 7,000 homes across the city
East Rise (The Valley, Sheffield)	20 flats/maisonettes (with plans to demolish 40 more)	Sustainability and investment plans being developed as prelude to stock transfer. Aim to reduce by c10,000 homes across city in 10 years
Bridgefields (High Moor, Blackburn)	Two streets c75 homes	About 150 homes on Bridgefields. 1,100 overall in town over two years
Borough View (Southside, Redcar and Cleveland)	116 street properties (mixed tenure)	Demand and supply study suggested demolition of 1,200 older properties and replacement with 500 newer homes, in neighbourhood alone. Wider plans for borough
Southmead (Kirkside East, Leeds)	4 houses	No plans as yet

Note: No accurate data for Valley Top (Fairfields, Caerphilly).

Source: Interviews with housing managers (2001)

housing stock to housing associations or companies, favoured by the government, offered the possibility to fund the larger-scale demolition programmes that were necessary. However, these programmes had not yet been implemented. I discuss them in more detail in Chapter Eleven.

Economic growth and economic divergence

As housing markets diverged, so did the economic position of the areas. In terms of job growth, most were in a better position in 2001 than in 1999. Our interviews with employment advisers, economic development staff and labour market analysts suggest genuine labour market improvement. But, in the context of a national trend of service sector growth and manufacturing decline, some areas were doing much better than others.

On the one hand, central city and some inner-city job markets were reviving. Retail, financial and professional services, IT and entertainment sectors were generating jobs in city centres, accessible to those in deprived inner-city areas and replacing, to some extent, the industrial works, factories and warehouses of the manufacturing era. East-Docks in East London saw the most significant local growth, with the opening of a major new exhibition centre and associated hotels, night clubs and bars. The city centres of Nottingham, Sheffield, Newcastle, Leeds and Birmingham saw growth in retail and service industries, and city business parks attracted call centres and distribution centres.

Whether or not local people would get these jobs was another issue. There was a pattern of in-commuting to highly technical jobs, one that was likely to persist whatever the aggregate skills profile of the local community, simply because people travel further for well-paid and high-skilled work. The former shipyard area in Newcastle's Shipview, for example, was developing as a centre for marine and offshore technologies, with a cluster of over 150 companies, and ultimately, several thousand jobs. Aside from managerial and scientific positions, even production and engineering jobs in these companies tended to be highly specialised and skilled, such as robot manufacture. Even in less-skilled work, labour markets could not be expected to be local. In East-Docks, firms operating in the new exhibition industry brought in experienced stand-assembly workers from as far afield as the Midlands in the absence of a pool of trained workers locally. And in the least skilled and least well-paid jobs, for which long distance travel was uneconomic, there could be a local source of competition. In cities with large university populations, such as Newcastle, Sheffield and Nottingham, students, increasingly needing to support themselves through their studies, provided competition for work in restaurants and bars, for part-time administration and office work and as cleaners or labourers.

However, at least in the cities, there was consistent evidence of job growth. Outside the cities, the pattern was more variable. Retail development on out-of-town sites, wholesale and distribution and telesales sites provided significant work opportunities on industrial sites formerly populated by manufacturing and engineering firms, but only where the infrastructure and location were favourable. Aside from Blackburn, there was certainly new job creation in Knowsley, continuing a pattern that began in the late 1990s. The biggest growth was in call centres, which altogether accounted for about 4,000 jobs. Existing call centres expanded, and a major new one located on the industrial park close to Overtown. A large call centre also contributed to job growth near Fairfields in Caerphilly. As newly developed strategic business sites came on stream, other parts of the borough also saw growth, with hundreds of new jobs particularly in high-tech industries such as aerospace and defence communications.

However, for places with inaccessible locations and/or an out-of-date infrastructure for modern business, the chances of the new economy generating work on the same scale as previously were small. Growth in Beachville in Thanet and in Southside in Redcar and Cleveland was slower than in the other areas. Both of these areas had peripheral locations which meant that they were not a first choice location for inward investment. They faced difficult dilemmas about where to position themselves economically. In Beachville, new business parks were being developed, and slowly being occupied, but longer-term prospects looked better for strategies to capitalise on the area's distinctive assets – its coast and countryside, for a limited revival of the tourist industry, and more fundamentally, its airport, which was expanding for freight use and being considered as a passenger terminal. Meanwhile, population growth continued to outstrip sluggish employment growth. As a local study concluded, "all is far from well in the local economy … a broader base is desperately needed" (Beatty and Fothergill, 2003a). In Southside, many of our respondents felt that the area had, in a sense, missed the boat for major new economic developments. One, an employment adviser, described the economy as "about 10 years behind places like Sunderland. Here all the big firms are still shedding jobs whereas in others, they've gone and to some extent been replaced. Here, there hasn't been much replacement, no call centres, for example". It was difficult to see where major new job growth would come from, leaving the economic future of the area uncertain. "We have to decide where we're heading, if really we want to be mainly a dormitory for other areas, in which case it's not a very attractive dormitory and we need to sort that out" (community leader and member of LSP).

Meanwhile, the loss of manufacturing jobs continued. In every area where manufacturing was still a major sector of the economy, jobs were lost. Smaller firms struggled in export markets because of the strength of the pound and large firms continued to look to source production elsewhere. 'Branch plant syndrome' was now operating on a European or global level. For example, a long-established toy manufacturer in Beachville moved its production to China, and there were hundreds of job losses in Middle Row in Birmingham when a steering wheel manufacturer relocated to Hungary.

As we had seen in the 1990s, the study areas in general mirrored the economic fortunes of their wider travel-to-work areas. Local labour markets reflected broader trends. But the particular locational or infrastructure characteristics of local areas did mean that they were more or less well placed to take advantage of growth and more or less affected by continuing job losses. In particular, Fairfields, with its valley location, was least well placed to attract new jobs and least well connected to major industrial developments in more accessible parts of the borough. However, in the two-year period between our visits, its labour market did relatively well, with the expansion of the call centre mentioned earlier and a meat packing factory, both a few miles away in a nearby borough. While 2000/01 was a particularly bad period for manufacturing in the borough as a whole, a local job centre manager described Fairfields' economy in this period as 'buoyant'. Like High Moor in Blackburn, located close to a new motorway, Kirkside East in Leeds was particularly well placed for the economic development that was beginning to accompany the new A1/M1 link. By contrast, Beachville residents in Thanet were less well connected to the new business parks in the middle of the borough than people travelling from outside the area. So, while the trends driving labour market changes were not local, local factors *could* make a difference to area job prospects.

Overall, the indications from 2001 were further evidence of what had been clear in 1999. Britain's economic geography was changing. The number of jobs was growing, but their distribution did not replicate the jobs map of the industrial economy. Of all the disadvantaged areas that had suffered severe decline in the 1970s, 1980s and 1990s, some would be obvious and early winners from economic recovery, others would recover less well and more slowly, and some would continue to lose out. For some, the economic base had simply shrunk.

Summary

- The patterns of divergence between areas were clearer in 2001 than they had been in 1999.
- In inner London and inner Birmingham there was population growth, but mainly from asylum seekers and other incomers and homeless families. Social housing was under pressure and concentrations of poverty and social problems were maintained. However, there was also evidence of polarisation within the areas as higher-income households began to move in. House prices rose more than the national average.
- These and other inner-city areas were also accessible to job growth in central city areas, in retail, entertainment and financial and professional services.
- Outside inner London and inner Birmingham, most of the areas still faced a situation of very low demand for housing. Demand had not fallen further and on the whole, low demand was being well managed. However, the underlying lack of demand left unpopular neighbourhoods very vulnerable to rapid decline and intolerable living conditions.
- Some industrial areas outside cities were benefiting from job growth in call centres, warehousing and distribution, although manufacturing was still

declining. To attract new jobs, areas needed specific locational advantages. Those without such advantages showed little sign of economic recovery.

- It was evident that Britain was developing a new economic geography that would not replicate the jobs map of the past. Among the country's disadvantaged areas, some would be winners, but others would be losers.

Note

[1] It was impossible to confirm this figure, which should be treated with some caution.

New solutions?

Avoiding concentrations of poverty

The underlying drivers of neighbourhood decline and polarisation had moved on since 1999, but so too had policy. Local authorities and other agencies were getting their acts together over the management of disadvantaged areas (Chapter Nine) but, using new ideas, tools and powers handed to them by central government, they were also beginning to think more strategically and to look for new solutions to the bigger problems of housing and labour that were highlighted in Chapter Ten. The new approach to neighbourhood renewal was not just to manage the immediate problem but to avoid concentrations of the poor in the longer term. It was about flattening the hierarchy of areas, so that neighbourhoods that had traditionally been poor did not simply continue to attract only those with no choice. By 2001, new schemes to improve housing, mix tenure and reduce worklessness were beginning to be implemented. Our second round of visits gave us an opportunity to investigate their early progress.

Improving housing

In 1999, serious housing stock problems had affected about a third of the small neighbourhoods in our study. Nine of the areas had more than 50% council or housing association housing, giving us an opportunity to look at stock condition across a range of different types and ages of housing. The worst problems were in the more modern stock, built since the 1960s, with poor materials or design. Half of the neighbourhoods with this kind of stock needed major investment. In Caerphilly, Valley Top's 1980s homes were experiencing damp problems because external cladding had decayed. In Rosehill in Nottingham, heating systems were inefficient and homes were poorly insulated, making heating very expensive. The worst stock problems were in The Grove in Hackney, where some of the tower blocks were structurally defective, a third had no central heating, and many suffered from severe condensation. The council had estimated the repair bill at £45,000 per dwelling. By contrast, estates built in the 1930s and 1940s were generally sound. They needed modernisation, to windows, kitchens and bathrooms, rather than structural attention.

Quite apart from the self-evident need to provide a better standard of housing and thus avoid the knock-on effects on physical and mental health and child development, it was obvious that a low standard of housing could only serve to perpetuate poverty concentrations, since no one would choose to live in it unless they had to. But local authorities' capacity to improve their housing stock had historically been very limited. While most authorities had planned maintenance programmes, they had often had to rely on additional funding, from the SRB or Estate Action to make major improvements. The coverage of such programmes was necessarily partial.

By 2001 this was changing, as more authorities were pursuing options of whole stock transfer or private finance to bring investment into the housing stock and to enable the demolition necessary to bring supply in line with demand. In 1999, only one authority, Thanet, had transferred its housing stock. In 2001, five others had done so or were awaiting tenants' votes on the issue[1]. In another, Leeds, the city had been divided into six areas, each of which would make its own decision on stock transfer. The remaining authorities had either made a decision not to pursue stock transfer, or had not yet reached a decision.

The major advantage of stock transfer was that it offered an unprecedented opportunity to improve housing conditions. In Knowsley, limited local authority finances had meant that only 50 to 60 homes in the Overtown area could be substantially refurbished each year, aside from those included in Estate Action or the SRB programme. By comparison, stock transfer would enable "huge resources" (according to a housing manager) to be pumped in, with most properties eventually benefiting from new UPVC windows and kitchen or bathroom refurbishments. It would also enable the demolition of some 4,000 to 5,000 properties within five years, just to 'catch up' with the low demand problem.

Stock transfer was a financial boon, but it was not always widely welcomed, either by local authorities or tenants. In Labour-controlled areas, the provision of affordable housing by the local authority was an important political principle that was only reluctantly given up, and it was resisted by some councils, such as Nottingham, whose stock was in relatively good condition. Others felt that they really had no other option, and this message was conveyed to tenants, who were often concerned about the possibility of higher rents and the removal of housing management and finance from local democratic accountability. In Knowsley, for example, residents of a very run-down estate explained that the stock transfer vote could only go one way:

> "… it'll go ahead because there's no other option. People have just been told you either go on living as you are or you have the Knowsley Housing Trust." (residents, Crescent Road estate, Overtown, Knowsley)

On a local authority-wide scale, stock transfer *was* the only option. At neighbourhood level, attempts were being made to improve the stock through other funding streams, notably through the government's Private Finance Initiative (PFI). In East-Docks, the council had put together a PFI deal in which about 1,100 homes were to be improved and managed by a private company, over a

30-year period, while still owned by the council. In five years, all the homes would at least have a new kitchen and bathroom. But perversely only the better stock in the area was included, some of it already improved by SRB. The stock that needed improvement most would not offer a viable option for a private investor. The funding package involved the release of 11 small 'parcels' of land, mostly where council homes would be knocked down to make way for new homes for private sale. PFI was by no means a perfect solution, but others were scarce. In Riverlands, the council had decided to invest its own funds in an ambitious plan to refurbish the troubled Rosehill estate, and was making good progress. However, even here, it seemed that the ultimate success of the scheme would eventually depend on attracting further private finance (Box 11.1). Even at neighbourhood level, the sheer cost of improving council homes was a real stumbling block.

Mixing tenure

Apart from the improvement of the existing stock, the other major development since our first acquaintance with the areas was the open discussion of the social and economic value of mixed income and mixed tenure neighbourhoods and the development of specific plans to break up poverty clusters. Some authorities were already looking towards opening up council housing to a wider range of

Box 11.1: Ambitious housing schemes and funding problems

In Nottingham the council was using £12 million of its own funds to redesign the Rosehill estate. Rosehill was built on the Radburn design principle. Traffic circulated around the outside, while homes were grouped in cul-de-sacs joined by networks of winding pathways, overgrown and with poor visibility and lighting. Garages, parking areas, play areas and open spaces were away from houses and not overlooked. People with cars could drive to the outside of the estate and walk into their homes, so there was hardly any pedestrian movement within it, contributing to increased fear of crime, and allowing young people to gather unsupervised in public spaces. In 1999, Rosehill was a highly unpopular estate. In 2001, work had already begun on revamping it close by close, turning entrances onto the roads, enclosing private rear gardens and shutting off alleyways, as well as replacing doors and windows. The aim was "to create some of the best social housing in the city, if not in the country" (neighbourhood manager). But the overall success of the scheme was threatened by lack of public finance. The biggest thorn in Rosehill's side was its unpopular block of flats and bedsits, which attracted a transient and problematic population. After extensive consultation and option appraisal, the neighbourhood management board decided that the only option would be to demolish these and replace them with a conventional street layout – a scheme costing more than the Housing Corporation allowance for the whole of the city. As in Bridgefields in 1999, the feasibility of the redevelopment rested on success in attracting a private developer who would participate in a mixed tenure development.

people, not just the very poor. Three of the 12 were involved in the government's pilot of choice-based lettings systems, and at least two others were considering such a scheme. Under these schemes, all homes available for rent would be widely advertised, with prospective tenants bidding for those they were interested in. Newham's scheme abolished all points criteria and need assessments and moved directly to a date order system. In Sheffield and Blackburn, the choice element was operating alongside a needs assessment system.

The changes in lettings systems were very new, but some authorities were already trying to implement much more radical plans to mix tenure in specific neighbourhoods. Small mixed tenure schemes had been around for some years, encouraged by planning policy guidance (PPG3), and they were still happening. In Kirkside East, for example, a development of low-cost homes for ownership was being considered in place of some structurally faulty council maisonettes, achieving both income for the council and tenure mix. However, councils were becoming increasingly willing to discuss more radical measures to break up concentrations of social housing as the problems of low-income neighbourhoods gained more political currency. The idea that disadvantaged neighbourhoods were unworkable prompted local politicians to think about large-scale transformation rather than small scale change involving particular blocks. The language of transformation, terms like 'land values', 'sustainable social mix' and 'attracting aspiring residents', was increasingly being used, in place of a language of amelioration of living conditions for existing residents. In Leeds, for example, while there were no firm plans, a local councillor for the large social housing area of Kirkside East, doing better economically and well placed for new business developments on the east of the city, talked freely about the idea of achieving a broader mix of people in order to reduce social problems and improve the environment:

> "We've got to look at changing the social mix. It isn't happening naturally, so do we look at social engineering to create a different environment? You know it's a good location here – on the other side of the road you've got houses going for quarter of a million. It's potentially valuable land being dragged down by poor quality housing stock and by having the wrong people in it. You look at [another part of Kirkside East] and it's nice. You don't get people dumping rubbish and things like that because there are people here who've bought their houses and they won't put up with it – they'll be challenging you and ringing the council to get it mended. Now if you go to Southmead, it's different, it's like Beirut. You've got clusters of social problems. And 98% social housing. You've got to look at it and make a decision about whether it's the right mix of people."

Two authorities had gone much further. Newham Council was explicit about its objective to make East-Docks into a socially-mixed area: "a high quality residential environment [with a] mixed and sustainable tenure ... a residential area of choice" (London Borough of Newham, 2000). Most of the less good council stock not included in the PFI scheme, about 1,700 homes in all, was included in one of seven regeneration areas, otherwise known to residents as "clearance areas". At the end of 2000, the council announced plans to decant existing residents from these homes and sell them with vacant possession to a developer. The majority, 75%, would be demolished and replaced with private housing. The remainder would be extensively refurbished and returned to council ownership, thus creating a mixed tenure area of 49% social rented and 51% private ownership in the wider East-Docks area. Existing tenants would be rehoused around the borough in new social housing provision.

Newcastle City Council had similarly radical plans, bound up in the visionary Going for Growth strategy launched in 2000. Going for Growth was city-wide: a 20-year plan to create jobs and halt the outflow of population from the city itself to neighbouring areas. It was a comprehensive programme of economic development, physical regeneration and the creation of sustainable, vibrant, mixed-tenure neighbourhoods with adequate services, good transport links and pleasant environments. A total of 20,000 new homes would be built, some of them on greenfield sites at the edge of the city, but 6,600 would be demolished to make way for new developments close to the river. Master plans were issued for consultation with some areas marked for demolition, including part of the estate at Sunnybank. The housing market context here was quite different from that of inner London. All of the areas earmarked for demolition had substantial levels of empty properties. They were communities in decline. The City's strategy was a move to try and regenerate them permanently, rather than to manage a continuing decline.

Our interviews suggested that these strategic attempts to break up poverty concentrations and create sustainable mixed-tenure neighbourhoods were moving too fast. Laying down plans for the vibrant urban neighbourhoods of the future, politicians and city officials had overlooked the strength of existing communities and their commitment to their homes and neighbourhoods, however run down. They spoke of realising land values and getting rid of social problems, whereas residents spoke of the social value of their existing communities and their rights to stay in their homes. Newham Council's plans for East-Docks generated a vociferous and organised public response. An action group was formed, proposing an alternative scheme for social housing refurbishment, enabling all those who wanted to stay in the area. Some people felt that after years of allowing their neighbourhoods to run down economically, socially and physically, politicians were now, rather than investing in them, getting rid of them to attract people with more money and fewer difficulties.

"The council seems to think that no one wants to live in East-Docks. They do. They just want to live here in a different way – decent housing, less crime, more policing, things like that. They want to be able to have their friends and family around them." (resident, East-Docks)

"It wasn't him [council leader] who had his house bombed in the war was it ? It's like we've been here and lived through all of that and now they've suddenly woken up to the fact that now the land's valuable down here and we can just be shoved off. It's what I said would happen 15 years ago, they've finally realised the value of the land. We've got something that suddenly everyone wants, the docks, and that's the last thing they want, us sitting on all of that, so they're going to clear us off." (resident, East-Docks)

"… at a public meeting, [director of housing] said East-Docks' greatest asset is its land, and I said 'that may be your view, but to people who live here, its greatest asset is its people'. And a big cheer went up and they looked really taken aback. It's about a vision of a place with nice buildings and piazzas and cafes but what about the people who live here now? People are talking about clearance, cleansing…. East-Docks has been dumped on so many times. People have waited here and seen the money go elsewhere, and then all of a sudden there's some money being spent and they're being moved out … it's sad because of all the regeneration that's going on down here. Overall good things are happening. It seems like they're saying the people of East-Docks aren't good enough to be part of it. It's sad because it doesn't have to be like that. They could have taken it much slower and put residents in the driving seat. Everyone sees that it's got to change." (community worker, East Docks)

In Newcastle, the City's plans provoked "a massive reaction" (regeneration manager), a "horrendous backlash" (housing manager) when people saw their estates shaded on a map for demolition. A process of local consultation began, leading to revised district plans. A number of new residents' groups sprang up to campaign for the future of their communities. However, huge uncertainty remained. On Sunnybank estate, the new plan was to look towards mixed tenure and improved management and investment within three years. When we visited in 2001, the estate was shrouded in uncertainty and suspicion. Many residents believed that the council intended to sell the estate to a developer. Indeed rumour was rife that it had already been sold, for £1, although this was not in fact the case.

The determination of low-income communities, even those in severe decline, to fight for their right to remain, demonstrated that people could not just be moved around to facilitate neighbourhood renewal. There was a real tension between resident aspirations for community-led regeneration, and strategic plans to create sustainable urban neighbourhoods, with mixed tenure and a balance between housing supply and demand. Achieving social mix would be a slow process, not a rapid transformation.

Tackling worklessness and achieving economic inclusion

While housing issues hung in the balance, economic problems were being proactively tackled at the local level. In 1999, we had seen evidence of effective programmes to link local people to local jobs. These were much more widespread in 2001. Some programmes were government funded, such as the New Deals for the Unemployed, and the EZs. Others were local initiatives, arising from closer working between local authority economic development departments and employers, or between area-based regeneration programmes and the companies they were looking to attract. There was a burgeoning not just of funding but of good practice in this area of work; a wider recognition that training was most effective if linked to specific job prospects, that transport barriers could be overcome, and that tailored, individual attention was often needed.

Respondents across the 12 areas consistently reported that government-funded employment programmes were providing the kind of support that was needed by people who had been out of work for a long time. The New Deals provided a personal adviser, and funding to access the training that was identified. The New Deal for the 50+ group offered a £60 per week wage subsidy if a full-time job could be secured – a significant incentive to formalise work that was already being undertaken informally. New Deal advisers were given a discretionary fund (Adviser Discretionary Fund [ADF]) of up to £300 per person, and encouraged to use it flexibly to remove barriers to work, paying for work clothes, tools and equipment, or driving lessons. In one area, ADF had been spent to buy a client a bicycle to get to work, and in another to pay for sessions at a slimming club, for someone for whom low self-esteem was a real barrier to seeking work.

In 2000, new schemes were introduced that offered even more flexibility. Employment Service Action Teams were set up to target disadvantaged groups and areas, working with the unemployed regardless of whether they were claiming Jobseeker's Allowance. EZs provided a mandatory programme for people aged over 25 and out of work for more than 12 months. Both schemes responded flexibly to individual needs (Box 11.2). They enabled a different culture and approach. As one manager said: "you can just tear up the rule book and do what's best for the individual" (Action Team manager, Redcar and Cleveland). With schemes like this available, employment advisers consistently reported that it was always possible to find the funding to help remove barriers to employment.

Local schemes, funded by local authorities or by the SRB or European regeneration funding, were also in place to make sure that training was not offered in isolation but linked to specific jobs. Some simply involved local jobs fairs, which had a high rate of success. Others went further, offering customised training followed by a guaranteed interview or, in one case, a guaranteed job (Box 11.3). Where there were no big new employment developments on the

Box 11.2: Action Teams and EZs

Action Teams were present in 11 of the areas and typically worked from community venues. In Blackburn, for example, they had a mobile unit that visited different residential areas. Thanet's 18-strong Action Team operated from three shop front sites and community centres, while in Newcastle, each of the targeted wards had a dedicated adviser who was contactable by mobile phone as well as at pre-arranged 'surgeries'. Action Teams had no fixed budget per client and could be very flexible, taking risks to give people a chance of sustainable employment. In Beachville, a grant had been made to an artist to get some prints made of his work, to help start him up in business, and interim payments were occasionally made as bridging funds while people awaited their first pay packet.

Five of the areas had EZs. In Caerphilly, the EZ had seen 1,600 clients by mid-2001, with a 60% success rate in finding jobs, 87% of which had been retained for more than 13 weeks. The hub of the scheme was a close personal adviser relationship, but money was being used flexibly to change people's lifestyle and approach to work, as well as simply to find training or a job. Money had been provided for 50 people to buy cars. Groups of people were sent on intensive activity courses, blocks of customised, full-time training to break the lifestyle patterns of unemployment. For one group of women, intensive training for the catering industry had involved catering skills, food hygiene, first aid, and personal and communication skills, as well as sessions to boost self-confidence, such as having a makeover. £10,000 had been provided for a joint initiative with the council and ELWa[2] to create a call centre training facility.

doorstep, making the linkages with more distant labour markets was a key issue. In Birmingham, a new retail development came on stream in Solihull, several miles from Middle Row, but well linked by bus. The Employment Service and the developer set up 'The Hub', a recruitment centre for all the firms, linking in local training providers where additional skills were needed. A jobs fair labelled 'Bringing Solihull to Middle Row' was held in Middle Row, with information not just on jobs and training but on bus routes, times, and fares. In 2001 a new scheme, funded by the European Social Fund, was being piloted, to give people free bus passes for the first four weeks of a new job, to help establish the travel pattern and to ease the transition from benefit to employment. In Blackburn, transport was also a key factor enabling local people to get jobs on the redeveloped industrial estates. Because the estates had such good motorway access, there was a risk that jobs would be more accessible to car owners from outside the town than people living much nearer. The council's regeneration department persuaded the bus company to run a special bus service running from the town through the major housing estates in High Moor to the three industrial parks, convincing company officials that there would be sufficient business by taking them on a tour of the new business sites in the area.

The growth of new employment opportunities, combined with this intensive

Box 11.3: Linking local people to local jobs

East-Docks, Newham

Newham Council established an 'Access to Jobs' team in 1997 to promote local employment. In 1999, anticipating the development of the new exhibition centre in East-Docks, it gained European funding to employ a liaison officer specifically for this site. A jobs and training group was set up to identify the skill needs of potential employers and to put tailored training in place. For example, a specialist trainer trained the local training outlet in stand assembly, so that these courses could be provided locally on an ongoing basis. A recruitment centre was established at a community venue in the heart of East-Docks, to handle all of the recruitment for the development, and the company running the exhibition centre agreed to give preference to contractors willing to take on local labour. A jobs fair was held to recruit to the first 400 jobs, all of which were filled locally. All of these employees were offered pre-employment training looking at basic employability skills, as well as a module provided by the centre itself.

Kirkside East, Leeds

In Kirkside East, Leeds, a partnership between the City Council, training providers, and employers established the Job Guarantee scheme, first tried when a new Tesco store opened in 2000. Several months prior to the store opening, local people were invited to undertake interview or basic skills training. Job interviews were then held, focusing on appearance, body language and personal attributes, rather than work experience and skills. Successful applicants (all but six of those interviewed) were guaranteed jobs, following a customised 10-week training course of customer care, health and safety and retail training. A special training centre was set up at the local adult education centre, with Tesco tills and equipment. Transport to work and training was provided, as was fully funded childcare. Of 351 people initially employed, 147 were recruited through the partnership. A total of 243 were previously unemployed (Walton et al, 2002). In 2001 the scheme was being extended to other employers: a hotel, housing association and the health authority.

investment in removing obstacles to work, meant that unemployment continued to fall in all the study areas. The reductions were significant, such that in half the areas, the number of Jobseeker's Allowance claimants in April 2001 was half what it had been five years previously. Over the period from the start of the study in 1998 to 2001, unemployment in most of the areas fell faster, both in percentage point terms and in relation to its starting point, than the national average (Table 11.1), evidence that these areas which had been slower to benefit from economic recovery in the 1990s were finally beginning to catch up. Riverlands in Nottingham and Kirkside East in Leeds, the stronger economies, had kept pace with the national trend in the 1990s and continued to do so. Only a handful of areas such as Southside in Redcar and Cleveland and Middle Row in Birmingham, where job growth was still sluggish or skill problems very severe, continued to fall behind national trends.

Table 11.1: Change in claimant unemployment (1998-2001)

	1996	Unemployment as % of 1996 level 1998	2001	Fall 1998-2001 as % of 1996 figure
West-City (Hackney)	100	69	46	23
East-Docks (Newham)	100	66	45	21
Overtown (Knowsley)	100	80	60	20
Riverlands (Nottingham)	100	62	47	15
Shipview (Newcastle)	100	74	48	26
The Valley (Sheffield)	100	78	58	20
High Moor (Blackburn)	100	63	48	15
Middle Row (Bimingham)	100	76	63	13
Fairfields (Caerphilly)	100	68	45	23
Southside (Redcar and Cleveland)	100	74	60	14
Kirkside East (Leeds)	100	68	50	18
Beachville (Thanet)	100	67	50	17
England and Wales	**100**	**61**	**44**	**17**

However, just as falling unemployment earlier in the decade had masked more complex labour market adjustments, falling unemployment in this period did not mean that the government's investment in employment and training initiatives had solved the economic problem.

Despite a falling claimant count, our interviews revealed continuing underlying concerns about labour market developments. The problems raised by our Bridgefields respondents were replicated elsewhere. One described a 'twin-track' economy, with a gulf opening up between highly skilled and well-rewarded jobs at the upper end of the labour market and poorly paid and insecure jobs, offering no progression, at the other. It was a gulf that was difficult for people to jump, because the structure of the labour market offered few chances to develop. One experienced Employment Service employee noted:

> "… a huge growth in agency work. I remember when I first started, we weren't actually allowed to take vacancies from agencies, now they're virtually all agency ones. It's difficult because it means that people don't get any training or progression, just a series of short-term jobs. Also it's a less good process for people. Agencies usually don't give any feedback if you're not successful, so people don't know what they've got to improve. People somehow seem to have a bit less power in the job-seeking process." (employment adviser, Riverlands, Nottingham)

Low pay was mentioned as a problem by several respondents, but more frequently they mentioned this issue of the dominance, in service industries, of low-skilled and temporary work: jobs that provided an income but a weak sense of identity or security. A culture of disposability was becoming embedded in the labour market. Apart from its impact on the low-pay, no-pay cycle, to which I alluded in Chapter Three, this shift also had the effect of alienating some people from the labour market altogether. The 'no-work' patterns that had been established during a period of low employment were very difficult to break when the economy seemed to offer few good options. While this was evident in 1999, it had become all the more visible in 2001 as the numbers of people out of work overall had dropped even further.

> "You still have a concentration of people who don't see the labour market as providing something that they want. I would say there's probably been a big growth in the informal and illegal economies. You're seeing people who are obviously sustaining themselves in that way – working-class lads walking around with £1,000 worth of gear on. And what's significant is that these people actually *aren't* important to the economy. They're not needed in the labour market because the city's labour requirements can be met by other people, women and students." (economic analyst, Newcastle)

> "The 'improver' market [for training] is dominated by women but the unemployment register is four to one male. A lot of the work that's coming through is 'women's jobs' and that's a problem. Some working-class males can't find the opportunities that they're looking for." (adult education worker, Kirkside East, Leeds)

> "Good employment, what I'd call a career, isn't out there. There's lots of bitty jobs about. And a lot of people with low aspirations, but it's hard to have aspiration when there's no real jobs. You can't make a career out of bitty jobs." (youth worker, Beachville, Thanet)

> "We're now getting down almost to the bottom of the barrel. People who are just turning over, getting the odd short-term contract or signing off for a bit to avoid the programme or who go on the programme and fail to attend – it's things like drugs, alcohol, debt, criminal records, behavioural problems, whether you'd class it as attitude or what, we sometimes just feel we're beating them with a big stick." (employment adviser, Kirkside East, Leeds)

So while economic growth continued, structural changes ensured that two problems persisted for low-income areas. For a few, outside the cities, there were genuine problems with the number of jobs. For the remainder, the problems were about the ability of the labour market to deliver inclusion; its tendency to trap the low-skilled in an uncertain cycle of low pay or no pay; and its inherent unattractiveness particularly to young men for whom alternative lifestyles and alternative economies offered better propositions. These broader problems of economic structure had not been addressed in government policy. Given these broader problems of economic structure, intensive and inventive supply-side labour market initiatives could only go a certain way to tackling what was, in essence, a problem of labour demand.

The persistence of poverty and exclusion

Because the economic structure was constantly recreating exclusion, many of our respondents in the 12 areas found it difficult to be convinced that, overall, the problems of relative poverty and social exclusion were diminishing or, indeed, would diminish significantly in the future. The time lag in the production of official statistics made it impossible to assess, at the time of writing, whether official measures showed any significant trends over this two-year period. In a sense, one could hardly expect them to. Investment in social programmes, working with people, takes time to reap its rewards. The social services manager in Beachville, Thanet, for example, was confident that the increase in preventative services for families would lead to a drop in the number of child protection registrations, but probably not for at least five to seven years. But the broader question was whether the new public investment in disadvantaged areas, combined with economic growth, showed signs of reducing problems in the longer term.

It was rare to find professional respondents who were not upbeat about increases in funding and the new facilities and services that were being provided. But they often volunteered two broader concerns. One was about the non-working poor, and the way in which they seemed to be getting left behind by rising inequality. The other was about labour market exclusion, not unemployment per se, but the alienation from formal work of young people who could not see it offering them anything worthwhile. In the face of this, the government's initiatives seemed destined to have only a limited impact:

> "Definitely more people are working. You can see that by the number of cars on the street. But that does tend to mask the problem for those who can't work, like the single elderly. Life is still a real struggle." (vicar, East-Docks, Newham)

> "There's no real change for the people we see. People are struggling more on benefits than they used to. People are getting poorer, I'd say. There's a widening gap between the cost of living and your benefits and it's becoming more obvious when we've got all these substantially priced properties all around." (church worker, High Moor, Blackburn)

> "SRB has made some difference but it hasn't cured anything. It doesn't really address some of the underlying issues, such as poor educational attainment and unemployment. People want money and

the well-paid manual jobs aren't around any more in this area. Plus the ugly hand of drugs stymies any attempt at regeneration. Being a junkie's a full-time job." (local authority officer, Southside, Redcar and Cleveland)

"These [young African Caribbean] kids are possibly right in their view of the world. They know what's going on [lack of job prospects] and they don't see themselves fitting into that bigger picture. We're doing what we can at local level but it needs bigger changes." (community worker, Riverlands, Nottingham)

While our qualitative interviews in 1999 had revealed a picture of decline and despondency, those in 2001 told a story of optimism and new opportunities to make positive changes, tinged with concern about continuing social problems and uncertainty about whether society's economic and social structure would continue to generate social exclusion, at the same time as government policy was battling against it.

Summary

- By 2001, we were able to observe the implementation of initiatives to improve housing, reduce concentrations of poverty and tackle the economic problems of the areas.
- Transfer of the council housing stock was happening, or being considered, in half the areas, as the only way to bring major new investment into social housing. The money was welcomed and offered a real prospect of change after many years of under-investment. It also offered a major opportunity to bring supply in line with demand. However, as a principle, it was sometimes resented.
- In the absence of stock transfer, funding housing improvements at neighbourhood level was difficult. The PFI was being used in one case.
- Local authorities were also looking to reduce poverty concentrations by changing the tenure mix of neighbourhoods. Two had radical plans for demolition and mixed tenure redevelopment. These had caused widespread local opposition. Others were piloting choice-based lettings schemes.
- The number and range of schemes to help unemployed people into work and to link local people to local jobs had improved since 1999. Flexibility to tailor interventions to individual needs was the key to their success. Unemployment had fallen in all the areas, in most cases more than the national average. However, as in 1999, there were concerns about the ability of the labour market to offer worthwhile employment to those with low skills. Low pay and insecure work were trapping people in poverty or excluding them from the labour market despite supply-side initiatives.

- The overall picture in 2001 was more optimistic than in 1999, and there were prospects of tackling housing demand and supply problems in the longer term. However, it was not clear that the wider inequalities in society that were driving social exclusion had been sufficiently addressed.

Notes

[1] Tenants in Birmingham subsequently voted against stock transfer.

[2] ELWa: Education and Learning Wales, the joint name for the National Council for Education and Training for Wales and the Higher Education Funding Council for Wales.

TWELVE

The end of Poverty Street?

Structural causes of decline

The stories of these 12 areas and neighbourhoods demonstrate very clearly the structural origins of neighbourhood 'degeneration', but also the importance of space and place. What had made the areas poor in the first place, and kept them persistently poor, was the fit between their 'intrinsic' or 'hard to change' characteristics – location and topography, housing stock and economic structure – and the demands of the economy and the housing market. The most fundamental causes of area change were, in this sense, "externally induced" (Galster, 2001, p 2118). They were 'macro' causes, originating way beyond the neighbourhood, but the particular spatial distribution of their impacts was also determined by 'micro' explanations: by the characteristics of the areas themselves and their particular fit with economic and housing demands.

Working-class areas in the inner cities and in industrial towns and villages were originally poor, in the 1800s, because they were created to meet a demand for industrial workers. Close to coal mines, shipyards and inner-city factories and warehouses, they were always at the bottom of the housing market. The large overspill council housing estates that were created from the 1930s to rehouse these workers from inner-city slums were also poverty clusters from their inception, although they initially offered a higher standard of homes sought after by the better-off working class as well as the extremely poor. Regardless of their housing market status, they at least met a demand for labour, giving them an intrinsic economic value that diminished as the structure of their industries was transformed and labour demand evaporated in the second half of the 20th century.

Other areas, a minority in the inner cities, like Middle Row in Birmingham or The Valley in Sheffield, started life with a higher market value, housing the professional and business classes, but lost their status over time as preferences changed and the middle classes deserted the Victorian properties and inner-city locations they had once demanded. Formerly prosperous, they became home to new waves of the disadvantaged, often immigrants who could not gain access to housing elsewhere. Even these patterns, however, were established by the 1960s. Only Beachville, the coastal resort in Kent, had a more recent decline, when air travel changed people's holiday preferences, ending the mass demand for English seaside holidays.

Nevertheless, although the areas were already poor by the 1960s, it was the period between the 1970s and the late 1990s in which they became increasingly dislocated from labour markets. This was both a spatial dislocation, as traditional industries declined and new job growth took place outside the major cities and industrial areas, and a mismatch between the skill base of their residents and the job requirements of modern industry. Population continued to be lost, leaving a shortfall in demand for the areas' housing, and enabling a process of residential sorting, whereby people could choose not to live in the least popular areas. Meanwhile, changes in housing preferences and in housing policy undermined demand for the social housing stock that made up the bulk of the accommodation. As preferences for homeowning were met by the Right to Buy and by the release of greenfield land for private housebuilding, tenants leaving the social housing sector were replaced in smaller numbers. Newcomers were predominantly disadvantaged, as the basis for council house allocation was changed to give priority to the homeless and those in urgent housing need. As demand diminished and council housing became mainly a tenure for the poor, sorting also occurred within the sector, leaving the least popular estates with effectively no demand. When we first visited the areas in 1999, most of the social housing estates we saw outside London had no waiting list. At best, it was just possible to find tenants to replace those who left, but the situation was finely balanced. There was no opportunity to balance lettings to achieve a workable social mix, and tenants widely reported that their areas had become dumping grounds for society's most needy, vulnerable or dysfunctional individuals. Private housing in these areas also had very low market value, and in the most extreme cases was being abandoned by people who had no prospect of selling. On the inner London estates, preference for council housing was also low, but demand was high, fuelled by large numbers of refugees. The vast majority of lettings were to homeless applicants.

Thus, what created and maintained Poverty Street was the lack of value of some areas in relation to broader societal structures. Disadvantage originally had an uneven spatial distribution because the features of certain areas were less desirable or necessary than those of others. Changes in the national economy and the housing market in the second half of the 20th century combined to residualise areas that were already poor.

The sharp end of social change

The declining economic value of inner-city and industrial areas and the diminishing demand for their housing ensured that the geography of poverty in England and Wales remained relatively resilient to change. The poverty map that was drawn by the IMD in 1998, showing clusters of poor areas in inner London, the metropolitan areas of the Midlands and the North, mining villages and coastal towns, looked very similar to the one drawn by the Censuses of 1971, 1981 and 1991. Only the continuing decline of coastal resorts during the late 1980s and 1990s added to the picture. Urban and industrial areas continued to be relatively poor.

But this did not fully explain the widening of the gap between areas from the 1970s onwards. Poor areas became relatively poorer in this period not just because the implications of economic and housing market changes were inherently spatial, but because, in general, the poor were becoming relatively poorer and more excluded. The consequences, for those at the bottom, of the increasing polarisation and fragmentation of society, were felt most in the places where the poor were concentrated.

Two broad changes were taking place. First, income inequality was rising, partly because of changes in the economic structure and partly because of public policy. Quite apart from rising unemployment and economic activity in the 1970s and 1980s, the decline in manufacturing and growth in services also affected those who were in work. There was less demand for full-time low-skilled or semi-skilled male employment, and more demand for part-time low-skilled jobs and, at the other end of the scale, for high-skilled full-time workers. The relative value of having skills and higher-level educational qualifications increased, with rising earnings polarisation between low-skilled, part-time and temporary work and high-skilled, full-time and permanent work. The massive expansion of women's employment and of higher education brought more middle-class women into the labour market, in both full- and part-time jobs. Working-class women, who could not afford childcare, either took part-time low-paid jobs or sometimes gave up work if male partners lost their jobs, rather than losing out on household benefits. The number of no-earner households increased as well as the number of two-earner households. The failure of successive governments to ensure that benefit payments kept pace with earnings resulted in an increasing gulf between non-working households and those with someone in employment. Even the New Labour government's increases in benefit rates went only a small way towards closing the gap that had arisen since the 1970s[1]. Carr-Hill and Lavers (2000), repeating Rowntree's analysis of the costs of basic family diets, found that present-day families dependent on social security have a standard of living no higher than those enjoyed by similar families in 1950. While the gains at the top were huge, the gains at the bottom of society were negligible.

Second, the social world was changing. Employment changes had an impact way beyond their economic one. The loss of traditional industries which had provided stable employment for large numbers of men in industrial communities denuded the physical and social fabric of neighbourhoods. Apart from loss of income and the stress of living in poverty, many people faced a debilitating loss of self-esteem and identity. Their skills and their traditional roles in family and community were literally redundant, and for communities, the social life based around work and work-based social organisations was completely disrupted. Families and relationships were placed under enormous strain, and many young people grew up with insecurity and little sense of their place in the world. But the impact of these changes was particularly powerful because they were not taking place in isolation. Not only were the social structures of large firms and trades unions breaking up, so too were other social supports, such as the traditional family, church and geographical community. In society as a whole, technological advance and the demands of new employment structures promoted the values of mobility and transferability rather than those of permanence and long-term commitment, and under the political leadership of the Conservative governments from 1979-97, the values of freedom of choice and individual opportunities and rights were promoted at the expense of the values of mutualism and social welfare. Global companies and global communications brought other value shifts. Brands increasingly became a source of identity, high-tech or designer products a status symbol. In a world of fragmenting social structures and technological change, the growing dominance of the values of individualism and materialism offered huge opportunities and rewards for people with the abilities, resources and confidence to take advantage, but left others increasingly vulnerable. Society became "atomised at top and bottom" (Toynbee, 2002).

The fall-out from these changes impacted throughout society. Stress and mental health problems increased, as did alcohol and drug abuse, and the strain on family and community relationships. But the impact was most strongly felt in those areas which had had the most profound shock to their economic and social structure, where opportunities to participate in the new economy were most limited, and where people had the fewest resources to access the material goods and lifestyles that were being promoted as the new norm. The poorest areas saw the biggest drugs outbreaks, the highest rates of mental illness, the most widespread anti-social behaviour, the highest rates of teenage pregnancy, and the most vibrant illegal economies. They were at the sharp end of social change.

Management failure

The extreme concentrations of poverty that developed in the poorest neighbourhoods made them almost impossible to manage within the normal structures and resources of public services. Problems were more numerous, more complex and consistently recurring, and it was difficult for services to keep up. When we visited in 1999 it was clear that the failure of public sector services, under pressure to provide a basic level of service provision, such as carrying out prompt housing repairs, cleaning up litter, or putting teachers in front of classes, created a sense of resentment, anger and demoralisation for residents. Relationships between residents and service providers were often tense and fraught. The strain of operating in this environment took its toll on public service organisations, which sometimes found it hard to recruit staff, suffered low morale and high rates of sickness, and found their budgets stretched by having to cope with crime and vandalism. Staff in some services, like schools, found their time occupied by non-core tasks, such as dealing with welfare issues, because of the extra demands that the areas threw up.

There were, of course, shining examples of good practice in extraordinarily difficult circumstances, and most neighbourhoods did benefit from slightly enhanced resources, such as an extra litter picker, youth project or weekly refuse collection. Some neighbourhoods, like Saints' Walk in Knowsley, were hauled back from decline or, like Sunnybank in Newcastle, held back from its brink by bursts of additional investment (like Estate Action or extra policing), or by enhanced services provided in a coordinated way and responsive to residents' needs. The individual contributions and commitment of public sector workers in these situations were sometimes highly praised by residents. However, these outstanding examples should not be allowed to obscure the overall picture, which was that until the late 1990s, successive governments failed to recognise and make provision for the vast additional demands that were placed on services by the concentrations of poverty and exclusion that social and economic progress had produced.

The problem was not just the level of service that was needed but the style of its provision. From the mid-1980s onwards, public services came under intense pressure to improve their value for money, efficiency and accountability. Compulsory Competitive Tendering was intended to produce value-for-money services by specifying the service to be provided and selecting the most competitive bidder, but in doing so it produced pared-down services with no slack. Efficient services were achieved by targeted work in special short-term projects, and accountability by the introduction of targets and performance indicators which, by necessity, focused on 'hard' rather than 'soft' outcomes. The result was that permanent staff were cut in favour of short-term project staff or sessional workers and generic frontline workers like police constables, caretakers and housing officers were removed so that manpower could be diverted to specialist and mobile squads or so that demands for service could be met in apparently more efficient ways by centralised units. Community and youth workers, whose role involved the building of confidence and capacity, were made to justify their existence in terms of hard outputs, and often cut altogether.

This mode of service delivery was not what was needed in areas of concentrated poverty. These, even more so than more ordered neighbourhoods, required frontline supervision and enforcement, people on hand to notice and remedy problems, and permanent, area-based staff with the time to build relationships of confidence and trust, support people over extended periods while they coped with complex problems, and help restore the self-esteem that economic and social exclusion was constantly eroding. The failure of national and local government to design and deliver differentiated services in areas of exceptional need was another link in the vicious circle of neighbourhood decline.

Social interaction and neighbourhood stigma

In the face of decline, the support of friends, family living locally and other neighbours was highly valued. Many people spoke of 'the community' or 'the people' as an asset of their neighbourhoods and a reason to stay. Poverty, because it limited travel opportunities and the ability to buy goods and support services, promoted local interactions and mutual support. Geographical community retained its strength and value while in more affluent areas it had declining importance relative to communities of interest operating over a wider arena. Many areas retained a core of families whose association with the neighbourhood spanned several generations. Especially, but not exclusively, among these, there were strong informal networks of friendship, mutual aid and exchange of goods. Informal local economies of unpaid work, cash-in-hand work and trade in stolen goods were well established. There was also, in most areas, a range of small-scale community groups, running social activities and trips, youth clubs and pensioners' lunches, or running bigger ventures like community halls, food cooperatives and credit unions, and lobbying for better services from public agencies.

However, while local ties were strong, they did not provide a bridge to other beneficial networks outside the neighbourhood, an asset that was becoming increasingly important as labour markets were becoming less localised and geographical mobility was increasing. On the contrary, barriers to intra-neighbourhood networks seemed to be growing as the socioeconomic distance between neighbourhoods grew. 'Postcode stigma' appeared to be a reality in the job market and awareness of it damaged the confidence of some young residents, particularly, in operating outside their home neighbourhood.

Local networks also came under strain as the social composition of areas changed and existing communities needed to absorb new and different people. There were tensions between the desire, on the part of newcomers and existing residents, to maintain community, and the uncomfortable unfamiliarity of cultures and behaviours. The growing proportion of vulnerable and chaotic households, whose behaviour could be anti-social and difficult to influence, created a particular pressure. Public and social space became contested, forcing people to withdraw to smaller networks of trust and familiarity, groups that were valuable to their members but exclusive to others.

Shrinking networks made it easy for vulnerable people to become isolated in areas that others described as friendly and inclusive. They also diminished people's capacity to act collectively to sustain and enforce behavioural norms. As it became harder to challenge anti-social behaviour or damage, neighbourhood environments declined. Litter and damage multiplied and levels of disorder grew, fuelling the cycle of abandonment and increasing poverty concentration, and enhancing neighbourhood stigma. Interaction between neighbourhoods as well as within neighbourhoods became increasingly difficult.

'Regeneration': not up to the job

The growing problems of the poorest neighbourhoods were recognised by central government from the late 1960s onwards in the form of successive area-based regeneration programmes: the Urban Programme, CDPs, UDCs, City Challenge and the SRB. By its nature, this was 'special funding' and was not distributed evenly or consistently over time. Certain areas received bursts of funding for specific purposes, while others were not included.

Despite their partialness, these area funding programmes constituted a significant attempt to tackle neighbourhood problems, contrasting sharply with the policy regime in the United States, where growing poverty concentrations were allowed to develop without these kinds of interventions. It is impossible to assess how much worse deprived neighbourhoods would have become without the input of regeneration policy. Nevertheless, it is easy to see in hindsight that policy was inadequate for the job of neighbourhood renewal.

The first round of programmes was launched before the oil crash of 1973/74, in the era of post-war prosperity. At this stage, the scale of Britain's economic decline and the outcome of its restructuring were not fully anticipated. Confident that the market would deliver work and prosperity, politicians designed regeneration programmes essentially aimed at redressing the social problems of the poor: community projects, housing and environmental improvements and welfare provision. The CDPs were an early attempt to manage area problems by better coordinated service delivery. These programmes did not recognise or attempt to tackle the economic causes of decline.

Under the Conservative governments of the 1980s and early 1990s, the focus switched to the economic revitalisation of the areas, through Urban Development Corporations. Again, these had only a limited coverage. Importantly they were local programmes, aimed at attaining a better match between certain poor areas and the demands of the new economy. They did not address the broader problems of structural economic decline that underpinned the problems of the poorest areas more generally. They were generally successful in attracting inward investment and achieving physical transformation. Some, like London's Docklands, were spectacularly so. But the assumption was that benefits would 'trickle down' to local populations, and social and welfare programmes were neglected. Although the foundations for economic revival were laid, many people in the poorest neighbourhoods were largely unaffected, even in places like London's East-Docks where rapid economic development was taking place close by. Broader trends in housing demand dragged the areas down at the same time as extra investment was going into pulling their economies up.

The SRB was an attempt to roll economic and social projects into one overall regeneration programme. Most SRB programmes incorporated job creation programmes, education and training, housing and environmental improvements and projects to tackle social problems or build communities. All the SRB programmes in the study areas had tangible benefits. Their injection of funding, their local focus and their partnership approach also enabled them to be a catalyst for better management and joined-up working in the longer term. But they could never expect to 'regenerate' the neighbourhoods. Again, they were local programmes, not linked to wider strategies, and not supported by macro-economic policies that could protect the areas from the impact of structural decline. SRB funding was only for a maximum of seven years and in some cases was largely absorbed by expensive housing refurbishment programmes. Local politicians, professionals and residents knew the limitations of SRB. They treated it as a valuable extra funding stream and used it either to put a brake on rapid decline, to hold on to conditions and build a platform for future recovery, or, in exceptional cases, to provide a bridge to new economic opportunities that were already on the doorstep.

Moreover, there were also implementation problems with regeneration. Residents often felt disempowered in decision-making processes. It felt as though things were being 'done to' them rather than 'with' them. In some cases, it was transparent that, far from bending mainstream services to match SRB resources, local authorities and other agencies were swallowing up SRB to fund services and capital projects that they could not otherwise afford. Good projects were established but could not necessarily be sustained beyond the life of the programme. Competitive bidding induced a bidding and programme management culture, rather than a long-term strategic approach.

Despite these implementation problems, regeneration programmes brought more benefits than disbenefits. They could not, however, tackle the roots of the problem. They were essentially 'micro' solutions and could never, on their own, achieve the regeneration of neighbourhoods crippled by social change and their redundancy in economic and housing markets. As Carley and Kirk (1998) have argued, area regeneration programmes made a contribution to managing deprivation, in some cases very effectively, but they did not resolve the problem.

A concerted response

By the end of the 1990s the problems of the poorest areas and neighbourhoods had become very clear. The accounts of our 12 case studies up to that point paint a bleak picture of social polarisation and policy failure. These areas of concentrated poverty had high levels of health and social problems and large proportions of households workless and dependent on state benefits. People who lived in them often felt stigmatised by the outside world and deprived of the opportunities and advantages that they might expect elsewhere. Although reasonable conditions had been maintained in some areas, others, like Bridgefields, had intolerable living environments, strewn with rubbish, disturbed by anti-social behaviour, crime and drug dealing, and lacking decent housing, shops or services.

The election of the New Labour government brought a new political determination to act. In many ways, the new government learned the lessons of the past, tackling problems simultaneously at a number of levels: through better day-to-day management; giving more decision-making power to people in poverty; increasing the resources directed to poor areas through special initiatives and through the NRF; linking social welfare programmes to wider economic developments with the creation of the RDAs; and encouraging the repopulation of cities and implementing housing policies that might in the long run lead to better tenure mix and a greater dispersal of poverty. For the first time, closing the gap between poor neighbourhoods and the rest became a task of mainstream agencies, not just of short-life regeneration partnerships. LSPs were tasked with developing strategies for neighbourhood renewal and would be accountable for raising standards in the poorest neighbourhoods to acceptable levels or bringing them closer to the national average.

No one pretended that these policies would transform the areas overnight. It would be a long process, at least 10 or 20 years. But by 2001, the scale of the effort was certainly evident. Facilities and services were improving with extra investment and neighbourhood conditions were not getting any worse. The interlinked problems of poor neighbourhoods were being tackled in a more coordinated way, and there was a genuine change of culture among public sector employees who were enthusiastic about working in a joined-up way and convinced of its benefits. Attempts were being made to broaden participation and strengthen local democracy. Although it would take time to work through, and although enhancing participation and bending mainstream programmes were by no means unproblematic, in broad terms the government's agenda was hitting the ground as it was intended.

However, while policy was better conceived and determinedly implemented, it was, like its predecessors, vulnerable to wider economic and social changes.

Economic growth and divergence

The critical issue, as ever, was the direction of economic change. Would growth be sufficient to pull up even the poorest areas?

The picture in 2001 was certainly more optimistic than it had been for some time. While the broader economic context throughout the 1970s and 1980s and even into the mid-1990s had been one of continuing industrial decline in cities and outlying industrial areas with service sector growth mainly in smaller towns and cities, the mid to late 1990s saw the beginning of revival in the economies of the large ex-industrial cities, driven by the growth of the service sector. Manufacturing continued to decline, but the overall position for the most disadvantaged areas in the cities was net growth, either very locally or close by. They were beginning, once again, to have an intrinsic value in the market for labour.

Inner London was undergoing the most dramatic transformation. West-City was close to the City and easily accessible to the West End, while East-Docks was close to Docklands and, since 1999, linked to central London by the Jubilee Line extension. New local employment was being generated with the exhibition site and associated hotels and entertainment venues, and the area was also close to Stratford, which would have its new European rail terminal within another five years. These developments brought new economic opportunities for the existing population, and the critical issue was not labour demand but ensuring that local people were linked to local jobs, which were also easily accessible to people from further afield. Even away from London, by 2001 all of the cities we studied were generating service sector growth in excess of manufacturing sector losses.

Opinion is divided over whether these signs of growth can be said to constitute a revival of city economies. On the one hand, it was clear that some service-based jobs, in sectors such as retail, hospitality, entertainment, care, education, IT, finance, business support services and media, needed to be located near people, in towns and cities. High-technology science-based services were particularly likely to be based in large cities (Begg et al, 2002). On the other hand, Breheny (1999) warned that service sector growth in cities was not as strong as expected and is still vulnerable to decentralisation to cheaper locations. Meanwhile, with improved technology, the remaining manufacturing industries would require fewer employees, diminishing the demand for labour in areas where these industrial sectors remained in significant numbers. Recent research has shown a trend for high-tech manufacturing to locate in small cities close to London rather than in areas of traditional manufacturing (Begg et al, 2002). Breheny (1999) suggested that this pattern of development, on the current scale, constitutes only a very limited city revival. Real revival would involve much bigger inner-city job growth, an agenda overlooked by the Urban Task Force:

> The cities can tick over as they are; with disappearing manufacturing jobs, slow growth in services generally and strong performance in some small sectors; with attractive and apparently buoyant downtown areas; with the retention or even attraction of young professionals living centrally in regenerated environments; with an underclass of people excluded from the workplace and trapped in the inner cities. (Breheny, 1999, p 18)

The bigger problem, however, was outside the cities. Some kinds of firms, in much more limited numbers, such as call centres or storage, packing and distribution firms, would employ significant numbers outside major centres of population, because of their needs for greater space, and areas with good business infrastructure and transport links would be successful in attracting them. Overtown in Knowsley, for example, was seeing a growth in call centres. Planners in Beachville were hoping that the development of its airport both as a freight centre and ultimately as a passenger terminal, would be the spur to economic revival, along with the re-shaping of tourism in the town geared towards day trips and short breaks. There was also potential for these areas to regain economic value, although the future was uncertain.

However, the changing spatial pattern of labour was leaving other areas out in the cold, failing to make an economic recovery that would replace jobs in anything like the numbers demanded by the labour intensive industries of the past. They were losing manufacturing jobs and were intrinsically unattractive locations for the service industries that were replacing them. Such areas were in transition to a smaller employment base, sustaining a smaller population, some of whom would work outside the area. In the case of the South Wales mining valley, Fairfields, this had been clear many years ago, because of the location and topography of the area. It was also becoming clear for Southside in Redcar and Cleveland, located slightly away from the main North-South transport routes and with large tracts of contaminated industrial land.

Moreover, even in areas where there was job growth, it was not clear that the transition to a service sector economy would bring significant benefits to many of those who were poor. The spectre of widespread and enduring worklessness was gone, but replaced instead by a cycle, for many, of periods of low pay and no pay. Low-paid employment was becoming a more widespread problem than unemployment. By 2000/01, almost half of all adults and children below the low-income threshold[2] were in households where one or more adults was working, whereas only 10% were in unemployed households (Kenway and Palmer, 2002). For a minority, dropping out of the formal labour market was a more attractive option than low-paid work. Economic exclusion was taking a different form, but not disappearing.

Social exclusion and population change

These changes meant that, both in poor areas that were now beginning to do better economically and those that were not, large numbers of people remained on relatively low incomes. They were either non-working poor or people who were economically active but churning in and out of low-paid work. According to respondents in our study areas, more people were in work, but the problems of poverty were not significantly diminished. Feelings of exclusion, and the behaviours of exclusion, like crime, anti-social behaviour, buying and selling drugs, drinking and drug taking, early pregnancy, persistent truancy, child abuse and neglect and so on, were still very much in evidence and, according to some people, worsening. To some extent, this was because long-term, intergenerational, social exclusion would take time to break. More and better services, delivered in a more accessible way, were creating opportunities for change and in every area there were examples of individuals who had made lasting changes in their lives and of widening participation in programmes that would make a difference: adult education, early years activities, community health promotion activities and so on. But it was also a cycle that was still reproducing itself, as the structures of economy and society continued to alienate and exclude some of its members. For some people with lower abilities or opportunities, the very focus on paid work and academic attainment was excluding in itself.

In inner-city areas, particularly in London, the problem was exacerbated by an increasing influx of immigrants, many of them refugees, whose household resources were extremely low and who were often not equipped with the skills to compete for higher-paid jobs in the labour market, and were additionally disadvantaged by discrimination. Even if some existing residents did well, the pool of poverty was constantly being topped up.

Established patterns of low-value housing

During the late 1990s, public policy began to focus not just on reducing poverty, per se, but on breaking up its spatial concentration, to achieve greater social integration and minimise area effects. But this was difficult to achieve, because of the established spatial pattern of high- and low-value housing and the operation of the housing market. Unable to access higher value housing, those on lower incomes are obliged to rely on social housing or the cheaper end of the private sector. These homes are clustered together, in social housing estates or areas of Victorian street terraces.

By 2001, twin-track policies to encourage greater tenure and income mix were being actively pursued. One was to open up social housing to a wider range of people, thus avoiding the continuing concentration of the needy and vulnerable on the least popular estates. The other was to attempt to revitalise inner-city neighbourhoods by promoting city living, encouraging middle- and high-income households back into central and inner-city areas.

This was easier to achieve in some areas than in others. Predominantly private sector areas had more elasticity in the housing market than those dominated by social housing. As housing markets in London showed, areas of Victorian and Edwardian housing in inner-city areas retained a potential value if preferences for urban living, and city economies, revived. There was already evidence of rising market values for private sector housing in most of the inner-city areas in our study.

But the potential for revival did not extend to all areas of low-value private sector housing. In smaller towns like Blackburn, centrally located jobs and shops could easily be accessed from areas on the edge of town. Victorian workers' cottages in central areas, with no gardens or parking space, and often in poor condition, had little intrinsic value, especially in the context of low housing demand generally in the sub-region. Moreover, in some areas, like parts of Blackburn and Birmingham, inner-city private housing areas had become predominantly associated with Pakistani Muslim communities, with over 70% of their populations being from this ethnic background. Such areas were becoming increasingly segregated. For one ethnic group, a disadvantaged one, these areas could be relatively popular because of their cultural familiarity and relative freedom from racist attack, while being relatively unpopular in the wider housing market. But many homeowners were on low incomes and could not afford to invest in the stock, leading to its continuing decline and devaluation.

In any case, most intensive poverty clusters in England and Wales continued to be in areas of social housing. Even where spare land or unwanted council homes enabled new homes to be built for ownership, shared ownership or private renting, these would not necessarily be sought after, given the stigma attached to the areas. While the example of West-City (where City professionals were prepared to pay in excess of £200,000 for an ex-council flat) demonstrates that in situations of extremely high housing demand, blocks of social housing could start to have a more even tenure mix, this was not necessarily a phenomenon that would happen so readily outside the capital. Even if it were, it could only occur on a gradual basis. The drastic plans of Newcastle and Newham Councils for the wholesale social engineering of deprived areas by demolishing existing social housing areas and replacing them with private or mixed-tenure developments were unacceptable to local people, because of the disruption to communities and the social impact of displacement. Moreover, the poor had to live somewhere. Unless space could somehow be found for them in higher-income communities, new immigrants, homeless families and those who could not afford private sector prices would have to be housed where homes were available for them – in clusters of social housing. Without a radical equalisation of the housing market or a drastic reduction of the number of people living in poverty, the spatial pattern of poverty established by the distribution of housing would take decades rather than years to change.

Policy limitations and realistic futures

Compared with the efforts of its predecessors, the neighbourhood renewal policies of the current government are a huge advance. But the analysis of the problem of neighbourhood decline that I have presented here suggests that their impact will be limited.

I have argued throughout this book that what determines neighbourhood fortunes is the 'fit' between their characteristics and the demands of the wider society. Places with a good fit are rewarding to the people who live in them, providing incomes from work, desirable environments, and access to other amenities. Over time, they also attract more people, and more advantaged people. Places that fit less well are less rewarding. Their residents are more likely to live in poverty, because of weak labour demand. Over time, people with choice move away and are replaced by people with no choice. The least advantaged people end up in the least advantaged places. Clearly, then, there are two ways to tackle spatial concentrations of poverty. One is to remove the differences between people and the other is to remove the differences between areas.

Removing individual differences is an egalitarian agenda with well-rehearsed policy components: reduction of inequalities in wages and salaries; wealth and income taxes to redistribute wealth; protection of the weak through generous benefits; elimination of racial discrimination; provision of compensatory access to health and education and so on. As others have pointed out (see discussion in Chapter Seven), the New Labour government has gone some way down this road with its tax and benefit policies and its cross-cutting interventions for groups at high risk of social exclusion. However, it has not attempted a fundamental redistribution of wealth nor challenged the operation and values of the international economic system that is producing these inequalities. Simply for this reason, the success of policies to tackle neighbourhoods where clusters of people are socially excluded must be limited, since the mechanisms causing their exclusion are going largely unchecked.

It is far beyond the scope of this book to propose an entire policy programme for the eradication of social exclusion, but there are two clear issues that emerge from my findings as central to the problems of poor neighbourhoods. The first is the contribution of low-paid and insecure work to the poverty trap and to the alienation of young and older people from paid work. If people in areas of traditionally low-skilled employment can only expect to obtain low-paid or fragile employment, these areas will inevitably continue to be relatively poor, and to be beset by problems of social exclusion. The second is the importance of ethnicity and immigration in shaping neighbourhood trajectories. The disadvantages faced by many people from minority ethnic groups are among the key drivers of neighbourhood poverty, even in prosperous cities and regions. We cannot expect to achieve neighbourhood renewal unless we can have a sensible debate about the implications of international migration. We need to able to trace and understand settlement patterns of different groups, and understand how the presence of different ethnic groups affects local housing markets and economies, social networks and interactions between areas, service needs and service performance. Discrimination on racial grounds may well turn out to be one of the biggest drivers of socioeconomic segregation. Ethnicity cannot be treated as marginal to the problem of disadvantaged areas, while we concentrate on deprivation or poverty. In some areas it is critical.

However, it is the second approach to spatial inequality that has been more my focus in this book: the attempt to remove differences between places so that some places do not have such a poor fit with labour or housing demand, and cease to draw in the most disadvantaged households on a continuous basis. The government has set about this task with gusto, determined that no one should be disadvantaged by where they live. In one sense, it has addressed the issue of 'fit' by looking to get rid of the characteristics that people do not want: large areas of council housing, poor quality housing, crime and anti-social behaviour and poor facilities and services. Neighbourhoods tailored more to people's needs and demands will ultimately be more mixed and more sustainable. This will take time to do, and one can question some of the underlying approaches, such as the willingness to displace communities to achieve social mix and rising land values, and the application of private finance and private sector models of service provision. However, in respect of housing, services and the physical environment, the importance of 'fit' is recognised and visible in policy.

What is not so evident, however, is the application of a concept of 'economic fit'. Economic fit seems to be pursued, on the supply side, by a range of welfare-to-work and educational initiatives and, on the demand side, by local economic development nested within regional economic strategies. Area regeneration appears to be premised on the understanding that, with these interventions, everywhere can be restored to its former level of economic viability, albeit with jobs of a different kind. Ostensibly, it is an agenda of growth and regeneration for everywhere.

But is this realistic? The evidence from the 12 study areas is that the change in Britain's economic structure is having spatial as well as sectoral implications. It is not necessarily the case that all areas can be revitalised in time and with sufficient overall economic growth. Some fit less well with the requirements of the modern economy than they did with the industrial economy. Large cities or areas with a previously high degree of employment specialisation face a particularly hard task to adapt to structural economic change (Begg et al, 2002). Some are doing so slowly but others, because of their specific spatial characteristics, such as location, topography and transport infrastructure, are failing to do so and may continue to fail. The change in Britain's economic structure may mean that some places are simply economically redundant. The ensuing pattern of population distribution, along with housing preferences, will trap some areas in a position of no or very low housing market value, which is unlikely to change regardless of housing market interventions. If areas have no economic viability, it will be impossible to eliminate the disadvantages that they impose on their residents.

In a similar vein, Begg et al (2002) have argued that the regeneration of individual cities should not be approached in isolation but in the context of the wider urban system. Different cities perform different economic roles. Some will be in competition. It is unrealistic to aim to regenerate all cities, because some will be in decline while others grow. Managing decline as well as growth should be on the policy agenda. The same applies to deprived areas within cities and regions. For some places, in areas of economic growth, the challenge will be to achieve managed development that ensures that the benefits of growth are evenly spread: linking local people to jobs, and ensuring affordable housing, affordable shops and the provision of community services as well as private sector growth. It is the 'trickle-down' issue all over again. Other areas may be in a 'holding' position, where economic development can be stimulated while building a more attractive and sustainable residential environment – the classic 'regeneration' approach of many SRBs. Finally, for a small minority of areas, the challenge will not be renewal but the management of a transition to smaller communities with a different purpose.

The timescale of managed decline may be longer – 20 or 30 years rather than 10 – and its content different. Housing tenure and housing allocations will need to be closely managed to protect communities from the 'dumping' of households that cannot be managed elsewhere. Rather than giving up on areas that have a limited future, in order to protect others, we need to recognise and respond to their additional vulnerability. We will need to be willing to invest in physical improvements that will only be temporary, and in the permanent provision of additional services and facilities in order first to hold on to neighbourhood conditions and second, in recognition that clusters of poverty without a broad economic base will need a higher level of ongoing provision. Managing area decline will need to be seen as a legitimate cost of economic growth.

I conclude, somewhat depressingly, that we will not see an end to what I have called in this book 'Poverty Street'. Poor areas will always exist. They have been a feature of this country at least since the Industrial Revolution and will continue to be so. Cities, throughout their history, have been residentially segregated (Marcuse, 1993). Since choice will always enable the better-off to choose where they live, the poor will always be concentrated, to some extent, in the least favourable locations. What is more at issue is the extent of that concentration, and the depth of the contrast between areas. Both of these can be minimised by smoothing the gradient between areas (making sure that areas fit with the demand for housing and for labour) and smoothing the gradient between people. On the first point, there are some promising measures in place. Tenure mixing will help, but will take a long time, and may lead just to smaller pockets of poverty rather than to their removal. Better housing, better environments and better services will reduce the gradient of choice and encourage social mix, and they will also limit the extent of the disadvantage that poorer areas confer on their residents. But clusters of poverty will inevitably remain and, as long as there are big differences between rich and poor, the areas where the poor are concentrated will continue to manifest the kind of problems described in this book. That is why we also need action to smooth the gradient between people as well as places. Ultimately, we will not bring an end to the problems of 'Poverty Street' either by reducing residential segregation or by improving management and services, unless we are also prepared to challenge seriously the inequalities in our economy and our society that are the real causes of relative poverty and of social exclusion. Moreover, clusters of socioeconomic problems will remain in a minority of areas because, in economic terms, restructuring has pulled the rug out from beneath them. Historically poor but economically viable, they now face the prospect of economic redundancy. Managing the long-term transition of these areas is, in some respects, a bigger challenge than managing the area 'regeneration' on which our policy aspirations have focused to date.

Notes

[1] To match rises in earnings since 1977, a single person's Jobseeker's Allowance in 2000 would need to have been £87 per week, rather than its current £53 (Carr-Hill and Lavers, 2000).

[2] The low-income threshold used in this analysis is 60% of median household income after housing costs. As a guideline, in 2000/01 this represented £84 per week for a single adult and £225 for a couple with two children.

Bibliography

Agulnik, P., Burchardt, T. and Evans, M. (2002) 'Response and prevention in the British welfare state', in J. Hills, J. LeGrand and D. Piachaud (eds) *Understanding social exclusion*, Oxford: Oxford University Press, pp 155-77.

Alcock, P., Craig, G., Lawless, P., Pearson, S. and Robinson, D. (1998) *Inclusive regeneration: Local authorities' corporate strategies for tackling disadvantage*, Sheffield: Centre for Regional Economic and Social Research, Sheffield Hallam University.

Aldridge, S. (2001) *Social mobility: A discussion paper*, London: Cabinet Office, Performance and Innovation Unit.

Allen, J. and Cars, G. (2001) 'Multi-culturalism and governing neighbourhoods', *Urban Studies*, vol 38, no 12, pp 2195-209.

Anastacio, J., Gidley, B., Hart, L., Keith, M., Mayo, M. and Kowarzik, U. (2000) *Reflecting realities: Participants' perspectives on integrated communities and sustainable development*, Bristol/York: The Policy Press/Joseph Rowntree Foundation.

Atkinson, A.B. (1998) 'Social exclusion, poverty and unemployment', in A.B. Atkinson and J. Hills (eds) *Exclusion, employment and opportunity*, CASEpaper 4, London: CASE, London School of Economics and Political Science, pp 1-20.

Atkinson, R. (2000) 'Narratives of policy: the construction of urban problems and urban policy in the official discourse of British government 1968-1998', *Critical Social Policy*, vol 20, no 2, pp 221-32.

Atkinson, R. and Kintrea, K. (2001) 'Disentangling area effects: evidence from deprived and non-deprived neighbourhoods', *Urban Studies*, vol 38, no 12, pp 2277-98.

Atkinson, R. and Moon, G. (1994) *Urban policy in Britain: The city, the state and the market*, London: Macmillan.

Audit Commission (2002) *Policy focus: Neighbourhood renewal*, London: Audit Commission.

Barry, B. (2002) 'Social exclusion, social isolation and the distribution of income', in J. Hills, J. LeGrand and D. Piachaud (eds) *Understanding social exclusion*, Oxford: Oxford University Press, pp 13-29.

Beattie, D. (1992) *Blackburn: The development of a Lancashire cotton town*, Halifax: Ryburn.

Beatty, C. and Fothergill, S. (1998) 'Registered and hidden unemployment in the UK coalfields', in P. Lawless, R. Martin and S. Hardy (eds) *Unemployment and social exclusion: Landscapes of labour inequality*, London: Regional Studies Association, pp 116-40.

Beatty, C. and Fothergill, S. (2003a) *Seaside towns research project: A case study of Thanet*, Sheffield: Centre for Regional Economic and Social Research, University of Sheffield.

Beatty, C. and Fothergill, S. (2003b) *Seaside towns research project: Economic change in Britain's seaside towns*, Sheffield: Centre for Regional Economic and Social Research, University of Sheffield.

Beatty, C., Fothergill, S., Gore, T. and Green, A. (2002) *The real level of unemployment 2002*, Sheffield: Centre for Regional Economic and Social Research, University of Sheffield.

Begg, I., Lever, W. and Boddy, M. (2002) *Urban competitiveness: Policies for dynamic cities*, Bristol: The Policy Press.

Benington, J. and Geddes, M. (eds) (2001) *Local partnership and social exclusion in the European Union: New forms of local social governance?*, London: Routledge.

Bennett, T. (1998) *Drugs and crime: The results of research on drug testing and interviewing arrestees*, Research Study 183, London: Home Office.

Benwell CDP (Community Development Project) (1978) *Permanent unemployment. Final report series No 2*, Newcastle: Benwell CDP.

Beynon, H., Hudson, R., Lewis, J., Sadler, D. and Townsend, A. (1989) 'It's all falling apart here: coming to terms with the future in Teesside', in P. Cooke (ed) *Localities: The changing face of urban Britain*, London: Unwin Hyman, pp 267-95.

Birmingham City Council (2001) *Ethnic groups in the labour market*, Birmingham: Birmingham City Council Economic Information Centre.

Blackaby, D., Leslie, D., Murphy, P. and O'Leary, N. (2000) 'White/ethnic minority earnings and employment differentials in Britain: evidence from the LFS', *Oxford Economic Papers*, vol 54, pp 270-97.

Borough View Renewal Team (2000) *Area renewal – Building foundations*, Internal report.

Bowman, H. (2001) *Talking to families in Leeds and Sheffield: A report on the first stage of the research*, CASEreport 18, London: CASE, London School of Economics and Political Science.

Bowman, H., Burden, T. and Konrad, J. (2000) *Attitudes to adult education in disadvantaged areas*, York: Joseph Rowntree Foundation.

Bradshaw, J. and Sainsbury, R. (2000) *Experiencing poverty*, Aldershot: Ashgate Publishing.

Bramley, G. (1997) 'Poverty and local public services', in D. Gordon and C. Pantazis (eds) *Breadline Britain in the 1990s*, Aldershot: Ashgate, pp 192-212.

Bramley, G. and Evans, M. (1998) *Where does public spending go? A pilot study to analyse the flows of public expenditure to local areas*, London: DETR.

Breheny, M. (ed) (1999) *The people: Where will they work? Report of TCPA research into the changing geography of employment*, London: Town and Country Planning Association.

Brennan, A., Rhodes, J. and Tyler, P. (1998) *Evaluation of the Single Regeneration Budget Challenge Fund: A partnership for regeneration. An interim evaluation*, London: DETR.

Bridge, G. (2002) *The neighbourhood and social networks*, CNR Paper 4, Bristol: Centre for Neighbourhood Research, University of Bristol.

Buchanan, J. and Young, L. (2000) 'Examining the relationship between material conditions, long-term problematic drug misuse and social exclusion: a new strategy for social inclusion', in J. Bradshaw and R. Sainsbury (eds) *Experiencing poverty*, Aldershot: Ashgate Publishing, pp 120-43.

Buck, N. (2001) 'Identifying neighbourhood effects on social exclusion', *Urban Studies*, vol 38, no 12, pp 2251-75.

Buck, N., Gordon, I., Pickvance, C. and Taylor-Gooby, P. (1989) 'The Isle of Thanet: restructuring and municipal conservatism', in P. Cooke (ed) *Localities: The changing face of urban Britain*, London: Unwin Hyman, pp 166-97.

Buck, N., Gordon, I., Hall, P., Harloe, M. and Kleinman, M. (2002) *Working capital: Life and labour in contemporary London*, London: Routledge.

Burgess, E. (1967) 'The growth of the city', in E. Burgess, R. Park and R. McKenzie (eds) *The city*, Chicago, IL: Chicago University Press, pp 1-46.

Burnett, J. (1986) *A social history of housing 1815-1985*, London: Methuen.

Burningham, K. and Thrush, D. (2001) *'Rainforests are a long way from here': The environmental concerns of disadvantaged groups*, York: York Publishing Services for the Joseph Rowntree Foundation.

Burns, D. and Taylor, M. (1998) *Mutual aid and self-help: Coping strategies for excluded communities*, Bristol/York: The Policy Press/Joseph Rowntree Foundation.

Burns, D., Forrest, R., Flint, J. and Kearns, A. (2001) *Empowering communities: The impact of Registered Social Landlords on social capital*, Edinburgh: Scottish Homes.

Byrne, D. (1999) *Social exclusion*, Buckingham: Open University Press.

Campbell, M. (2001) 'Missing links', *New Start*, 20 July.

Campbell, M., Carley, M., Kearns, A., Wood, M. and Young, R. (2000) *Regeneration in the 21st century: Policies into practice: An overview of the Joseph Rowntree Foundation Area Regeneration Programme*, Bristol/York: The Policy Press/Joseph Rowntree Foundation.

Carley, M. and Kirk, K. (1998) *Sustainable by 2020?: A strategic approach to urban regeneration for Britain's cities*, Bristol/York: The Policy Press/Joseph Rowntree Foundation.

Carley, M., Kirk, K. and McIntosh, S. (2001) *Retailing, sustainability and neighbourhood regeneration,* York: York Publishing Services for the Joseph Rowntree Foundation.

Carr-Hill, R. and Lavers, B. (2000) 'New Labour, new poor', in J. Bradshaw and R. Sainsbury (eds) *Experiencing poverty,* Aldershot: Ashgate Publishing, pp 181-99.

Castells, M. (1997) *The power of identity,* Oxford: Blackwell.

Champion, A.G., Atkins, A., Coombes, M. and Fotheringham, S. (1998) *Urban exodus: A report for the CPRE,* London: Council for the Protection of Rural England.

Clarke, J., Gewirtz, S. and McLaughlin, E. (2000) *New managerialism, new welfare,* London: Open University/Sage Publications.

Coates, K. and Silburn, R. (1970) *Poverty, the forgotten Englishmen,* Harmondsworth: Penguin.

COI (Central Office of Information) (1989) *Urban regeneration in Britain,* London: HMSO.

COI (1995) *Urban regeneration,* London: HMSO.

Coleman, J. (1988) 'Social capital in the creation of human capital', *American Journal of Sociology,* vol 94 (Supplement), pp S95-S120.

Collard, S., Kempson, E. and Whyley, C. (2001) *Tackling financial exclusion: An area-based approach,* York: York Publishing Services for the Joseph Rowntree Foundation.

Cooke, P. (ed) (1989) *Localities: The changing face of urban Britain,* London: Unwin Hyman.

Dale, A., Williams, M. and Dodgeon, B. (1996) *Housing deprivation and social change: A report based on the analysis of individual level Census data for 1971, 1981 and 1991 drawn from the Longitudinal Study and the Samples of Anonymised Records,* London: The Stationery Office.

Daley, P. (1998) 'Black Africans in Great Britain: spatial concentration and segregation', *Urban Studies,* vol 35, no 10, pp 1703-24.

Darton, D., Hirsch, D. and Strelitz, J. (2002) *Tackling disadvantage: A 20 year enterprise,* York: Joseph Rowntree Foundation.

Das, J., Rao, V. and Woolcock, M. (2003) *Social networks and risk management strategies in poor urban communities – What do we know?,* mimeo, World Bank.

Davies, N. (1998) *Dark heart: The shocking truth about hidden Britain,* London: Vintage.

Davies, W. and Herbert, D. (1993) *Communities within cities: An urban social geography,* London: Belhaven Press.

Dean, J. and Hastings, A. (2000) *Challenging images? Housing estates, stigma and regeneration,* Bristol/York: The Policy Press/Joseph Rowntree Foundation.

DETR (Department of the Environment, Transport and the Regions) (1996) *Urban trends in England: Evidence from the 1991 Census*, London: DETR.

DETR (1998) *English House Condition Survey 1996*, London: The Stationery Office.

DETR (1999) *Unpopular housing: National Strategy for Neighbourhood Renewal. Report of Policy Action Team 7*, London: DETR.

DETR (2000a) *Neighbourhood management. Report of Policy Action Team 4*, London: The Stationery Office.

DETR (2000b) *Measuring multiple deprivation at the small area level – The Indices of Deprivation 2000*, London: DETR.

DETR (2000c) *Towards an urban renaissance: The Report of the Urban Task Force*, London: DETR.

DETR (2000d) *Quality and choice: A decent home for all*, Housing Green Paper, London: DETR.

DfEE (Department for Education and Employment) (1999) *Social exclusion and the politics of opportunity: A mid-term progress check*, London: DfEE.

Dickens, A. (1857) 'Londoners over the border', *Household Words*, 12 June.

Docherty, I., Goodlad, R. and Paddison, R. (2001) 'Civic culture, community and citizen participation in contrasting neighbourhoods', *Urban Studies*, vol 38, no 12, pp 2225-50.

DoE (Department of the Environment) (1977a) *Unequal city: Final report of the Birmingham Inner Area Study*, London: HMSO.

DoE (1977b) *Policy for the inner cities*, London: HMSO.

Dorn, N., James, D. and South, N. (1987) *The limits of informal surveillance – Four case studies in identifying neighbourhood heroin problems*, London: Institute for the Study of Drug Dependency.

Douthwaite, R. (1992) *The growth illusion: How economic growth has enriched the few, impoverished the many and endangered the planet*, Dublin: Lilliput.

Duffy, B. (2000) *Satisfaction and expectations: Attitudes to public services in deprived areas*, CASEpaper 45, London: CASE, London School of Economics and Political Science.

Duffy, K. (1995) *Partnership and participation: The experience of Poverty 3 in the UK*, London: DSS.

Economist, The (2001) 'The redundant male', 8 September.

Elam, G., Ritchie, J. and Hulusi, A. (2000) 'Eking out an income: low income households and their use of supplementary resources', in J. Bradshaw and R. Sainsbury (eds) *Experiencing poverty*, Aldershot: Ashgate Publishing, pp 217-31.

Elias, P. and Bynner, J. (1997) 'Intermediate skills and occupational mobility', *Policy Studies*, vol 18, no 2, pp 101-24.

Ellen, I. and Turner, M. (1997) 'Does neighbourhood matter?: assessing recent evidence', *Housing Policy Debate*, vol 8, pp 833-66.

Evans, H. (2001) *Sprouting seeds – Outcomes from a community based employment programme*, CASEreport 8, London: CASE, London School of Economics and Political Science.

Evans, M., Noble, M., Wright, G., Smith, G., Lloyd, M. and Dibben, C.(2002) *Growing together, growing apart: Geographic patterns of change of Income Support and income-based Jobseeker's Allowance claimants in England between 1995 and 2000*, Bristol/York: The Policy Press/Joseph Rowntree Foundation.

Fainstein, S. (2001) *Competitiveness, cohesion and governance: A review of the literature*, mimeo, Rutgers University, New Brunswick.

Ferrie, J.E. (2001) 'Is job security harmful to health?', *Journal of the Royal Society of Medicine*, vol 94, pp 71-6.

Field, S., Mair, G., Rees, T. and Stevens, P. (1981) *Ethnic minorities in Britain: A study of trends in their position since 1961*, Home Office Research Study No 68, London: Home Office.

Fieldhouse, E.A. (1999) 'Ethnic minority unemployment and spatial mismatch: the case of London', *Urban Studies*, vol 36, no 9, pp 1569-96.

Fleckney, P. (1997) *'Riverlands' – New and updated booklet of facts and figures*, Nottingham: P. Fleckney.

Fordham Research (2000) 'Redcar and Cleveland Borough Council supply and demand study', unpublished.

Forrest, R. and Kearns, A. (1999) *Joined-up places? Social cohesion and neighbourhood regeneration*, York: York Publishing Services for the Joseph Rowntree Foundation.

Forrest, R. and Kearns, A. (2001) 'Social cohesion, social capital and the neighbourhood', *Urban Studies*, vol 38, no 12, pp 2125-45.

Galster, G. (2001) 'On the nature of neighbourhood', *Urban Studies*, vol 38, no 12, pp 2111-24.

Gans, H. (1962) *The urban villagers*, New York, NY: Free Press.

Geis, K. and Ross, C. (1998) 'A new look at urban alienation: the effect of neighbourhood disorder on perceived powerlessness', *Social Psychology Quarterly*, vol 61, no 3, pp 232-46.

Giddens, A. (1994) *Beyond Left and Right*, Cambridge: Polity Press.

Giddens, A. (1998) *The third way: The renewal of social democracy*, Cambridge: Polity Press.

Glennerster, H. (1995) *British social policy since 1945*, Oxford: Blackwell.

Glennerster, H., Lupton, R., Noden, P. and Power, A. (1999) *Poverty, social exclusion and neighbourhood: Studying the area bases of social exclusion*, CASEpaper 22, London: CASE, London School of Economics and Political Science.

Graham, J. (2000) *Drug markets and neighbourhood regeneration*, mimeo, CASE, London School of Economics and Political Science.

Gray, J. (1998) *False dawn: The delusions of global capitalism*, London: Granta.

Green, A. (1996) 'Aspects of the changing geography of poverty and wealth', in J. Hills (ed) *New inequalities: The changing distribution of income and wealth in the UK*, Cambridge: Cambridge University Press, pp 265-91.

Green, A. and Owen, D. (1998) *Where are the jobless?: Changing unemployment and non-employment in cities and regions*, Bristol/York: The Policy Press/Joseph Rowntree Foundation.

Gregory, I., Southall, H. and Dorling, D. (1999) *A century of poverty in Britain 1898-1998: A geographical analysis*, mimeo, University of Bristol and Queen Mary's College, London.

Hall, S. and Mawson, J. (1999) *Challenge funding, contracts and area regeneration: A decade of innovation in policy management and coordination*, Bristol/York: The Policy Press/Joseph Rowntree Foundation.

Harloe, M., Pickvance, C. and Urry, J. (eds) (1990) *Place, policy and politics: Do localities matter?*, London: Unwin Hyman.

Hastings, A. and Rao, M. (2001) 'Doctoring deprived areas cannot rely on exceptional people', *British Medical Journal*, vol 323, pp 409-10.

Healey, P. (1998) 'Insititutionalist theory, social exclusion and governance', in A. Madanipour, G. Cars and J. Allen (eds) *Social exclusion in European cities*, London: Jessica Kingsley Publishing, pp 53-74.

Hedges, B. and Clemens, S. (1994) *Housing Attitudes Survey*, London: DoE.

Hill, D. (2000) *Urban policy and politics in Britain*, London: Macmillan.

Hills, J. (1995) *Inquiry into income and wealth Vol 2*, York: Joseph Rowntree Foundation.

Hills, J. (2000) *Reinventing social housing finance*, London: IPPR.

Hills, J., LeGrand, J. and Piachaud, D. (eds) (2002) *Understanding social exclusion*, Oxford: Oxford University Press.

HM Treasury (1999) *Access to financial services: Report of Policy Action Team 14*, London: HM Treasury.

HMIC (HM Inspectorate of Constabulary) (2001) *Open all hours: An HMIC thematic inspection report on the role of police visibility and accessibility in public reassurance*, London: The Home Office.

Home Office (2000) *Neighbourhood wardens: Final report of Policy Action Team 6*, London: Home Office.

House of Commons Select Committee on Education and Employment (2000) *Fourth Report*, HC (99-00) 60, London: The Stationery Office.

Howarth, C., Kenway, P., Palmer, G. and Street, C. (1998) *Monitoring poverty and social exclusion: Labour's inheritance*, York: Joseph Rowntree Foundation.

Husband, C., Baldwin, P., Simpson, S. and Mellors, C. (2000) *Managing social cohesion and young people's entry into the labour market: Final report to the ESRC* (www.regard.ac.uk/research_findings/L130251036/report.pdf).

Hutton, W. (2002a) 'The class war destroying our schools', *The Observer*, 26 May.

Hutton, W. (2002b) *The world we're in*, London: Little, Brown.

Jargowsky, P. (1996) *Ghettos, barrios and the American city*, New York, NY: Russell Sage Foundation.

Jencks, C. and Mayer, S. (1990) 'The social consequences of growing up in a poor neighbourhood', in L. Lyon and C. McGeary (eds) *Inner city poverty in the United States*, Washington, DC: New York Press, pp 111-84.

Katz, B. (2002) *Smart growth: The future of the American metropolis?*, CASEpaper 58, London: CASE, London School of Economics and Political Science.

Keane, F. (2000) *A stranger's eye*, London: Viking.

Kearns, A. and Parkinson, M. (2001) 'The significance of neighbourhood', *Urban Studies*, vol 38, no 12, pp 2103-10.

Keen, L. and Scase, R. (1998) *Local government management: The rhetoric and reality of change*, Buckingham: Open University Press.

Kenway, P. and Palmer, K. (2002) *What do the poverty numbers really show?*, Policy Analysis No 3, London: New Policy Institute.

Kiernan, K. (2002) 'Disadvantage and demography – chicken and egg?', in J. Hills, J. LeGrand, and D. Piachaud (eds) *Understanding social exclusion*, Oxford: Oxford University Press, pp 84-96.

Kintrea, K. and Atkinson, R. (2001) *Neighbourhoods and social exclusion: The research and policy implications of neighbourhood effects*, Urban Change and Policy Research Group, Discussion Paper No 3, Glasgow: University of Glasgow.

Kleinman, M. (2000) 'Include me out? The new politics of place and poverty', *Policy Studies*, vol 21, no 1, pp 49-61.

Knowsley Borough Council (1999) 'Beyond the millennium. Overtown Housing Management District. Operational Plan 1999/2000', Internal document.

Lambert, C., Hammond, J., Malpass, P. and Stewart, M. (1999) *Hartcliffe and Withywood Study: Progress towards sustainable regeneration*, Bristol: University of the West of England.

Lee, P. and Murie, A. (1997) *Poverty, housing tenure and social exclusion*, Bristol/York: The Policy Press/Joseph Rowntree Foundation.

Lee, P. and Murie, A. (1999) *Literature review of social exclusion*, Edinburgh: Scottish Office.

Leeds City Council (1998) 'Housing strategy 1999/2000 to 2000/01', Internal document.

Levitas, R. (1998) *The inclusive society: Social exclusion and New Labour*, London: Macmillan.

Llewelyn-Davies (1997) *The London study: A socio-economic assessment of London*, London: Association of London Government.

London Borough of Newham (2000) *Minutes of Cabinet Committee 11 Dec 2000*.

Lovering, J. (1995) 'Creating discourses rather than jobs: the crisis in the cities and the transition fantasies of intellectuals and policy makers', in P. Healey (ed) *Managing cities: The new urban context*, London: Wiley, pp 109-26.

Lovering, J. (1997) 'Global restructuring and local impact', in M. Pacione (ed) *Britain's cities: Geographies of division in urban Britain*, London: Routledge, pp 63-87.

LSE (London School of Economics) (1976) *British cities: Urban population and employment trends 1951-1971*, London: LSE.

Lupton, R. (2001) *Places apart? The initial report of CASE's areas study*, CASEreport14, London: CASE, London School of Economics and Political Science.

Lupton, R. and Power, A. (2002) 'Social exclusion and neighbourhoods', in J. Hills, J. LeGrand, and D. Piachaud (eds) *Understanding social exclusion*, Oxford: Oxford University Press, pp 118-40.

Lupton, R., Wilson, A., May, T., Warburton, H. and Turnbull, P.J. (2002) *A rock and a hard place: Drug markets in deprived areas*, Home Office Research Study 240, London: The Home Office.

Macaskill, M. (2000) 'Black market takes over in slum towns', *Sunday Times*, 30 April.

McCulloch, A. (2001) 'Ward-level deprivation and individual social and economic outcomes in the British Household Panel Study', *Environment and Planning A*, vol 33, pp 667-84.

McKenna, F. (2000) 'Who'll benefit from the cash in hand economy?', *New Start*, 14 April.

McKnight, A. (2002) 'Low-paid work – drip-feeding the poor', in J. Hills, J. LeGrand, and D. Piachaud (eds) *Understanding social exclusion*, Oxford: Oxford University Press, pp 98-117.

Madanipour, A. (1998) 'Social exclusion and space', in A. Madanipour, G. Cars and J. Allen (eds) *Social exclusion in European cities*, London: Jessica Kingsley Publishing, pp 75-94.

Mander, D. (1996) *More light, more power: An illustrated history of Shoreditch*, London: London Borough of Hackney/Sutton Publishing.

Marcuse, P. (1993) 'What's so new about divided cities?', *International Journal of Urban and Regional Research*, vol 17, no 3, pp 355-65.

Marsh, A., Ford, R. and Finlayson, L. (1997) *Lone parents, work and benefits*, DSS Research Report No 61, London: The Stationery Office.

Massey, D. (1994) *Space, place and gender*, Cambridge: Polity Press.

Massey, D. and Denton, N. (1993) *American apartheid: Segregation and the making of the underclass*, Cambridge, MA: Harvard University Press.

Meegan, R. (1989) 'Paradise postponed: the growth and decline of Merseyside's outer estates', in P. Cooke (ed) *Localities: The changing face of urban Britain*, London: Unwin Hyman, pp 198-234.

Meegan, R. and Mitchell, A. (2001) '"It's not community round here, it's neighbourhood": neighbourhood change and cohesion in urban regeneration policies', *Urban Studies*, vol 38, no 12, pp 2167-94.

Michael, L. (1992) *Bygone 'Shipview'*, Newcastle: Newcastle-Upon-Tyne City Libraries and Arts.

Morris, L. (1993) 'Is there a British underclass?', *International Journal of Urban and Regional Research*, vol 17, no 3, pp 404-17.

Moser, C. (1999) *Improving literacy and numeracy: A fresh start*, London: DfEE.

Mumford, K. (2001) *Talking to families in East London: A report on the first stage of the research*, CASEreport 9, London: CASE, London School of Economics and Political Science.

Mumford, K. and Power, A. (2003) *East Enders: Family and community in East London*, Bristol: The Policy Press.

Murray, C. (1996) 'The emerging British underclass', in R. Lister (ed) *Charles Murray and the underclass: The developing debate*, London: Institute of Economic Affairs, pp 19-51.

National Assembly for Wales (1999) *A better Wales? A consultation paper on values, service priorities and spending plans*, Cardiff: National Assembly for Wales.

National Assembly for Wales (2001) *Better homes for people in Wales*, Cardiff: National Assembly for Wales.

NRU (Neighbourhood Renewal Unit) (2002) *Collaboration and coordination in area-based initiatives*, London: Neighbourhood Renewal Unit.

Noble, M. and Smith, G. (1996) 'Two nations? Changing patterns of income and wealth in two contrasting areas', in J. Hills (ed) *New inequalities: The changing distribution of income and wealth in the UK*, Cambridge: Cambridge University Press, pp 291-320.

Oatley, N. (2000) 'New Labour's approach to age-old problems: renewing and revitalising poor neighbourhoods – the National Strategy for Neighbourhood Renewal', *Local Economy*, vol 15, no 2, pp 86-97.

ONS (Office for National Statistics) (1996) *Social focus on ethnic minorities*, London: The Stationery Office.

ONS (1999) *Social trends*, London: The Stationery Office.

ONS (2000) *Psychiatric morbidity among adults*, London: The Stationery Office.

OPCS (Office of Population Censuses and Surveys) (1994) Census 1991: *Key statistics for local authorities*, London: HMSO.

Page, D. (2000) *The reality of social exclusion on housing estates*, Findings N120, York: Joseph Rowntree Foundation.

Park, R. (1952) *Human communities*, New York, NY: Free Press.

Parker, H., Bakx, K. and Newcombe, R. (1988) *Living with heroin: The impact of a drugs 'epidemic' on an English community*, Milton Keynes: Open University Press.

Parker, H., Bury, C. and Egginton, R. (1998) *New heroin outbreaks among young people in England and Wales*, Crime Prevention and Detection Paper 92, London: Home Office.

Parker, T. (1983) *The people of Providence*, London: Hutchinson.

Peach, C. (1996a) 'Does Britain have ghettos?', *Transactions of the Institute of British Geographers*, vol 21, pp 216-35.

Peach, C. (ed) (1996b) *Ethnicity in the 1991 Census Volume 2*, London: The Stationery Office.

Philo, C. (ed) (1995) *Off the map: The social geography of poverty in the UK*, London: Child Poverty Action Group.

Pitts, J. (2000) 'Neighbourhood destabilisation, youth crime and the destabilised school', in J. Bradshaw and R. Sainsbury (eds) *Experiencing poverty*, Aldershot: Ashgate Publishing, pp 251-66.

Plant, M. and Miller, P. (2000) 'Drug use has declined among teenagers in the UK', *British Medical Journal*, vol 320, p 1536.

Powell, M. (ed) (2002) *Evaluating New Labour's welfare reforms*, Bristol: The Policy Press.

Power, A. (1996) 'Area-based poverty and resident empowerment', *Urban Studies*, vol 33, no 9, pp 1535-64.

Power, A. (1997) *Estates on the edge: The social consequences of mass housing in Northern Europe*, New York, NY: St Martin's Press.

Power, A. and Bergin, E. (1999) *Neighbourhood management*, CASEpaper 31, London: CASE, London School of Economics and Political Science.

Power, A. and Mumford, K. (1999) *The slow death of great cities: Urban abandonment or urban renaissance*, York: Joseph Rowntree Foundation.

Power, A. and Tunstall, R. (1995) *Swimming against the tide: Polarisation or progress on twenty unpopular council estates 1980-1995*, York: Joseph Rowntree Foundation.

Price Waterhouse (1997) *Mapping local authority estates using the 1991 Index of Local Conditions*, London: DETR.

Purdue, D. (2001) 'Neighbourhood governance: leadership, trust and social capital', *Urban Studies*, vol 38, no 12, pp 2211-24.

Putnam, R. (2000) *Bowling alone: The collapse and revival of American community*, New York, NY: Simon and Schuster.

Rahman, M., Palmer, G. and Kenway, P. (2001) *Monitoring poverty and social exclusion 2001*, York: York Publishing Services for the Joseph Rowntree Foundation.

Ramsay, M. and Partridge, S. (1998) *Drug misuse declared in 1998: Results from the British Crime Survey*, Research Study 197, London: The Home Office.

Rex, J. and Moore, R. (1967) *Race, community and conflict: A study of Sparkbrook*, Oxford University Press for the Institute of Race Relations.

Robson, B., Bradford, M., Deas, I., Hall, I., Harrison, E., Parkinson, M., Evans, R., Garside, R., Harlington, A. and Robinson, F. (1994) *Assessing the impact of urban policy*, London: HMSO.

Robson, B., Parkinson, M., Boddy, M. and MacLennan, D. (2000) *The state of English cities*, London: DETR.

Rogers, R. and Power, A. (2000) *Cities for a small country*, London: Faber and Faber.

Sampson, J. (1999) 'What "community" supplies', in R. Ferguson and W. Dickens (eds) *Urban problems and community development*, Washington, DC: Brookings Institution Press, pp 241-92.

Schoon, N. (2001) *The chosen city*, London and New York, NY: Spon Press.

Sennett, R. (1998) *The corrosion of character*, New York, NY: W.W. Norton & Co.

SEU (Social Exclusion Unit) (1998) *Bringing Britain together: A National Strategy for Neighbourhood Renewal*, London: Cabinet Office.

SEU (1999) *Teenage pregnancy*, London: Cabinet Office.

SEU (2000a) *National Strategy for Neighbourhood Renewal: A framework for consultation*, London: Cabinet Office.

SEU (2000b) *Minority ethnic issues in social exclusion and neighbourhood renewal*, London: Cabinet Office.

SEU (2001a) *A new commitment to neighbourhood renewal: National strategy action plan*, London: Cabinet Office.

SEU (2001b) *Preventing social exclusion*, London: Cabinet Office.

Shaw, M., Dorling, D., Gordon, D. and Davey Smith, G. (1999) *The widening gap: Health inequalities and policy in Britain*, Bristol: The Policy Press.

Sheffield City Council (2001) *Aiming for excellence: Sheffield's Housing Revenue Account Business Plan 2001*.

Skyers, S. (2001) Unpublished PhD thesis, London School of Economics and Political Science.

Smith, C., Rundle, S. and Hastings, R. (2002) *Police service strength: Statistical Bulletin 10/02*, London: Home Office.

Smith, D. and Macnicol, J. (1999) 'Social insecurity and the informal economy', Paper presented at the Annual Conference of the Social Policy Association.

Smith, G. (1999) *Area-based initiatives: The rationale for and options for area targeting*, CASEpaper 25, London: CASE, London School of Economics and Political Science.

Spence, N., Gillespie, A., Goddard, J., Kennett, S., Pinch, S. and Williams, A. (1982) *British cities: An analysis of urban change*, Urban and Regional Planning Series Volume 26, Oxford: Pergamon Press.

Taylor, I., Evans, K. and Fraser, P. (1996) *A tale of two cities: Global change, local feeling and everyday life in the North of England: A study in Manchester and Sheffield*, London: Routledge.

Taylor, M. (1995) *Unleashing the potential: Bringing residents to the centre of regeneration*, York: Joseph Rowntree Foundation.

Thomas, D. (1991) *Community development at work: A case of obscurity in accomplishment*, London: Community Development Foundation.

Townsend, P. (1979) *Poverty in the United Kingdom*, Harmondsworth: Penguin Books.

Townsend, P., Corrigan, P. and Kowarzik, U. (1987) *Poverty and labour in London*, London: Low Pay Unit.

Toynbee, P. (2002) 'After the jubilation must come the reckoning', *The Guardian*, 5 June.

Toynbee, P. (2003) *Hard work: Life in low pay Britain*, London: Bloomsbury.

Tunstall, R. and Lupton, R. (2003) *Is targeting deprived areas an effective means to reach poor people? An assessment of one rationale for area-based funding programmes*, CASEpaper 70, London: CASE, London School of Economics and Political Science.

Turok, I. and Edge, N. (1999) *The jobs gap in Britain's cities: Employment loss and labour market consequences*, Bristol/York: The Policy Press/Joseph Rowntree Foundation.

Van Kempen, R. and Ozuekren, A.S. (1998) 'Ethnic segregation in cities: new form and explanations in a dynamic world', *Urban Studies*, vol 35, no 10, pp 1631-56.

Wallace, M. (2001) 'A new approach to neighbourhood renewal in England', *Urban Studies*, vol 38, no 12, pp 2163-6.

Wallace, M. and Denham, C. (1996) *The ONS classification of local and health authorities of Great Britain*, London: The Stationery Office.

Walton, F., Hill, C. and Campbell, M. (2002) *The Tesco job guarantee programme: An assessment. Report prepared for the Leeds Employer Coalition*, Leeds: Policy Research Institute, Leeds Metropolitan University.

Wilson, A., May, T., Warburton, H., Lupton, R. and Turnbull, P.J. (2002) *Heroin and crack cocaine markets in deprived areas: Seven local case studies*, CASEreport 19, London: CASE, London School of Economics and Political Science.

Wilson, W.J. (1987) *The truly disadvantaged: The inner city, the underclass and public policy*, Chicago, IL: University of Chicago Press.

Wilson, W.J. (1997) *When work disappears: The world of the new urban poor*, New York, NY: Alfred A. Knopf.

Young, M. (1999) 'Some reflections on the concepts of social exclusion and inclusion: beyond the third way', in A. Hayton (ed) *Tackling disaffection and social exclusion: Education perspectives and policies*, London: Kogan Page, pp 210-23.

Young, M. and Willmott, P. (1957) *Family and kinship in East London*, London: Routledge and Kegan Paul.

Index

NOTE: Letters following page numbers show that information is in a figure (*f*), note (*n*) or table (*t*).